Europe
at the Margins

The **European Science Foundation** is an association of its 56 member research councils, academies, and institutions devoted to basic scientific research in 20 countries. The ESF assists its Member Organisations in two main ways: by bringing scientists together in its Scientific Programmes, Networks and European Research Conferences, to work on topics of common concern; and through the joint study of issues of strategic importance in European science policy.

The scientific work sponsored by ESF includes basic research in the natural and technical sciences, the medical and biosciences, the humanities and social sciences.

The ESF maintains close relations with other scientific institutions within and outside Europe. By its activities, ESF adds value by cooperation and coordination across national frontiers, offers expert scientific advice on strategic issues, and provides the European forum for fundamental science.

This volume arises from the work of the ESF Scientific Programme on Regional and Urban Restructuring in Europe (RURE).

Further information on ESF activities can be obtained from:

European Science Foundation
1, quai Lezay-Marnésia
F-67080 Strasbourg Cedex
France

Tel. (+33) 88 76 71 00
Fax (+33) 88 37 05 32

Europe
at the Margins
New Mosaics of Inequality

Edited by
COSTIS HADJIMICHALIS
Aristotle University of Thessaloniki, Greece

DAVID SADLER
University of Durham, UK

JOHN WILEY & SONS
Chichester · New York · Brisbane · Toronto · Singapore

Copyright © 1995 by the European Science Foundation

Published in 1995 by John Wiley & Sons Ltd,
Baffins Lane, Chichester,
West Sussex PO19 1UD, England
Telephone National Chichester (01243) 779777
International (+44) (1243) 779777

Other Wiley Editorial Offices

John Wiley & Sons, Inc., 605 Third Avenue,
New York, NY 10158-0012, USA

Jacaranda Wiley Ltd, 33 Park Road, Milton,
Queensland 4064, Australia

John Wiley & Sons (Canada) Ltd, 22 Worcester Road,
Rexdale, Ontario M9W 1L1, Canada

John Wiley & Sons (SEA) Pte Ltd, 37 Jalan Pemimpin #05-04,
Block B, Union Industrial Building, Singapore 2057

Library of Congress Cataloging-in-Publication Data

Europe at the margins : new mosaics of inequality / edited by
 Costis Hadjimichalis and David Sadler.
  p.   cm.
 Includes bibliographical references and index.
 ISBN 0-471-95635-X
  1. Marginality, Social — European Union countries. 2. Equality —
 European Union countries. I. Hadjimichalis, Costis. II. Sadler, David.
 HN380.5.Z9M264 1995
 305'.094 — dc20   94–44563
                                                              CIP

British Library Cataloguing in Publication Data

A catalogue record for this book is available from the British Library

ISBN 0-471-95635-X

Typeset in 10/12pt Palatino by Mayhew Typesetting, Rhayader, Powys
Printed and bound in Great Britain by Bookcraft (Bath) Ltd

This book is printed on acid-free paper responsibly manufactured from sustainable
forestation, for which at least two trees are planted for each one used for paper
production.

Contents

About the Contributors   vii

Preface   xi

Part I   INTRODUCTION   1

1   Integration, Marginality and the New Europe   3
    C. Hadjimichalis and D. Sadler

2   New Aspects of Marginality in Europe   15
    E. Mingione

Part II   GENDER, RACE, CULTURE   33

3   Women of the South after, like before, Maastricht?   35
    D. Vaiou

4   New International Migrations and the "European Fortress"   51
    E. Pugliese

5   The Creation of Socio-spatial Marginalisation in Brussels: a Tale of Flexibility, Geographical Competition and Guest-worker Neighbourhoods   69
    C. Kesteloot

6   Culture and Marginality in the New Europe   87
    K. Robins and A. Aksoy

Part III   CAPITAL, LABOUR, STATE POLICIES   105

7   Remote Rural Areas: Villages on the Northern Margin   107
    J. Oksa

8   New Forms of Transport and Communication, New Patterns of Disadvantage   123
    J. Gaspar

9   Old Industrial Places and Regions: the Limits to Reindustrialisation   133
    D. Sadler

10   Growth at the Margins: Contract Labour in a Core Region   149
    J. Allen and N. Henry

11 Housing the "Guestworkers"   167
    J. van Weesep

Part IV CONCLUDING COMMENTS AND OPEN QUESTIONS   195

12 Where Have Urban Movements Gone?   197
    C. G. Pickvance

13 Thinking about the Edge: the Concept of Marginality   219
    A. Bailly and E. Weiss-Altaner

14 Open Questions: Piecing Together the New European
    Mosaic   237
    C. Hadjimichalis and D. Sadler

Index   245

About the Contributors

Asu Aksoy is a researcher based in Istanbul, having previously worked in the UK on communications, new technologies and corporate decision-making. She is presently conducting research on technology, communication and socio-economic development in Turkey.

John Allen is Senior Lecturer in Economic Geography at the Open University. He is author of *Landlords and property* (with Linda McDowell, 1989) and editor of *The economy in question* and *Uneven re-development* (with Doreen Massey, 1988) and *Political and economic forms of modernity* (1991). Research interests include housing and labour markets. He is currently working on the nature of occupations in the contract services industries.

Antoine Bailly is Professor and Director of the Department of Geography at the University of Geneva, past president of the Association de Science Régionale de Langue Française, and president of the Western Regional Science Association. He is the author of books in economic, regional and urban geography, and has undertaken research into the development of service activities in Europe and North America.

Jorge Gaspar is Professor in Geography and Planning at the University of Lisbon. He was co-ordinator of one of the four working groups of the European Science Foundation's "Regional and Urban Restructuring in Europe" programme, 1990–94. He has been involved in various regional planning projects, including the Lisbon and Tagus Valley Regional Co-ordinating Commission, and is general co-ordinator for the evaluation of the Portuguese Regional Development Plan (1994–99). He has published widely in the field of regional planning, and is a member of Academia Europaea.

Costis Hadjimichalis is Associate Professor in the Department of Urban and Regional Planning at the Aristotle University of Thessaloniki. His research interests include regional labour markets, flexible specialisation, the informal sector and regional social movements. Major books include *Industrialisation and uneven development* (with Dina Vaiou, Exandas, in Greek), *Uneven development and regionalism: state, territory and class in southern Europe* (Croom Helm) and *Regional development and policy* (editor, Exandas, in Greek). He is a member of the editorial boards of *Synchrona Themata*, *Antipode* and *European Urban and Regional Studies*.

Nick Henry is Lecturer in Geography at the University of Birmingham. His research interests are in regional development and the nature of growth regions, with a special emphasis on high technology and service industries.

Christian Kesteloot is Research Associate of the National Fund for Scientific Research and part-time Senior Lecturer at the Institute of Social and Economic Geography at the Catholic University of Leuven. He has published on the relationship between economic development and urban structures in west European cities, particularly Brussels, on foreign minorities in Belgium, and on theory in human geography. He is editor of *Les fractionnements sociaux de l'espace belge, une géographie de la société belge*, a social geography of Belgium written by a group of radical geographers called Mort-Subite (also the brand of an excellent Belgian beer and the name of a famous Brussels café where they used to meet). He is a member of the editorial board of *Espace, Populations, Sociétés*.

Enzo Mingione is Professor of Urban and Regional Sociology at the Faculty of Political Sciences in the University of Messina. He has published extensively in both Italian and English. Major books include *Fragmented societies* (Blackwell, 1991), *Beyond employment* (co-edited with Nanneke Redclift, Blackwell, 1991) and *Social conflict and the city* (Blackwell, 1981). He is a member of the editorial boards of *Inchiesta* and *International Journal of Urban and Regional Research*, and recently was guest editor for a special issue of the latter on the theme of "New urban poverty".

Jukka Oksa is a rural sociologist working in the Karelian Institute of the University of Joensuu. His research interests are rural villages and rural policies in remote north European regions. He has recently published *Russian Karelia in search of a new role* (1994).

Chris Pickvance is Professor of Urban Studies at the University of Kent at Canterbury. His research interests are in housing, local government, urban protest and urban and regional policy. He is currently working on a project on "Environment and housing movements in Hungary, Russia and Estonia". He is co-editor of *Place, policy and politics: do localities matter?* (with Michael Harloe and John Urry, Unwin Hyman, 1990) and of *State restructuring and local power: a comparative perspective* (Pinter, 1991).

Enrico Pugliese is Professor and Chair of the Department of Sociology at the University of Naples. He has previously held visiting professorships at the University of Missouri and at Columbia University, New York, and worked as Professor of Economic Sociology at the University of Salerno. Recent books include *Sociologia della disoccupazione* (Il Mulino, 1993) and *Razziste e solidari* (Eddriesse, 1993). He has published articles in many international journals including *Social Research, International Journal of Urban* *and Regional Research, International Journal of Political Economy,* and *Sociologie et société.*

Kevin Robins works in the Centre for Urban and Regional Development Studies at the University of Newcastle, where he has been involved in a programme on information and communication technologies. He is author of *Geografia dei media* (Baskerville, 1993) and co-editor of *The regions, the nations and the BBC* (with Sylvia Harvey, British Film Institute, 1993).

David Sadler is Lecturer in Geography at the University of Durham. His research interests include processes of international economic restructuring, state policies and the geography of uneven development in Europe. Recent books include *The global region: production, state policies and uneven development* (Pergamon, 1992), *Approaching human geography: an introduction to contemporary theoretical debates* (with Paul Cloke and Chris Philo, Paul Chapman, 1991) and *A place called Teesside: a locality in a global economy* (with Huw Beynon and Ray Hudson, Edinburgh University Press, 1994). He is editor of *European Urban and Regional Studies.*

Dina Vaiou is Assistant Professor in the Department of Urban and Regional Planning at the National Technical University of Athens. Her current research interests include feminist critiques of spatial analysis, the changing nature of local labour markets (with a special emphasis on informal activities and patterns of work), the impacts of integration on women in southern Europe, and the ways in which gender forms part of these processes. She is a member of the editorial boards of *European Planning Studies, Gender, Place, Culture* and *European Journal of Women's Studies.*

Jan van Weesep is Professor of Urban Geography and Urban Policy at the University of Utrecht, and director of the urban research programme of its Faculty of Geographical Sciences. His research interests cover the geography of housing, including the various dimensions of social segmentation. He has recently co-edited *Government and housing* (1990) and *Urban housing for the better-off: gentrification in Europe* (1991). Within the ESF's RURE programme, he was co-editor of *Competition between European cities* (Avebury, 1995).

Eric Weiss-Altaner is Professor in the Department of Urban Studies at the University of Quebec at Montreal. He has published widely on demography and inequality, mainly in America.

Preface

This book arises from the European Science Foundation's scientific programme entitled "Regional and Urban Restructuring in Europe", known affectionately to participants over its life span from 1990 to 1994 as RURE. The ideas and work on the margins of the new Europe reported here developed from discussions within our working group and among other colleagues in RURE. It became evident at an early stage that the majority of projects in the programme as a whole (of which there were about a dozen) either took for granted the "positive" aspects of European integration, or were preoccupied with important special themes (such as migration, for instance, or the role of large corporations), and thus paid less attention to those places and social groups which seemed to be missing out. RURE was not alone in this; issues to do with the uneven distribution of the costs and benefits of the Single Internal Market programme of what was to become the European Union (EU), and of political liberalisation in eastern Europe, were frequently submerged in a generalised "Europhoria" during the late 1980s and early 1990s. The starting-point for this project was therefore a critical concern for the process of building a new Europe, looking mainly at the "losers" as one way of painting a fuller picture of the whole story.

It was clear from the beginning, however, that it was not possible to cover all issues relevant to this vast topic. We therefore chose a selective focus, based on a combination of our interests and those of members of our working group, as well as specialist non-RURE scholars whom we invited to participate in the book. Particular attention is paid here to EU countries and regions, and those social groups in residence or attempting to enter. This is also an outcome of the process of gathering together contributions within the constraints of time, resources, and the state of existing research. We have not tried to be complete in our coverage, in other words, but we hope that the various dimensions of change recorded and analysed here shed new light on processes of restructuring as seen from, and experienced in, the margins (although this is most certainly not to deny the significance of linkages with other places and processes).

As editors we are particularly grateful for the collaborative atmosphere in our working group and in RURE in general. Almost all of the chapters have been discussed on several occasions in various venues. We would like to thank the European Science Foundation for making this possible (and in particular John Smith for his cheerful support and encouragement); the co-directors of RURE, Arie Shachar and Sture Oberg and the chair of our working group, Jorge Gaspar, for providing a stimulating environment in which to work; and the RURE co-ordinator Anders Malmberg for making sure this happened. We gratefully acknowledge the innovative work of the contributors to this volume, and thank them both for their effort and their patient response to what probably seemed a never-ending stream of requests, suggestions and revisions. Special thanks are due to Enzo Mingione and Chris Pickvance who read and commented helpfully on draft versions of our introductory and concluding comments. We must also apologise to those who were on time with their manuscripts for a slight delay in finally completing the whole project caused by receipt of the last chapters.

While we are happy to take final responsibility for the contents, the last word should be with our contributors. We hope that they, and readers of this book, feel that the issues raised here can form part of an invigorated debate on the kind of geography which might be constituted from future social, economic, political and cultural priorities in the emergent new Europe. One measure of the success or failure of this collective venture should be its contribution to such a broader debate.

Costis Hadjimichalis and David Sadler
Thessaloniki and Durham

ACKNOWLEDGEMENTS

Grateful acknowledgement is made to the following sources for permission to reproduce the photographs shown on pages x, 247 and the reverse of the part title pages.

Page x   © Costis Hadjimichalis
Page 247 © Epsilon
Part I   © Costis Hadjimichalis
Part II   © Epsilon
Part III   © Derek Hudspeth, Department of Geography, Durham University, UK
Part IV   © Costis Hadjimichalis

Part I

INTRODUCTION

1 Integration, Marginality and the New Europe

COSTIS HADJIMICHALIS
Aristotle University of Thessaloniki, Greece

DAVID SADLER
University of Durham, UK

Since the mid-1980s, dramatic and far-reaching economic, social and political changes have taken place in Europe. On some accounts at least, a new continent is rapidly being fashioned, epitomised in the creation of a Single Internal Market within the European Union (EU) as part of its "1992" programme, and the transformations taking place in eastern Europe and the former Soviet Union. These developments also embrace novel and increasingly complex cultural dimensions. The scope of such changes has been particularly broad, leading some to suggest that they represent the emergence of an epochal shift in Europe's global role. Whether or not such observations are an accurate portrayal of recent events in a long-term historical context (and this is an important question, to which we return below), it is impossible to escape the forceful reality of scenes such as the dismantling of the Berlin Wall, or the signing of the Maastricht Treaty.

INTEGRATION/DISINTEGRATION

The dominant image in such a world, and an increasingly significant part of political discourse, is one of *integration*. This is central to the future of the member states of the EU as part of economic and monetary union. It is also commonly voiced as the appropriate path for widening of the EU, to embrace former members of the European Free Trade Association and — eventually, perhaps — those states in eastern Europe which survive the next few years relatively intact, or with some measure of internal stability. Such observations are further reinforced — if somewhat symbolically — by the comparisons which were drawn between Jacques Delors, former President of the Commission of the EU, and earlier architects of European

Europe at the Margins: New Mosaics of Inequality. Edited by Costis Hadjimichalis and David Sadler
© 1995 European Science Foundation. Published in 1995 by John Wiley & Sons Ltd

co-operation such as Jean Monnet and Konrad Adenauer. In this new era, it seems that there is a newly emergent (by no means uncontested, but certainly highly influential and probably dominant) consensus, extolling the virtues of a certain closely defined agenda. From such a perspective, regional and national variation even becomes part of the conceptual apparatus of integration. The resolution of uneven development and incorporation of regional differentiation has been encapsulated in the problematic notion of "Europe of the regions", a celebration of difference as part and parcel of a drive towards uniformity and equality. In this way, it is argued, the twin "problems" of uneven regional development and widely differing regional political cultures can be subsumed within this broader project of *harmonisation*.

Beneath the veneer of consensus, however, lies an undercurrent of tension which it is increasingly difficult to ignore. The implications of the "1992" programme and the Maastricht agreement, and the prospect of further enlargement, are sharpening the differences between EU member states over some important policy questions. At the geographical margins, the ultimate composition of the "new map" of Europe is far from clear, particularly in countries such as former Yugoslavia which has fallen apart at the seams under the weight of ethnic and religious conflict, and in the former USSR, which has undergone political disintegration. A neo-liberal thrust to the "integrationist" agenda sidelines other significant questions to do with heightened inequality emerging from contemporary economic restructuring. This is evident all too clearly on the streets of big cities, in rural areas, in the differential exclusion of certain groups from the formal economy, in gender inequalities, and in growing ethnic, racial and religious tensions. In these processes too, geography has a part, as the new Europe on closer examination begins to look increasingly fractured, rather than more closely integrated. These questions — to do with differentiation, marginalisation and exclusion — form the starting-point of this book.

The objective of this volume then is to explore in more detail and depth the ways in which the new Europe is associated with the reproduction and, indeed, intensification of differentiation and inequality. Our concern is with the regions, cities and social groups which seem at first sight to be "missing out" on the margins of contemporary restructuring in Europe. These places and peoples are at the peripheries of dominant economic, political and cultural systems. They all carry the image and stigma of a marginality which becomes closely associated with — indeed a defining characteristic of — their actual identity. In that sense, we are exploring the *representation* of marginality just as much as the *production* and *reproduction* of that phenomenon in its various guises. In the rest of these introductory remarks, we go on to explore some of the implications of this chosen focus.

ISSUES AND PROCESSES

Arguably the most significant of these implications is to state that we do not advocate a stress upon marginalised groups and places *per se*, somehow divorced from the broader global context of social relationships within which marginality and exclusion take place. Far from it: it is impossible, we would argue, to understand how particular groups become marginalised or excluded from employment, access to particular citizenship rights, or whatever, *without* such a framework. While competition and integration have had some positive and beneficial results, these are structurally related to processes of marginalisation and exclusion. The reproduction of inequality is an inevitable constitutive element in, rather than an optional consequence of, developments within the international workings of capitalism as a system of production and reproduction. Such questions to do with the connection between global or universal processes, and the particularities of local circumstances — especially in the economic sphere — have been and are being explored elsewhere (see Amin and Thrift, 1994). In the ongoing process of global integration, the three mega-regions of the world — North America, Europe and East Asia — have formed a new hierarchy, leaving most of the rest of the world in a relative backwater. The new Europe is less dependent on the Third World now than at any time in the previous century. For the poorer countries this process — and particularly the Single European Market — will present a new challenge: the "Europe" of 1992 and the Maastricht Treaty is not cut off from its surroundings but designed to dominate them instead (Mayo, 1989; Lipietz, 1993). We focus here, however — as do the chapters in this volume — upon certain manifestations of inequality and segmentation, on particular processes which marginalise some social groups and places, *within* Europe. We do this in order to shed further light on the overall dynamics of contemporary economic, social and political restructuring. These views from a particular perspective are therefore important not just in their own right, but for the wider understanding which they can bring.

Secondly, most of the chapters in this book focus upon certain fault lines within contemporary European society. This should not be taken to suggest that each point of fracture — gender, class, ethnicity, the state, location and so on — exists independently from the others. Rather, our perspective visualises each of these different bases for division and exclusion inter-acting in a variety of ways at particular moments. For some, the intersection of certain axes of inequality can reinforce their disadvantaged position within society, and it is for such groups that ideas of integration and harmonisation have a particularly hollow ring. Neo-liberal ideologies pay special attention to theories and models of European integration which assume the adequacy of competition alone in explaining the evolution of different national societies. Evidence suggests that, on the contrary, historical and geographical conditions in Europe are *not* linked in a single linear evolutionary path, in which peripheral or marginalised societies must somehow "catch up" with the advanced ones, and that "competition" is in this context a concept which conceals as much as it reveals. Neo-liberal accounts, for instance, tend to neglect the real impact of decentralised market structures and cultural differences, and instead pursue an absurd, oppressive search for administrative and legal "barriers" and "rigidities" to explain the survival of distinct national and regional markets and cultures. Part of this book's agenda, therefore, is to map precisely how and why certain dimensions in the constitution of society interact in the construction of inequality, particularly with respect to processes of economic and cultural transformation and changing class and gender relations. Only in such ways, we would suggest, might it be possible to begin to devise appropriate policy responses.

Thirdly, we aim to identify in this book not just the *intensification* of processes leading to inequality and marginalisation (which, we argued above, has occurred in the ideologically constrained drive towards European integration), but also an important element of *continuity*. Socially and spatially uneven development is far from novel. What is important in the last decade or so, however, is the precise way in which new forms of differentiation have been enabled to emerge, and old ones have taken on an even more sharply divisive edge. The interaction between new and old processes is important for an insight into the reasons for, and scope of, contemporary transformations. It is in this sense that we intend closely to examine whether or not the "new Europe" is that much of a radical break with the past. We may pose the question, for instance, whether national-istic ideas of the 1930s against "inferior people" have an immediate link with current "Eurocentrism", xenophobia and a general shift to the extreme right (Amin, 1989). Will North–South and West–East contradictions inevitably become more and more explosive, thereby engendering, among other things, a covert but aggresive racism and sexism against anything which does not follow "proper" north-western European behavioural and cultural stereotypes? This also sheds further light on the particularity of the agenda around which the new map of Europe has been tailored; the precise ways in which "integration" came to have such salience, and the reasons why it took the ideological form that it did. At the risk of anticipating our concluding remarks, it should suffice to say here that we would not argue against the potential of European integration *per se*, but rather take issue with the particular kind of path which has been adopted, and the highly uneven consequences which have followed from that choice.

Finally, we are aware that the term "marginality" has been used in a problematic way in the past, especially in connection with urbanisation processes in the Third World. We will not repeat the critique of the ideological assumptions of "marginality theory". It has been sufficiently summarised by Perlman's (1979) criticism of the myth of marginality and by Castells (1983) writing on the social dimension of marginality. The ideology of "marginality theory" (best expressed by social research and policy recommendation by DESAL (1969) in Chile) merges and confuses in a single dimension the positions occupied by individuals and groups in different dimensions of the social and spatial structure: occupational, locational, class, stratification of private and public consumption, income distribution, cultural and power-political (see also Castells, 1983). Assuming the empirical covariation of the low-level positions occupied in these dimensions, "marginality theory" proposes an explanation of society in which rural migration and locational marginality appear as unexplained independent variables affecting people living on the urban margins.

The term has been used more carefully in current French literature modified under the wider concept of the "return of dangerous classes" (Jazouli, 1992; Jacquier, 1992; Zehraoui, 1992). Such French sociologists suggest that second-generation young migrants are the most marginalised groups, being excluded from both schools and the labour market. Analysing degradation and exclusion in suburban areas (les banlieues) of Paris and other major cities, they conclude that social and spatial exclusion are outcomes of economic restructuring, social changes in traditional family structures and policies of the state such as urban measures.

We aim to avoid old perceptions of marginality as well as those of its pure spatial variations, reviewed and criticised by Bailly and Weiss-Altaner in Chapter 13 of this volume. There is no deterministic relationship between centre and margins, where control lies in the former and dependency in the latter. On the contrary, the power of the term is in the way it can be used both as an indication of exclusion/inclusion of certain social groups and areas in the process of development and restructuring, as well as in a symbolic sense to denote a strategy of positional superiority, of prestige and status. As Bailly and Weiss-Altaner argue, marginality's range of reference spans both the physical and the social, thereby heightening the concept's attractiveness for thinking at the same time about social and spatial dimensions of exclusion/inclusion but not reducing everything in one process. Following a similar line of argument, Shields (1991) criticises positivist perceptions of marginality (in for instance imaginary maps) and addresses the importance of language as a medium and mediator. He argues that the social definition of marginal places and spaces is intimately linked with the categorisation of objects, practices, ideas and modes of social interaction as belonging to a "lower culture". To be in, on and around the "margin" implies exclusion from the "centre" (although there is no necessary or direct correlation here with geographical notions of core and periphery). In this way, margins become signifiers of everything "centres" deny, repress or exclude, almost a kind of subculture. Thus, marginality depends on the perception of some groups or places as outsiders, as having the smell and feel of "otherness".

While margins are in a position of exclusion, however, they can also be a source of power and critique. They can produce counter-hegemonic alternatives which contribute to a radical consciousness of resistance. We aim to keep this dynamic interpretation, and the contributors to this book develop a clear focus on critical social responses to different forms of marginality, both formal and informal. In this way our conception of marginalisation is not one where certain marginal places or groups necessarily play a passive or inactive role. While recognising the structurally determined constraints on individual actors and groups, particularly those in certain social and/or spatial positions, we intend to stress instead the active ways in which challenge and contestation can contribute both to the process of restructuring and to the interpretation of such processes. As Pickvance (Chapter 12) makes clear in this volume, there is no automatic or even predictable relationship between those at the margin and their action to challenge this position. Pro-activity is a contingent characteristic with no mechanical relation to those deprived and excluded.

THE STRUCTURE OF THE BOOK

As explained above, it would be impossible to cover extensively in one volume all possible forms of social and spatial marginalisation in the new Europe. The book therefore focuses on a limited number of themes, which firstly are related directly with — although not exclusively derived from — the ongoing process of European integration and, secondly, seem to have attracted relatively less attention from researchers and policy-makers despite their very real significance. A common denominator in all the chapters is their focus on marginality from both social and spatial perspectives at one and the same time. The contributors rightly emphasise that social and spatial attributes should not be separated analytically. What matters more is the manner of their combination.

The book itself is structured into four parts. In the introduction, Mingione expands upon some of the ideas which we have advanced in this chapter. The chapters in Part II focus most on what might be described as the ways in which gender, race and culture form part of processes of marginalisation in particular places, or are starting points in a consideration of the margins from a European perspective. Those in Part III discuss issues mostly related to capital restructuring, changing forms of labour relations and organisation, and state policies, and how these affect particular regions and cities. This part explicitly discusses policies of nation states and the EU which are, in contradictory ways, contributing to instead of reducing marginalisation. Then Part IV re-examines different uses of the concept of marginality, and explores the role of social agents in relation to various forms of exclusion and marginalisation. A short chapter with "open questions" relevant to further research and policy formulation concludes the book.

In his introductory chapter Mingione explores the links between poverty and marginality, and argues that poverty is no longer just associated with rural areas and the working class, but with broader changes in employment and welfare systems, and in the contradiction between globalisation and localisation. He points out that marginalisation trends are not mechanically connected to particular conditions affecting individuals, but largely depend on different systems of social integration that have come about in various parts of Europe. He identifies different models of welfare capitalism based on a persistent complementarity of state and family responsibility for social integration and the provision of welfare. Mingione concludes that a truly common European social policy is likely to remain "subsidiary" in the foreseeable future. A homogenising trend towards optimal quality levels — defined on the basis of social justice — is extremely unlikely, because of political and budgetary constraints.

The second part addresses issues of gender, race and culture. Chapter 3 deals explicitly with gender issues. Vaiou writes on women of the south and their unequal integration into the EU, concentrating on two interrelated issues: the notion of "social partnership" heavily promoted by the EU, but which does not correspond to the experience of work of the majority of women in the south, and the idea that increased mobility of labour is bound to follow the establishment of Economic and Monetary Union (EMU), arguing that this is impossible in the case of women in the south due to their particular role in the family and in regional labour markets. She uses data from a four-country research project (on Marche, Catalunya, Lisboa and Anatoliki Makedonia) to show that women of the south will bear the cost of EMU *in situ*, where they are already disadvantaged by the fact that they live in the less developed regions of the EU. Vaiou concludes that the unequal terms of integration for women are not a matter of "bad" or unfortunate policies that can be corrected by piecemeal reform; they are structural features of uneven development in which winners and losers are mutually determined.

In Chapter 4 Pugliese addresses the question of international migration and focuses on those European states which until 1975–80 could still consider themselves as source countries, namely Italy, Spain, Greece and Portugal. He uses the well-known metaphor of a "European fortress" to highlight the designation of new barriers which have been set up to defend the "civilised world" from the "new barbarians" (for instance, the Schengen agreement). Pugliese considers immigrants as part of the "new poor" and as forming the marginal workforce *par excellence*. For immigrants, insecure employment and racial and ethnic discrimination form the structural bases for their social marginality. In the past, immigration to an industrial society meant not only working in a factory, but also being part of the working class and of industrial conflict; to change from rural to urban/industrial life. Today, new immigrants are located in precarious, unprotected jobs in regions with both high and low unemployment, with both a rural and industrial specialisation. He concludes that chances of upward mobility for migrants are more limited than before, while the establishment of defence mechanisms against forms of exploitation and poor working conditions is even more difficult.

The theme of foreign immigrants settled in a major urban centre is discussed also in Chapter 5 by Kesteloot. He writes about guestworker neighbourhoods in Brussels which are concentrated in the inner city, abandoned by the Belgian population. Such ethnic neighbourhoods are places where informal economic activities developed since the late 1980s, in a pattern similar to that found elsewhere, for instance in New York, London, Chicago or Los Angeles. Networks of informal work are already well structured in these places and became an important human resource for the development of a flexible economy. Brussels being a tertiary city, flexible working practices were typically found in relatively low-paid office work, such as printing, copying, mailing services and security. Kesteloot describes the structural necessity of this type of work for the operation of the Brussels economy of commercial administration and national and supranational government. Thus, a few kilometres away from the office of the President of the Commission of the EU, the new European order seems to be dependent on the reproduction of a marginal foreign population, the equal rights of whom are not yet recognised by the EU.

The final chapter of this part, by Robins and Aksoy (Chapter 6), offers a general critique of exclusion practices, focusing on the question of culture. They argue that what motivates European identity is a desire to exclude non-Europeans, who are "brutes" compared to the "civilised and demo-cratic" refinement which is proper to Europe. Linking their discussion with foreign immigrants, they make a distinction between "citizenship-in-Europe" and "citizenship-for-Europeans". Robins and Aksoy use the case of Bosnia to address the issue of religion as a major criterion for exclusion, Islam and Christian Orthodoxy constituting the "other" that cannot belong to the essential Europe. They conclude by suggesting that what is at issue is the way in which the establishment of a European Union is at the same time constructing the cultural marginality and peripherality of those who are excluded. The mystification of origins, the xenophobia and the racism that have been characteristic of nationalistic sentiments, must be examined closely in this production of culture.

The third part of the book focuses on capital, labour and state policies, and starts with Chapter 7 by Oksa, who discusses social and spatial marginality in remote villages of the far north, in Finland. He identifies marginalisation as entailing a lack of resources for social mobility, becoming cut off from meaningful social contacts, or being excluded from policy-making processes. Remote and rural location has strengthened all these mechanisms and local people have tried to find ways to cope with them. One of these, Oksa describes, is the formation of telecottages, the introduction of new infrastructures based on information technology. Through these new telematic mechanisms, local people are fighting against marginalisation by increasing urban–rural interaction in new ways.

The Finnish case is in sharp contrast with rural southern Europe. While in the former farmers and other people enjoy relatively high incomes (compared to European agriculture as a whole), high levels of mechanisation, and efficient and adequate welfare services (even paid holidays for farmers!), in the latter, as discussed by Gaspar and Vaiou, the majority of farmers (and especially women) are still very poor, fighting for basic amenities and for their survival as farmers. These differences show clearly the contextual value of the concept of marginalisation and its different use in various moments and places.

Gaspar (Chapter 8) deals explicitly with infrastructure as means to decrease or increase marginality. He discusses European high-speed train and natural gas networks, and indicates that the main winners will be the principal urban agglomerations, which will experience both relative and absolute improvements to their competitive position. In the regional context of the Iberian peninsula, this is clearly to the disadvantage even of Portugal's most densely populated areas. Inside Portugal the same pattern is particularly clear in the settlement system: there is a reinforcement of the urban network of main towns at the expense of remote rural areas in the interior. He concludes that the most peripheral regions of Europe — in Ireland, Greece, the Iberian peninsula and southern Italy — tend to maintain their relative infrastructural deficit. This means a loss of opportunities and greater disadvantage compared to more developed regions.

Questions of marginality are not confined to rural areas, however. Chapter 9 by Sadler deals with structural changes in the organisation of capital and labour, and policy issues, in Europe's old industrial places and regions. These are districts where the adverse impacts of international competition (in sectors such as coal-mining, steel production and shipbuilding) have been felt most sharply. He uses the example of north-east England to describe processes of more general, shared significance, particularly with respect to the limits to state policies of reindustrialisation. His argument is that rather than reduce inequality, such policies reproduce it in different ways. Low-order service sector growth, expanded use of part-time and low-paid work (especially by women), and insecure new small business formation, are the most important consequences in terms of labour market restructuring, rather than the more high-profile image of new inward investment. Like several other contributors, Sadler concludes that the reproduction of marginality is not a historical accident, but a structurally related outcome of particular economic conditions and political choices.

A similar view of a different problem is presented by Allen and Henry in Chapter 10 on contract labour in south-east England. The other side of growth in London (based on highly dynamic, technologically advanced sectors such as international finance and commerce) is the expansion of low-wage, unstable manufacturing and service sector activities. They discuss the "down side" of growth in contract services such as cleaning, catering, delivery and security. In this respect their chapter deals with similar issues to Kesteloot's on Brussels. They argue that the marginal status of contract labour depends mainly on the social representation of skills. Abilities required to do certain jobs are undervalued, while the exchange value of such work is denied. They conclude that the adoption of a low-wage strategy in some sectors enables others to achieve a competitive advantage in the UK as a whole.

The last chapter of Part III deals with urban problems. In Chapter 11 van Weesep focuses on one particular aspect of marginality in three western European countries: the quality of guestworker housing. He compares and evaluates the housing systems in the Netherlands, Germany and Switzerland in relation to guestworker demands and those of the indigenous low-income population. The housing systems differ markedly among the three countries: in the Netherlands a vast social rental sector exists, whereas the Swiss system is market-driven. German housing lies somewhere between these two extremes. This situation influences the housing position of guestworkers, which is worst in Switzerland (where due to temporary stay restrictions it is difficult to improve their housing situation), better in Holland (where they occupy social housing left by local people) and somewhere in between in Germany (where they are facing competition from other underprivileged newcomers). He concludes that in all three countries indices of social and spatial segregation are increasing, but still these are not (yet?) as high as in the USA.

In Part IV, Pickvance (Chapter 12) addresses the important issue of social agency and its links to processes of marginalisation. He uses the case of urban movements to show that their image as representing the deprived, the underprivileged, the "underclass" is a long way from reality. There is no mechanical and automatic relation between social and spatial marginality and mobilisation or unrest. He makes the point that urban movements are not to be defined in terms of the social or spatial marginality of their members, but in terms of the "marginality" of their political form. Political exclusion of the marginalised takes place both from formal politics and from urban movements. In explaining the rise and fall of urban movements, Pickvance examines deprivation theory, consensus mobilisation theory, class theory and protest mobilisation theory. He concludes that there is no evidence that those experiencing the most deprivation, or at the lowest level of a class hierarchy, will be the most likely to take part in urban movements.

Bailly and Weiss-Altaner (Chapter 13) provide an elaborated account of the different uses of the marginality concept, bringing together the etymology of the term and its historical use. They point out that marginality evokes the geometric metaphor of centre and periphery, but argue against marginality's use as an economic and social dimension at a specific location. They propose a look inside and outside the social group, inside and outside the region. In so doing, they review the concepts of periphery and minority in relation to marginality from liberal and Marxist/radical viewpoints. Finally, in their conclusions they explore the wider use of the concept in a new era of international and supranational spaces.

Such issues are taken further by Hadjimichalis and Sadler in their final comments in Chapter 14, which summarise the emergent new mosaic of uneven development described in this book. We also conclude with some open questions for further investigation, reinforcing the point that this collection is intended to open up issues and to pose difficult questions, rather than to provide any definitive answers.

REFERENCES

Amin, A. and Thrift, N. (eds) (1994) *Globalization, institutions and regional development in Europe*, Oxford University Press.
Amin, S. (1989) *Eurocentrism*, Zed Books, London.
Castells, M. (1983) *The city and the grassroots*, Edward Arnold, London.
DESAL (1969) *La marginalidad urbana: processo y modo*, Santiago de Chile.
Jacquier, C. (1992) Le développement social urbain, *Les Temps Modernes*, no. 545–546 Jan, 165–179.
Jazouli, A. (1992) *Les années banlieues*, Seuil, Paris.
Lipietz, A. (1993) Social Europe, legitimate Europe: the inner and outer boundaries of Europe, *Environment and Planning D: Society and Space*, 11, 501–512.
Mayo, E. (1989) Europe against the world, *Marxism Today*, April, 11.
Perlman, J. (1979) *The myth of marginality*, University of California Press, Berkeley.
Shields, R. (1991) *Places on the margin: alternative geographies of modernity*, Routledge, London.
Zehraoui, A. (1992) Les cités des banlieues, *Les Temps Modernes*, no. 545–546 Jan, 209–215.

2 New Aspects of Marginality in Europe

ENZO MINGIONE
University of Messina, Italy

INTRODUCTION

Industrial capitalist societies are characterised by both heightened forms of social mobility and persistent social inequalities. Poverty and marginality are terms used to define those sectors of society that find themselves in serious difficulties (whether permanently or only temporarily), as compared with the conditions and life-chances of the majority of the population. Even at this very general level, considerable complications arise in three theoretical–methodological areas. The evaluation of whether a situation presents a greater or lesser difficulty is grounded in the assumption that modernisation also implies increasing individualism. It is indeed true that contemporary societies are based on increasing levels of individual responsibility for one's own destiny; however, this trend cannot be separated from the widely diversified social contexts in which all individuals act. Secondly, poverty and marginality are evaluated according to parameters that are historically and socially relative and, on the whole, arbitrary; this is so above all because they necessarily exclude any deeper consideration of the qualitative contexts in which different social subjects and groups are situated. Thirdly, the importance of these phenomena is linked to processes of social mobility within long time spans, difficult phases, life cycles and intergenerational transformations, while lines of research are able to discern only static conditions.

As will be seen in the rest of this chapter, the background against which processes of pauperisation are presently developing has changed compared with the typical scenario of industrial development, in which the fate of various social groups was tied to deruralisation and growing employment in a strongly expanding and progressively more concentrated and centralised manufacturing sector. For more than a century the debate on poverty centred on two dominant fronts: the backward rural or dependent growth contexts marking the destiny of subjects not as yet or insufficiently incorporated into the processes of industrial growth; and that of the

Europe at the Margins: New Mosaics of Inequality. Edited by Costis Hadjimichalis and David Sadler
© 1995 European Science Foundation. Published in 1995 by John Wiley & Sons Ltd

working class, that is, subjects overexposed to processes of commodification and poorly protected by the development of welfare systems.

Today the question is rendered complicated above all by changes occurring in employment systems, by structural decline in manufacturing/ industrial jobs even during phases of economic growth (which are increasingly based on capital-intensive investment), and by expansion of differentiated and polarised employment in services. Furthermore, the opportunities open to individuals and their life paths are complemented in diverse ways by welfare systems subjected to enormous strains by a persistent fiscal crisis and the complexity of the needs and interests of more complex societies, as well as by systems of primary sociality — family, community, kinship — that are increasingly fragmented and heterogeneous.

Finally, processes of marginalisation and, more generally, those of social mobility are set within a very uncertain framework, their prospects are difficult to manage and they are characterised by a multifactorial dynamic. From this standpoint, the use of the term "social exclusion" has become established, especially among EU experts, for defining the process of marginalisation as a phenomenon in which the disadvantages of a lack of access to tenured employment, social assistance and protection, education and health rights, and (sometimes) housing, cumulate. The end result is serious discrimination and a widening area of failed social integration. Even without using this term, which is in turn problematical given that it is centred on the concept of integration as formulated by the functionalist school, it is important to point out that this is precisely the "new" context in which the problem of social marginalisation in Europe is set.

THE ORIGINS OF TRENDS TOWARDS MARGINALISATION IN EUROPE

In order to understand the new forms of marginalisation in contemporary Europe, we must look at some important transformations which began in the late 1960s. The crisis of corporative-welfare strategies may be seen as one of the main signs of the present transitional phase, in which tension has been building up between the regulatory structure that matured during the Fordist era, characterised by growing importance of interest groups and associative organisations, and the new fragmented features of current societies (Mingione, 1991). Local, ethnic and subnational attachments are challenging the social order everywhere, but to a varying extent and in different ways, depending on the particular variant at work and on the specific fragmentation patterns shaping each society. The present legitimation crisis is affecting social systems that are decreasingly characterised by conflict and unable to change radically, while at the same time locked into slow processes of deterioration. These changes are also giving rise to new processes of pauperisation, to which both the economic and the political wings of the establishment are finding it difficult (or are even unwilling) to respond.

There are at least three major areas in which the present transitional phase is producing important socio-economic tensions:

1. The employment structure is moving towards a fragmented polaris- ation between high-income and low-income forms of paid employment. The possible consequences of this transformation differ depending on the modes of social integration of the emerging forms of the division of labour (we shall come back to this below).

2. The reshaping of welfare systems is a consequence of the increasing complexity of current societies and of the political instability induced by the decreasing capacity to govern this new complexity by means of the associative political order that matured within the system of national democracies as definitively consolidated in the Fordist– welfarist age.

3. The contradictions between present trends towards a new more radical phase of globalisation and the increasing importance of local, sectional and particularistic interests, on the one side, and the nation-bounded regulatory system with monopolistic access to political power but facing declining efficacy of socio-economic regulation, on the other.

The reciprocity-based side of social mixes has become more important and more visible. Models of industrial development are generally evaluated by looking at macro-indicators for, on the one hand, levels of official employment, wages and productivity of labour and, on the other, the welfare system. This leads to the idea that the family wage of the male breadwinner, complemented by welfare services and possibly supplemen- ted by secondary incomes of women, is all that has to be taken into account in order to understand the life strategies of different social groups. Social reality, however, has always been more complicated in that it is shaped by the different *modes of social integration* of an extremely varied division of labour and by the long-term, often intergenerational, mobility strategies of families in which resources and property may or may not be pooled and invested, leading to highly diversified outcomes and behaviour options. It is the fact that the very pillars on which Fordist social systems rest (that is rising tenured and standardised employment in large manufacturing firms and quasi-universalistic state welfare programmes) are gradually crumbling that makes the present situation so difficult to grasp in its entirety. This is particularly true with regard to marginalis- ation, where the combination of access to expanding tenured family-wage employment for adult male breadwinners with work-related social security and welfare provisions has constituted the bulwark against pauperisation for almost a century. Let us briefly see how transformations in employment, welfare and national regulatory systems are both setting in motion and affecting new marginalisation trends.

While remaining extremely uneven across countries and regions, the European employment system has changed substantially in the last two decades along two major structural lines: the decline of manufacturing employment in medium-sized and large concerns and the increase in a diversified range of service jobs. This transformation has given rise to three major consequences in terms of social marginalisation trends: direct loss of jobs; difficult entry into employment for young people and females; and an increasing number of individuals in poorly tenured and low-paid employment, not earning sufficient to support a family and a life strategy. These three consequences are unequally distributed across regions, local areas and social groups and, taken together, they outline a complicated map of social disadvantage.

Job losses in manufacturing and building have hit traditional male breadwinners everywhere, but disproportionately in some older industrial regions, starting with the Midlands in the UK, northern Germany and in particular the Ruhr basin, northern France, parts of Belgium and the Netherlands, and, more recently, north-western Italy. In some cases, the impact has inevitably been severe given the totally inadequate compensatory effects of new welfare measures (mainly retraining and re-employment schemes aimed at preventing long-term unemployment or occupational downgrading) and of the expansion in advanced service employment. Deindustrialisation has also had devastating consequences in some less developed regions, like southern Italy, where it comes on top of chronic economic problems.

The extremely heterogeneous range of new service jobs has created difficulties everywhere for new entrants into the job market, be they school-leavers or married women. The new jobs have proved inadequate both in quantitative and, even more so, qualitative terms for absorbing large numbers of potentially new workers. Job-search time has lengthened considerably, particularly for subjects with poor schooling or professional qualifications in need of a sufficiently tenured and well-paid job in order to maintain a family, whether partially or totally. Alternatively, these subjects are forced to accept a poorly paid provisional job, which is often informal and degrading, and risk remaining on the margins of official employment for the rest of their lives. A large number of poorly paid untenured jobs which are unacceptable to the local population attract new waves of migrants from underdeveloped countries, even to the traditionally out-migrating countries of southern Europe. This further complicates the picture of the marginalisation of work in Europe: what we now have is an unprecedented mix of long-term unemployed subjects in and out of inadequate forms of employment and migrants scattered throughout a variety of poorly paid untenured jobs in services, unlike their predecessors who filled the growing number of building, mining and manufacturing jobs (see also Pugliese, Chapter 4 this volume).

The new service-based regime of employment is extremely varied and selective. It lengthens the period of entry, making it more complicated for all subjects. A working career consists of several attempts at finding regular employment rather than slotting immediately into a tenured occupation. During the entry phase, any of life's typical accidents can render a person extremely vulnerable to marginalisation and downgrading, particularly in the case of weak subjects trapped in run-down areas. What is worse, however, is that this state of affairs leaves an increasing number of workers in forms of employment which are inadequate to support an autonomous life strategy. Furthermore, when these conditions are concentrated within specific regions or social groups and neither family, kinship and community arrangements nor state welfare programmes are able to reintegrate these subjects socially, marginalisation is the unavoidable outcome.

Transformations in employment have a particularly negative effect in regions characterised either by deindustrialisation or by a weak, more dependent industrial history, like southern Europe, Ireland, and eastern Germany. They have a devasting impact on people who cannot find a viable match between work and life strategies, for many reasons relating to both aspects, in more complex systems of social integration of heterogeneous employment positions. The increasingly wide variety of typologies of marginalisation is a further cause of difficulty, particularly from the point of view of social policies, where it is no longer viable to select just a few important areas for intervention.

This consideration leads immediately on to one of the problems besetting current welfare systems. Increasing complexity and the persistence of various forms of fiscal crisis may be considered the dominant parameters for the restructuring of welfare. Privatisation, in a variety of styles and forms, has been the most common, if not the only, response to crisis. It has progressively played down the universalistic philosophy of welfare state intervention without really solving new problems posed by the increasing pluralism of demands and scarcity of public resources. Existing welfare systems, more or less privatised depending on the country in question, are neither more efficient nor less expensive for their citizens, but they are certainly more patchy and less subject to public control than they used to be in the 1970s. Any attempt at responding to emerging problems encounters difficulty, suffocated as it is by tight budgetary restrictions and fierce competition from other, equally urgent and deserving, demands. Under these conditions the risks of marginalisation increase, particularly for social groups which have hardly any voice in society and even more for individual drop-outs who are totally neglected by public opinion until they become a problem of social order and, consequently, a target for repression rather than for other kinds of social policy.

European countries have responded in different ways to the welfare crisis, even if an emphasis on privatisation has been the most common reaction. The Single Internal Market, the Maastricht Treaty and the Social Charter of the Eleven will not substantially alter this trend. A common European social policy is likely to remain a marginal and "subsidiary" feature, and a homogenising trend towards optimal quality levels is extremely unlikely because of high costs and budgetary restrictions. In the meantime, growing internal competition and tighter EU control on member states' financial and fiscal policies is bound to restrict further the capacity for preventive intervention on the part of both nation states and local authorities. I shall return to this point later, when speaking specifically of the prospects for a unified European market in connection with the social conditions of disadvantaged groups.

Economic and cultural globalisation trends, the construction of multinational institutions (in this case chiefly the EU), and even more the persistent re-emergence of particularistic loyalties are reshaping the reality of social identity and citizenship. It is difficult for members of Western societies, socialised in the "conceptual order" of national capitalism where a country coincides with a society, an economy, an anthropological profile, to understand fully the destabilising impact of this transformation. Our image of the future is too often based on fantasies about a more or less remote past, but the reality will be unimaginably different. In order to have a vague idea of what is happening we must start from the assumption that the nation state constitutes the crucial stress point of the present transition.

From this perspective, it can be seen that emergent tensions are due to the fading away of the socio-economic project which underpinned national capitalist societies while, at the same time, its ensuing political form (nation state plus representative democracy and very limited political partici-pation) is still resisting in the guise of a historically unsurpassed form of élite formation, the articulation of power and the policy-making process. Nevertheless, the falling away of the socio-economic basis for the project is far from unproblematic. It is instead leading to the spread of tensions and contradictions.

The fact that an essential part of the socialisation process takes place within particular institutions (like the family) and is based on a well-defined transmission of local values, tastes and know-how needs to be reconsidered carefully. Modernisation has increased the range of communi-cation, information and geographical mobility. It has produced a certain degree of standardisation in consumption and working behaviour and permitted associations of similar social and economic interests well beyond the range of frequent face-to-face interaction. During a long phase of industrial history, this has greatly fostered the national level of identity formation and, more recently, the growing impact of its multinational and global levels; but it has never entailed a drastic attenuation, let alone the disappearance, of the local side to social identity formation. There is a strong impression that at present, as a result of globalisation trends, the particularistic features of social identity formation are being transformed in two opposite directions. On the one hand, they are weakened by the further impulse of globalisation (Bonanno et al., 1994) and by a new wave of standardisation which is, however, characterised by a high range of diversity of the kind that, for example, is controlled by flexible capitalist relations rather than by local traditions. On the other hand, the decline of the regulatory institutions in nation states may possibly bring about increasing opportunities to enhance the importance of the particularistic scale of social identity. The outcomes of current transformation tendencies reflect an increasingly complicated patchwork where globalisation is accompanied by the erosion of the socio-economic importance of the nation state, in contrast with its continued political centrality, and by a complex revival of new and old, conflicting particularistic fragments of identities (ethnic, linguistic, religious, communitarian).

Returning to the specific question of marginalisation trends, two points must be emphasised in particular. Social drop-outs and members of primary solidarity groupings who are particularly weak subjects are bound to find themselves in serious difficulty. The decline of the state's capacity to intervene on a universalistic scale will further penalise them. This picture calls to mind the idea of the two-thirds–one-third society, where the disadvantaged third is a derelict and forgotten stratum with no political voice, which sinks into a state of "subcitizenship". Our image of them is that of the beggars of the past, but they will be different. We do not as yet know how different.

SOCIAL INTEGRATION AND MARGINALISATION TRENDS IN CONTEMPORARY EUROPE

As indicated above, marginalisation trends are not mechanically connected to particular conditions affecting individuals, like unemployment, insufficient income and chronic forms of illness or handicap, but largely depend on the different systems of social integration that have come about in various parts of Europe. The crucial interconnected areas which it is important to discuss here are welfare systems and family and community support. I shall try in this section to outline the relationships between different systems of social integration and new marginalisation trends. My starting-point is the typology of "welfare capitalism" put forward by Esping-Andersen (1990), which I have reformulated in order to take into account both inter-European diversities and, specifically, the problems posed by new trends of marginalisation.

With the exception of Denmark (the Scandinavian model) and the UK (probably closer to the US model of pronounced individualisation and high exposure to market forces), all the European cases may be considered as variants of the German model of welfare capitalism, based on a persistent complementarity of state and family responsibility in providing for social integration and welfare. In the German model, two lines of division can be traced which produce four approximate subtypologies, depending on whether state intervention has traditionally been stronger (Germany, France and Benelux) or weaker (Italy, Spain, Portugal, Ireland and Greece) and whether households have been more (Baden-Württemburg, First and Third Italy, Catalonia, Rhône-Alpes) or less (northern Germany, the Parisian region, the Mezzogiorno, Andalusia) oriented towards the inno-vative family business. Starting from these assumptions, we already have six different typologies of social integration system for coping with new marginalisation trends in different ways and with different resources within the EU alone: the UK, Denmark, and the four variants of the German model of welfare capitalism. I shall look briefly at each of these with the limited aim of underlining the specific difficulties encountered in dealing with new marginalisation trends. To conclude, I shall make some overall observations on the role of the Single Internal Market and of the EU in the face of persistently diversified European systems of social integration in terms of social policies for combating poverty and social exclusion.

From the Esping-Andersen standpoint, the case of the UK may be considered a variant of the American model, not because of the lack of a welfare tradition, but because early radical deruralisation has, more than in any other case, weakened consanguinity relations and the economic importance of the family business and self-employment,[1] leaving indi-viduals vulnerable to labour market conditions as specifically comple-mented by welfare arrangements. New and strong tensions have resulted from a sharp decline in tenured employment for male breadwinners in manufacturing, particularly concentrated in the older industrial districts of the Midlands (Massey and Meegan, 1982), in combination with a con-siderable increase in the numbers of women working for a wage, though disproportionately in part-time and relatively poorly paid employment (Gallie, 1988), and with the wave of privatisation and "welfare disman-tling" reforms of the Thatcher governments. A set of social arrangements based on the combination of the family wage provided by the adult male breadwinner, the secondary complementary income of his partner and/or young adult children and state welfare provision has been undermined (on the side of the adult male family income) and further eroded by the concomitant possibility of women having to give up their part-time employment[2] and by government steps to dismantle welfare provisions.

As noted by some authors (Pahl, 1984, 1988; Morris, 1988, 1990), these transformations have led to a serious polarisation between work-rich and work-poor families, with the consequence that the latter find themselves in great difficulties, especially if socially isolated in regions more severely hit by deindustrialisation or belonging to a discriminated ethnic minority. In this last case, the social conditions are more disadvantageous for groups where kinship relations are weaker and there is a lack of orientation towards the family business (for instance, West Indians as against Asians). The crucial problem in the case of the UK arises from the fact that tensions produced by growth in new forms of the social division of labour, promoted by the expansion of the service-based regime of employment (Mingione, 1991; Sayer and Walker, 1992; Sassen, 1991; Fainstein et al., 1992), are rather poorly absorbed at the social level by family and community networks and by state welfare programmes. More than in other advanced industrial countries — also because of the radical nature of deindustrialisation — new social tensions are leading in the UK towards a two-thirds society where the marginalised one-third is the victim of labour-market disadvantages and social isolation, and has no voice in the political–institutional system.

The case of Denmark will be dealt with briefly and only with reference to what Esping-Andersen (1990) considered the most relevant difficulties besetting the Scandinavian model of welfare capitalism in the transition to a post-Fordist age. On the one side, what we have here is an amplified version of the fiscal crisis of the welfare state. The tax burden is already high and cannot be increased further to meet new needs deriving from expansion of the service regime of employment. The necessity to use public welfare programmes to cope with rising unemployment, increasingly diversified forms of flexible employment, the need for frequent retraining of workers and many other problems are overloading the welfare agenda at a time when room for manœuvre at the fiscal level is already very limited. On the other side, an increasing number and range of household typologies, particularly those headed by poorly educated and inadequately qualified workers (especially if they are women or recent immigrants with large families) require support and financial resources from the welfare state. If the fiscal crisis and/or the economic restrictions imposed by the Single Internal Market substantially modify the traditional Scandinavian capacity to respond to these tensions, new marginalisation tensions may very well break out.

The four variants of the German model of welfare capitalism are all based on the fact that the consanguinity facet of the family system has remained more important in terms of welfare provision and, consequently, of conditioning the life strategies of individuals and supporting and protecting weak subjects. This path of development is rooted in complex historical conditions that cannot be fully reconstructed here. The persistent diffusion of family farming and of the worker-peasant phenomenon (Villa, 1986) and, more generally, of the micro-family business and self-employment both in traditional and in innovative branches of the economy have certainly been among the crucial factors. It is a more or less typical feature of latecomer industrialisation and has become greatly revitalised as a precondition for relative economic success in the post-Fordist age, but only in cases where the family business or self-employment has retained innovative economic capacity and a sufficient degree of autonomy from processes of full proletarianisation or the expanding welfare-related redistribution of public resources (Bagnasco, 1977; Piore and Sabel, 1984). In the German model, public welfare systems have favoured the persistence of this feature in various ways, according to the different national case histories of development. One major way has been to expand monetary transfers to households and forms of protection of the family business against capitalist concentration and full proletarianisation to a relatively greater extent than in other models.

This has produced a parallel effect of, to some extent, discouraging married women from seeking paid employment outside the family concern: in all the variants of the model the activity rate of women remains, on average, 20% below that recorded in the American model (with more diffused marketable services) and in the Scandinavian model (with greater public provision of services). Some services have not been fully developed and a part of the burden/responsibility for looking after weak subjects — children, the sick, the handicapped, the elderly — is still borne by the family system (possibly compensated by monetary transfers). This burden falls nearly exclusively on adult women, both full-time housewives and those in employment.[3] These general characteristics have developed in different ways depending on the combination of two crucial factors: the presence or absence of a strong, well-organised and professionalised state and the more or less innovative and autonomous economic vocation of the family business.

The variant with a strong state and innovative family business has proved relatively able to face up to the post-Fordist transition and minimise exposure to marginalisation trends. The organised intervention of the state (in terms of retraining, unemployment schemes, a fixed minimum income, partial aid to households in difficulties) has favoured a higher degree of adaptation to the more flexible, fragmented and uneven labour market. It is chiefly the innovative vocation of the family business which has prevented social polarisation and the concentration of unfavourable conditions in discriminated social groups, mainly by promoting flexible arrangements and inter-household redistribution of resources between stronger and weaker subjects. A strong state is crucially important for supporting those subjects that fall into extremely and persistently difficult circumstances, either in the labour market (because of a poor level of skills and qualifications, or uneasy acceptance of work discipline) or in the household (whether socially isolated or critically overburdened with problems). The targeting by the state of specific areas for intervention has had the effect of dampening fiscal crisis, at least up to the moment when other difficulties have rekindled it, as in the case of Germany with the contemporary overlapping of the burden of the enormous social and economic costs of integrating the former GDR and the increasing problems produced by deindustrialisation in the north, where family businesses are less dynamic and responsive to the decline in wage income, alongside other problems in the south.

The variant based on a strong state and a less innovative family business has to face up to the possibility that the specialisation of welfare programmes might become, at the same time, both too expensive and insufficient to support adequately that part of the population hit by a serious deindustrialisation crisis in a fully proletarianised environment, where working-class households have little adaptive and sheltering capacity beyond their reliance on monetary incomes. Here, marginalisation trends prove more difficult to resist than in the previous case for the very reason that households and kinship networks have less resources with which to stimulate new advanced service economies and, as a consequence, are less able to integrate socially in the increasing fragmentation of the labour market. Emerging difficulties are reflected not so much in social polarisation (as in the UK) or in a general cost–welfare tension (as in the Scandinavian model) but rather in the fact that sections of the marginalised population, usually young individuals or families with poor occupational qualifications, slip through the fingers of welfare–family arrangements. This also implies increasing interregional tensions, particularly when the two variants characterised by more or less entrepreneurial family businesses are found within the same country where, by and large, the German model of welfare capitalism has been adopted. As family resources are highly diversified and the welfare state has developed a more specialised vocation for forms of emergency or complementary intervention, the competition for public welfare resources has become fierce and geographically divisive, particularly when less disadvantaged regions feel the heavy strain of supporting the more disadvantaged ones without any form of recompensation. This phenomenon is increasingly visible in the Italian case (Mingione, 1993) but could easily be extended to other countries, beginning with Germany.

The variant characterised by a weak state and dynamic innovative family strategies has also been able to deal relatively successfully with post-Fordist transition, at least until the recent worsening of the economic crisis. In many cases (for example northern Italy and Catalonia), the fact that public welfare provisions have not been particularly efficient has been compensated for in the short run by a higher rate of growth of flexible businesses in advanced services and by the development of local networks. The labour market has remained tight and family strategies have in general proved able to "micro-redistribute" the advantages and disadvantages of a less stable and increasingly heterogeneous employment structure.

However, in the medium term, this variant may have to pay the costs of the relatively low quality of some crucial welfare services, above all in education, professional training, labour market information, health and transport. Only in some cases, and only partially, have local authorities been able to compensate for the inefficiency of central state provision, as in the Emilia Romagna region (Capecchi, 1989). Hence, the prospect of an acceleration of deindustrialisation and a progressive extension of economic difficulties to a large area of micro-firms is real and very worrying. Moreover, we are speaking of regions which are all parts of countries that are already in trouble because of the negative impact of the post-Fordist transition in other regions where the family business is less dynamic and family strategies depend heavily on state monetary transfers.

The marginalisation syndrome in the fourth variant is a striking phenomenon, especially in the case of southern Italy, which offers a clearer picture of the typology than other less developed regions of Europe.[4] Mass youth unemployment, the large-scale diffusion of variegated forms of irregular and precarious employment,[5] high rates of urban poverty (Mingione and Morlicchio, 1993) and, in many cases, the persistence of rural poverty are among the main features of this syndrome. The traditional forms of intervention practised by weak states are under very heavy pressure and even risk extinction. They vary from country to country but are everywhere fundamentally based on income-support transfers in the hands of a patronage-oriented political élite. They are increasingly insufficient to prevent the pauperisation of a large part of the population, often viewed as an unfavourable alternative to economic policies designed to promote economic development, but at the same time considered necessary to ensure survival in the short run and to keep the less developed regions under political control. As already mentioned, this fact constitutes a very serious cause of political tension within Italy, and it may well extend to other countries. It will also be difficult to avoid the disaggregative potential in this situation from sooner or later involving the EU itself. We are not only talking of a Europe at two or more speeds — something which already exists and merely lacks official recognition — but rather of widely divergent socio-political perspectives that are increasingly incompatible with one another. In other words, economic integration accompanied by social and political disintegration, which up until a few years ago would have been considered an unmentionable heresy, is becoming a frightening possibility.

THE CHALLENGE OF SOCIAL MARGINALITY AND THE FUTURE OF EUROPE

The last point discussed above makes it necessary for us to look, at least briefly, at European social policies for dealing with poverty, marginalisation and uneven development. It is important to remember that, up to now, the EU has never claimed it has the power to put social policies into practice independently of individual member states, or displayed any serious intention of homogenising social policies as a further stage towards European integration. In fact, the "Structural Funds", the EU's major economic tools for implementing its redistribution programme, are under the control of member states while other minor programmes, like that to combat poverty, are intended as small-scale demonstration experiments, which, if successful, could at best be developed and expanded by member states or local authorities. EU officials and member state representatives stick to the line that any homogenisation of social policies cannot be part of the integration process since it would be too expensive, not realistically convenient and, even more importantly, interfere to an unacceptable degree with national sovereignty. Thus, the principle of the "subsidiarity" of European social policies, formulated by the British government, has now been accepted as the main strategic orientation of the EU. What this principle means is that the Union should limit itself only to interventions that cannot be achieved more effectively by individual member states or local authorities, without interfering *socially* with the welfare practices of its members.

Problems arise from the fact that both the constitution of the Single Internal Market, and the fiscal and economic restrictions and regulations imposed by the Union, strongly interfere with social policies, and so do — as I have emphasised — present transformations in employment and social structures. The weakening of national economic regulation, concomitant with new local tensions, is pushing the real prospect of economic integration with social disintegration to the forefront of the European agenda. The persistent financial storms that troubled the Community on the eve of the unified market may well be a sign that the matter needs to be reconsidered. On this question, I would like to develop some of the points raised above in a few final remarks that should be taken as a preliminary contribution to a wide-open debate.

Any discussion of the problems caused by social marginality in Europe must clearly remain within two common-sense boundaries. On the one side, there are the diverse traditional types of welfare capitalism which, as we have seen, are giving rise to different forms of marginality in different social contexts. Even if we are critical of the *laissez-faire* and "nationalistic" attitudes of European élites, this persistent and even increasing diversity must be taken into account. This does not mean that a homogenisation process is impossible, but rather that it should be based on different paths, welfare programmes and social protection schemes as required by local combinations of social arrangements and economic resources. On the other side, there is the general belief that economic integration together with social disintegration is hardly plausible. In other words, increasing divergence under conditions of social integration and the uncontrolled increase of various forms of marginality will seriously damage economic integration, starting with its political foundations.

The creation of the internal market may well be a necessary step in order to compete better on a global economic scale with other powerful blocs. It is also clear, however, that European economic integration *per se* is unable to create a large number of new jobs and is not counteracting the typical trends of the post-Fordist employment transformation. Therefore, we need to take into account the increasing difficulties faced by modes of social integration deriving from the uneven patterns of social and geographical redistribution of qualitatively diversified employment opportunities in different social contexts.

Deindustrialisation and the restructuring of manufacturing activities are continuing and will probably be intensified by further economic integration. The traditional industrial regions of central Europe will lose many manufacturing jobs, especially those less devastated by the first wave of deindustrialisation, like northern Italy, southern Germany and parts of France and Spain. Restructuring in the search for less costly and more flexible arrangements will "favour" the less developed regions of the Union only to a limited and selective extent, since new industrial investment is increasingly attracted to the east and to newly industrialising countries. Even the few regions benefiting from industrial relocation and new developments will face serious social difficulties in terms of the mode of social integration of a number of jobs which are too flexible to fit unproblematically into existing family and life strategies.

On the other hand, the further expansion on a continental scale of the service regime of employment will increase difficulties due to its geographical and social unevenness. In some globally important business and financial nodal points, particularly in southern Germany and large metropolitan cities, the expansion of advanced services will compensate for deindustrialisation but, at the same time, attract migrants from outside the EU to fill the worst working positions in personal and seasonal services and activities. These jobs are either strictly regulated and controlled, and end up becoming extremely expensive to maintain[6] or, alternatively, they cannot be filled permanently by either a local or a European migrant worker as their survival strategies are conditioned by inappropriate cost and cultural restrictions. As we have seen, this problem concerns all European social contexts to different extents. Outside the globally dynamic nodal points, however, the difficulties identified above will be aggravated by a combination of poor migrants in the worst service jobs and high rates of local unemployment and irregular employment. Conversely, the extension to every European region of a Scandinavian model of service provision (highly public and extensively regulated) appears unlikely due to both high costs and unfavourable socio-economic traditions (Flora, 1993), while severe and effective restrictions on immigration appear unrealistic on a continental scale given the present political situation. The uneven tripartition of the employment structure (the securely employed, the unemployed and irregularly employed, and Third World migrants in the worst jobs) is here to stay and requires a diversified policy on the part of the EU in order to prevent devastating social consequences. I shall return to this point in the concluding paragraph.

Some important patterns of socio-demographic transformation which cannot be fully analysed here for lack of space are worth at least mentioning. We have seen how householding processes, the mixes between conjugal and consanguineous family relations and various other reciprocity/community networks have continued to play a very important role in shaping the different models and variants of welfare capitalism. We must now take into consideration the impact of three consolidated changes in this complex area: the increased average length of life cycles, which raises the percentage of the elderly in the total population; the decline in the birth rate, which contracts the horizontal extension of consanguineous networks and, in combination with the previous factor, strengthens their vertical cohesion; and the increased instability and heterogeneity of conjugal life due to divorce, late marriages, the variety of cohabiting experiences and so on. The capacity of both the conjugal and con-sanguineous systems to provide support and social integration for weak social subjects has been seriously undermined. In the first case, new difficulties are immediately apparent: single-parent households, semi-abandoned children, and long-term socially isolated, unmarried or separated individuals are extremely vulnerable to marginalisation. At the same time, a more unstable conjugal system is less able to provide assistance to handicapped, drug-addicted, or mentally or chronically ill members. Even if less immediate,[7] the impact of the transformation of consanguineous systems is equally serious. Horizontal relations between siblings have up to now been one of the main factors fostering the adaptation of consanguineous relations in welfare societies that provide resources to look after the elderly and other weak subjects within a sufficiently large support network. The "verticalisation" of the system will certainly impoverish its supportive and networking capacity and, as a result, increase the demand for provision of welfare assistance from external social institutions, such as the welfare state, private associations, the market, and community organisations. It is also obvious that the impact of this transformation will be greater in the variants of the German model of welfare capitalism, where the consanguineous side of the family mix has remained more effective in supporting individual members in difficulties.[8]

In conclusion, economic integration accompanied by social disintegration would have a devastating effect. The EU needs urgently to reconsider the possibility of implementing a strategy of social intervention in at least three areas: immigration and regulation of the social conditions of work of immigrants; entry into paid employment and planning of working careers for young people within a less stable and more heterogeneous labour market; and provision of specialised aid in favour of subjects and households which suffer from particular forms of deprivation. This need not entail a homogenisation of social policies but, rather, paying careful attention to what are emerging as the most serious defects in the systems of social integration that have developed in the different European contexts, and providing for the redistribution of resources in order to ensure a minimum level of viability. In other words, one context may need more income support, another more public provision of some specialised services, and another a stricter regulation of some areas of employment. In a more economically integrated Europe, where the EU is imposing financial regulations and budgetary restrictions, the implementation of social policies cannot be left to the residual capacities of single member states or, even worse, to the limited capabilities of local authorities. On the contrary, it should be based on a process of negotiation and redistribution arising out of a consensus at the central Union level on the crucial importance of avoiding uncontrollable itineraries of social marginalisation. It is only this consensus which can act as a new springboard for building realistic forms of economic integration, which are not accompanied by devastating social disintegration.

NOTES

1. Recent research on the Italian case (Di Nicola, 1989; Mauri et al., 1992) confirms what was argued in the 1930s by the American anthropologist Linton (1936). He emphasised the superior capacity for support and adaptability of the consanguineous compared to the conjugal family, as the latter proves too limited and variable in order to face the increasingly heterogeneous difficulties to which weak members of the family, in particular children, the elderly, the handicapped or the chronically ill, are exposed for different reasons.

2. Both Pahl (1984, 1988) and Morris (1988, 1990) note that the lack of economic convenience of arrangements based on unemployment benefit for the breadwinner and income from secondary jobs (partially or totally deducted from the subsidy) has been one of the main factors promoting social polarisation, further amplified by the marginalisation of households hit by unemployment in terms of progressive isolation from social networks with sufficient resources to provide effective help.

3. These kinds of arrangement have a relevant impact both on the conditions of women and on the gender division of domestic work. As far as the latter is concerned, it usually proves more difficult to enter into negotiations for a partial reallocation of some of the burden to males, as the situation of women remains conditioned by a relatively high number of full-time housewives. It is not by chance that in these very contexts the debate on the "double presence" of women (in paid employment and in highly time-consuming domestic work) has been very intense (for the Italian case, see mainly Balbo, 1978, 1987, 1991; Bimbi 1977, 1986, 1991).

4. The Mezzogiorno offers a clearer picture of this typology, as it has been deeply conditioned by the patronage-oriented redistributive interventions of the state in terms of income support strategies (see Mingione, 1989, 1993).
5. This gives rise to an impressive combination of unemployment, underemployment and deregulated employment (see EEC, 1989).
6. As emphasised by Esping-Andersen (1990), the alternatives to a poorly regulated, but relatively cheap, service labour market (American model) are increasingly expensive, either in the case where services are mainly provided directly by the state (Scandinavian model) or in that where there is a highly regulated mixed economy (the variant of the German model characterised by a strong and efficient state).
7. The effects of a generation made up of a large group of single children born in the 1980s will be noticed only when they are in their forties and their parents are in their seventies (Lesthaeghe, 1991; Bimbi, 1991; Micheli, 1992). Moreover, due to delayed child-bearing, parents in this generation will be markedly older than in the case of previous generations.
8. The important role played by a consanguineous family system increasingly based on a strictly vertical intergenerational line, rather than on an extensive number of siblings, may eventually reduce the potential for geographical mobility. Recent surveys on the unemployed (IRES–CGLI, 1992) show that this is already occurring: the young unemployed will not accept a poorly paid job in a location which is outside the area of family and community support and where the social and economic costs of settling are too high and the loss of reciprocity support resources is not sufficiently compensated for by the prospect of a long-term monetary income.

REFERENCES

Bagnasco, A. (1977) Tre Italie: la problematica territoriale dello sviluppo italiano, Il Mulino, Bologna.
Balbo, L. (1978) La doppia presenza, Inchiesta, no. 32, 3–6.
Balbo, L. (ed.) (1987) Time to care. Politiche del tempo e diritti quotidiani, Angeli, Milan.
Balbo, L. (ed.) (1991) Tempi di vita, Feltrinelli, Milan.
Bimbi, F. (ed.) (1977) Dentro lo specchio, Mazzotta, Milan.
Bimbi, F. (1986) Lavoro domestico, economia informale, comunità, Inchiesta, no. 74, 20–24.
Bimbi, F. (1991) Doppia presenza, in Balbo, L. (1991) 56–62.
Bonanno, A. et al. (eds) (1994), The globalisation of the agricultural and food order, Kansas University Press, Lawrence, Kansas.
Capecchi, V. (1989) The informal economy and the development of flexible specialisation in Emilia-Romagna, in Portes, A. et al. (eds), The informal economy: studies in advanced and less developed countries, The Johns Hopkins University Press, Baltimore and London, 189–215.
Di Nicola, P. (1989) I mutamenti strutturali e culturali della famiglia in Emilia Romagna, in Donati, P. (ed.), Famiglia Anni '90. La condizione familiare in Emilia Romagna e i nodi della politica sociale, Morcelliana, Brescia.
EEC (1989) Underground economy and irregular forms of employment: synthesis report and country monographies, Brussels.
Esping-Andersen, G. (1990) The three worlds of welfare capitalism, Polity Press, Cambridge.
Fainstein, S., Gordon, I. and Harloe, M. (1992) Divided cities. New York and London in the contemporary world, Blackwell, Oxford.

Flora, P. (1993) Sozialstaat Europa, paper presented at 26th Deutscher Soziologentag, Düsseldorf, 28 Sept.–2 Oct. 1992.

Gallie, D. (ed.) (1988) *Employment in Britain*, Blackwell, Oxford.

IRES–CGIL (1992) *Caratteristiche e tipologia della disoccupazione in Italia: sperimentazione di strumenti di analisi e valutazione*, Ires, Rome.

Lesthaeghe, R. (1991) *The second demographic transition in Western countries: an interpretation*, IPD Working Paper, no. 2, Vrije Universiteit, Brussels.

Linton, R. (1936) *The study of man*, Appleton-Century-Crofts, New York.

Massey, D. and Meegan, R. (1982) *The anatomy of job loss: the how, why and where of employment decline*, Methuen, London.

Mauri, L., May, M.P., Micheli, G.A. and Zajczyk, F. (eds) (1992) *Vita di famiglia. Social survey in Veneto*, Angeli, Milan.

Micheli, G.A. (1992) La riproduzione sociale tramite la famiglia, in Mauri et al., pp. 35–78.

Mingione, E. (1989) Note per un'analisi delle classi sociali, in Catanzaro, R. (ed.), *Società, politica e cultura nel Mezzogiorno*, Angeli, Milan, pp. 43–77.

Mingione, E. (1991) *Fragmented societies. A sociology of economic life beyond the market paradigm*, Blackwell, Oxford.

Mingione, E. (1993) Regional inequalities and social identities: the case of Italy, *International Affairs*, **69**, 2, 305–18.

Mingione, E. and Morlicchio, E. (1993) New forms of urban poverty in Italy: risk path models in the North and South, *International Journal of Urban and Regional Research*, **173**, 3, 413–27.

Morris, L. (1988) Employment, the household and social networks, in Gallie, (ed.), *Employment in Britain*, Blackwell, Oxford, pp. 376–405.

Morris, L. (1990) *The workings of the household*, Polity Press, Oxford.

Pahl, R. (1984) *Divisions of labour*, Blackwell, Oxford.

Pahl, R.E. (1988) Some remarks on informal work, social polarisation and the social structure, *International Journal of Urban and Regional Research*, **12**, 2, 247–267.

Piore, M.J. and Sabel, C.F. (1984) *The second industrial divide: possibilities for prosperity*, Basic Books, New York.

Sassen, S. (1991) *The global city: New York, London, Tokyo*, Princeton University Press, Princeton, NJ.

Sayer, A. and Walker, R. (1992) *The new social economy*, Blackwell, Oxford.

Villa, P. (1986) *The structuring of labour markets*, Clarendon Press, Oxford.

Part II

GENDER, RACE, CULTURE

3 Women of the South after, like before, Maastricht?

DINA VAIOU
National Technical University, Athens, Greece

INTRODUCTION

The project of European integration has taken place since the end of the 1980s in a context of disintegration. War in the former Soviet republics and Yugoslavia, actual or threatened dismantling of states along ethnic or religious lines, rising nationalism and racism (to remain only in Europe): these are the downsides to integration in the European Union. The questions of "national frontiers" and of "territories" have re-emerged in (large parts of) Europe with renewed intensity. In this context, it seems that achievement of a "Europe without frontiers" is effected in contradictory ways: by introducing stronger restrictions in relation to the rest of Europe (outside the EU) and, at the same time, relaxing "borders" within the EU, so as to facilitate the free movement of capital, goods and people — but without quite removing barriers altogether.

The outer frontier, that which separates the EU from the rest of Europe, is held up (among other things) as a form of protection for the higher standards of living of those "within", on the basis of an argument that such standards would deteriorate if they were to be extended more broadly. Relaxing inner boundaries on the other hand creates and reinforces divisions between those who can move freely (and are therefore best placed to take advantage of the Single Market) and those who cannot. Marginalisation and poverty are not confined to areas beyond the outer frontier of the EU, but continue also to be the reality for large numbers inside it.

This chapter examines the prospects for women of the south in this project of selective integration, focusing on two interrelated themes. These are the notion of *social partnership*, heavily promoted by the EU in its recent documents and policies; and the idea that *increased mobility of people* (as well as of goods and capital) is bound to follow completion of Economic and Monetary Union (EMU) and the removal of customs barriers.

Europe at the Margins: New Mosaics of Inequality. Edited by Costis Hadjimichalis and David Sadler
© 1995 European Science Foundation. Published in 1995 by John Wiley & Sons Ltd

BEFORE (LIKE AFTER?) EUROPEAN INTEGRATION

The Maastricht Treaty brought again to the forefront of political and academic debate the fact that the economic benefits of a Single European Market will be very unequally distributed among regions and different social groups within the Union. It was for this reason that questions were raised about whether there should be two, three or or even more phases of integration. Southern Europe, to which this chapter refers, is one of the more disadvantaged areas, with the majority of its regions lagging significantly behind the EU mean on a number of important indices.[1] It is important to note here, however, that southern Europe is not a homogeneous entity. Even though many similarities do exist between different parts of the south, one cannot speak of a European south, especially if geographical and social inequalities within each country are taken into account.

Policies to ameliorate disparities have been developed, including restructuring of the European Structural Funds since 1989. As part of these measures, Action Programmes for Equality of Opportunities between men and women have been promoted. The goals of these programmes are broad and far reaching, but in practice they have been limited to developing a legislative framework for equality and supporting training schemes for women. Such initiatives maintain a partial focus on women-as-workers (or as unemployed), with a definition of (paid) work that does not correspond to the experience of work of the majority of women in the south.

In the EU as a whole, an important feature of recent decades is the growing participation of women in the labour force, reaching 40% in the mid-1980s. In northern European countries this has been accompanied by an increase in the number of part-time and temporary jobs and precarious contracts, mainly in the services where 67% of women's employment is concentrated (*Employment in Europe*, 1992). In southern Europe increasing participation rates of women are connected with the growth of self-employment and expansion of public services such as education, health and administration.

Women of the south are highly concentrated in the service sector, yet narrowly distributed in a few occupations, particularly sales persons, cleaners and caterers, primary-school teachers, secretaries and nurses. Trends for an increase in service employment offer prospects for growth in women's employment, but simultaneously reinforce tendencies for segregation into a handful of occupations. Women do not seem to have access to new jobs based on generalised use of new technologies. Rationalisation and modernisation in the service sector is a highly gendered process.

About one in four women works in industry, again in only a few branches (including textiles, clothing and footwear, toys, jewellery, food and tobacco processing). Practically all those branches face technical and administrative barriers (Conroy Jackson, 1990). Moreover they are highly concentrated in specific regions and in metropolitan areas. Thus macro-economic choices in the EU, in the context of competition with Third World countries, have a dramatic impact on women in areas with a productive structure based on such branches of production. Industrial policy is gendered too.

In agriculture, women's employment is concentrated in the more traditional and less mechanised crops (particularly olives, citrus and tobacco) where they cover over 50% of the hours of work per year. By contrast, women's contribution falls below 20% of the total hours of work in the cases of vegetable production in greenhouses and grain production. EU policies for restructuring Mediterranean agriculture affect women of the south more than men, because they are targeted at the traditional labour-intensive crops. The common agricultural policy is gendered as well.

A large part of women's work in the south, however, lies outside national and regional statistical measures. It is work that does not classify them as "economically active": for instance, agricultural labour in family farms, family helpers in small businesses, industrial homeworking, informal and/or temporary work in tourism, industry or personal services, and irregular work in the public sector or other areas of activity which employ a primarily female workforce.[2]

SOCIAL PARTNERS?

Women's involvement in "atypical" employment, and the terms of their integration in the formal labour market, place them a long way away from the image of "social partners" which is heavily promoted by the EU, and which is likely to be a continuing policy emphasis in the future. From the point of view of workers, the notion of "social partnership" presupposes formal labour relations and collective organisation through which rep-resentation will emerge. This picture has little to do with the work that women in the south engage in, which does not fall into this conceptual category, as will become clear from the discussion below.

The exact extent of atypical employment is impossible to assess, and relevant data have to be treated very cautiously. This is especially, but by no means exclusively, the case with respect to atypical employment that falls into the realm of "informal activities". These are, by definition, unrecorded.[3] The importance of atypical forms of employment is therefore usually assessed indirectly and from a variety of sectoral or local studies. The bulk of atypical — and largely unrecorded — work is quite hetero-geneous, sector-specific in its form and place-specific in its concentration. It is beyond the scope of this chapter to go into a discussion of different types of such work, but a number of points are important to keep in mind. The use of the term "atypical" (or "irregular") employment[4] in EU documents and policy recommendations characterises the activity of large numbers of people, mainly women, by juxtaposing it to an opposite form that is somehow "typical", or regular (see, for example, Meulders and Plasman, 1989). The "typical" employee working in large industrial or tertiary enterprises, on a formal contract in full-time work, and with social security and other fringe benefits is not, however, typical in southern Europe even for men. It is even less so among women. Despite very significant regional differences, productive activity is dispersed into a large number of small firms in all sectors, with growing numbers of self-employed. Over 70% of firms employ less than 10 people, while the average size of firm in commerce is less than two employees. Many are family enterprises, heavily dependent for their survival on unpaid family labour and on non-compliance with the regulatory system (see also Mingione, 1988). In this context "atypical" employment finds room to develop and, perhaps, become the "norm". Such patterns of diffuse production, and the forms of employment associated with them, are not exclusive to traditional or declining activities. They are also part of restructuring trends in many dynamic branches and regions (see Mingione, 1985; Hadjimichalis and Vaiou, 1990b). The Third Italy is probably the best known and most widely discussed example, but there are many more.

The cases that follow are illustrative but by no means unique. They are based on research in Marche in Italy, Catalunya in Spain, Lisboa e vale do Tejo in Portugal, and Anatoliki Makedonia in Greece — four very different contexts of work and everyday life in southern Europe (Vaiou et al., 1991b).

Marche, a region in the heart of the Third Italy, is close to or above the EU average on a number of indices and trends, such as GDP per capita, unemployment and women's participation rate. Like the rest of the Third Italy it is characterised by the interplay of industry and agriculture, and by diffused industrialisation involving small and medium firms. The average number of employees in manufacturing firms is just over five, and in commerce it is just under two. Manufacturing firms specialise in the production of consumer goods, mainly shoes and leather, clothing and textiles — which are highly feminised in their employment structures — and wooden furniture and musical instruments, where women make up less than 25% of the workforce. This type of industry is highly vulnerable to changes in fashion and shifting consumption patterns, and it is disadvantaged by the relative maturity of existing technologies. The service sector, oriented towards private services, accounts for around half of total employment in the region (Vinay and Melchiorre, 1991; see also Materazzi, 1991; Merelli et al., 1991; David and Vicarelli, 1991).

Catalunya, one of Spain's historic nationalities, is among the most dynamic regions in Spain, but slightly below EU average in terms of GDP per capita. It is a high-unemployment industrial region that was deeply affected by the economic crisis of the 1970s, especially in branches such as textiles and construction. A significant share of economic activity is diffused into small firms (70% of all firms employ less than 10 people). Since the mid-1980s, economic decline has slowed down, partly due to growth in the service sector and reindustrialisation linked to the influx of foreign capital in branches such as chemicals, food and drinks, transport equipment and tobacco. Job losses in textiles and wool have been responsible for a considerable reduction in women's participation in the labour force. The jobs lost have not been replaced by employment generated in the growing service sector or in the small-firm expansion that followed the closure of many enterprises (Solsona et al., 1991; see also Cruz Villalon, 1987; Garcia Ramón, 1988; Recio et al., 1988).

Lisboa e vale do Tejo is a recently created administrative unit which includes the metropolitan area of Lisboa, capital of a colonial empire for five centuries. The region is significantly below EU average in terms of GDP per capita but ranks first within Portugal. As might be expected, tertiary activities are predominant, representing 60% of regional employment and 64% of value added in the region. After the downfall of the dictatorship in 1974, left-wing governments, in their attempt to establish a "welfare state", favoured the expansion of social services (mainly health and education) in which a lot of women found jobs. Political and economic relations with the EU on the other hand encouraged location in the region of modern services (such as telecommunications and finance). Women do not have easy access to these new areas of employment (André et al., 1991; see also Ferreira, 1987; Commission for Equality and Women's Rights, 1991; Malheiros, 1990; Silva, 1983).

In Anatoliki Makedonia, a region in the north of Greece which is significantly below EU average in terms of GDP per capita, agriculture is still very important, accounting for around 46% of employment. The regional productive structure is based on a combination of intensive agriculture in the plains, tourism in coastal areas and industry around urban centres and on the main road network. Anatoliki Makedonia lags behind compared to "old" core areas of the country, but it has avoided the marginalisation of mountainous parts of Greece and of many small islands (Vaiou et al., 1991a; see also Centre for Spatial Research, 1990; Papayannakis et al., 1986; IPA, 1991).

In these different contexts many forms of "atypical" employment may be observed. Of these, "family workers" and "self-employed" appear in labour force surveys. Extensive use of family workers is very widespread in agriculture, in some areas where family farming predominates. In practice family farming means women's labour: in Marche, 42% of women's work is found in this category, whereas in Anatoliki Makedonia it reaches 76%.

Women's work exceeds 50% of total days of work in many crops (ORML, 1989; NSS, 1987). Family workers are very numerous in the traditional labour-intensive crops, mainly Mediterranean products (such as vines, olives and citrus) and tobacco.

Women's work in commerce also takes the form of family labour. The vast majority of businesses are very small (less than two employees per firm) and rely on unpaid family labour for their survival. This is also the case in many tourist businesses, such as restaurants, rooms to let, and tourist agencies. In these cases — where work is also seasonal — women become "housewives" when the season is over, or engage in agricultural work. Many women registered as housewives (that is, not part of the labour force) engage in a multitude of occupations through the year. They may be involved in farming for part of the year, in tourism during the season, in a family shop for some hours every day, and in homeworking, all without ever gaining the status of a "working person" (see Hadjimichalis and Vaiou, 1990a; Bimbi, 1986; CC.OO, 1987).

A trend that can be observed in both Marche and the region of Lisboa e vale do Tejo is that of increased numbers of self-employed women in agriculture (ORML, 1989; INE, 1989). This is associated with women's apparent entitlement to the farm when men find a job outside agriculture. It has in practice more to do with taxation and bureaucratic transactions than with any real transfer of control to women. This aside, self-employment is more prevalent among men than among women.

Reduced or irregular hours of work are common in many forms of temporary employment, such as "fixed term", "casual", "seasonal" or "work on call". Seasonal work is common in agriculture and in agro-industries (mainly tobacco and food processing). If employment is formalised (that is, with a written contract) there is a minimum number of working days that entitles workers to unemployment benefits for the rest of the year. Much of the seasonal labour in agriculture, however, is informal, without contract, especially during the harvest season. In the labour-intensive crops in Anatoliki Makedonia women represent over 80% of the labour used during the harvesting, selection and packing of fruit. In Catalunya the same types of jobs have recently been taken by immigrants from North Africa. In the Vale do Tejo, where the main crops are tomatoes and vines, women are also frequently employed in harvesting and processing the produce.

Following recent cuts in public expenditure, seasonal or temporary employment has become common in public services as well. In Marche and Catalunya young women are hired for three months or less once or twice a year in the postal and telephone service, in local government, and education in order to cover special needs without increasing the permanent workforce. In the region of Lisboa the "liberalisation" promoted by labour market policies resulted in a considerable rise in the number of temporary contracts involving mainly women. About 24% of employed women hold such contracts and many work with no contracts at all.

Large department stores and tourist facilities also operate on temporary or casual contracts. In Catalunya, chaining together temporary contracts is a common means for employers to cover permanent needs (and corresponding workplaces), with considerable savings on the part of the firms involved in terms of salaries and fringe benefit contributions (Miguelez Lobo, 1988). In the Italian department store chain "Standa" seasonal workers (usually the same ones) are hired at peak periods (for instance Christmas) when the stores are open from 8.30 in the morning until 8.00 in the evening. The company also employs women on part-time and part-year (six or seven months full-time) contracts (Vinay and Melchiorre, 1991).

"Homeworking" is an important part of the operation of a variety of branches in manufacturing, and involves primarily women. According to the Council of Europe (1989), in southern Europe women are 80–90% of the estimated 1.5 million homeworkers. Homeworking is the form of atypical employment which produces the worst working conditions for women, who work at home during the day, trying to combine household and caring tasks with paid work. They are paid on piece rates, which makes work very intensive. Working time cannot easily be separated from that devoted to other tasks. Sometimes materials used in the manufacturing of small articles (for instance toys, ornaments and shoes) are dangerous for both children's and adults' health. As a rule, homeworkers do not enjoy social security or other benefits and employers evade acknowledging their status as employees.

In Anatoliki Makedonia and Catalunya, homeworking is predominant in clothing which is an important branch in the regional productive structure (Recio et al., 1988; Hadjimichalis and Vaiou, 1990a). It used to be more common in Marche in the 1970s, but has become less frequent and more regulated since, both as a result of union and government controls and as a consequence of women's changing attitudes to work (Vinay, 1987). Homeworking in Marche accounts for 3.6% of regional employment in manufacturing, with higher figures in "feminised" branches where women's employment is concentrated (12% in shoes, 13% in musical instruments, 18% in other industries). Such data are, moreover, based on employers' responses to questionnaires and have to be treated as an understatement, like all quantitative data on atypical employment.

Many of the activities described above are informal in that they do not involve any contract and, quite often, employers do not abide by labour laws in terms of conditions of work, pay and social security. A number of studies indicate that this type of work is still prevalent in all sectors of economic activity and involves a predominantly female workforce. In agriculture, much of the seasonal labour is without contracts (up to 55–65% in Anatoliki Makedonia). The proliferation of family farming and of small family firms especially in tourism provides the preconditions for a significant volume of women's unrecorded and sometimes non-remunerated work. Subcontracting industrial production to homeworkers is a means of coping with international competition for many firms in clothing and food production, for instance. A number of services are also offered on an informal basis (Barthélemy et al., 1988). In the case of services, it is revealing to note the employment of paid domestic workers by households in which both partners are employed, in Lisboa and in Barcelona for example. In this case, women's growing participation in the labour force has contributed to the expansion of yet another area of women's informal work.

From the different cases and regional contexts reported here — as from many others in southern Europe — it becomes evident that, for women of the south (even in their limited definition as workers), the experience of work is very different from that on which the dominant philosophy of European integration is based. Women seasonal workers in Catalan or Makedonian agriculture, women who process fish in Anatoliki Makedonia with their feet in the water for eight hours a day, those who clean the villas where Japanese pensioners spend their holidays in the south of Portugal, part-year workers in the department stores of Marche or in the shopping centres around Lisboa, casual labourers in tourism and homeworkers in any town or region: all these women workers do not conform to the image of "social partners".

Those who "converse" with employers and state or EU bureaucrats (in the sense of taking part in a meaningful and structured dialogue about collective bargaining agreements, working conditions, health and safety issues and so on) are primarily men, whose relation to work is closer to the "norm". They are the ones who will shape the role of partnership, inevitably based on their own experiences. It is more than likely that all those women whose contribution is critical to the development of regions and cities in southern Europe but invisible and devalued, will be left out of the bargaining for better pay and improved working conditions, for social security entitlement and protection in the workplace, for restructuring and labour organisation priorities.

EUROPEAN CITIZENS ON THE MARGINS OF THE SINGLE MARKET

According to one elegant phrase, the Maastricht Treaty is "weak in matters of social policy". These include anything that is not directly part of the EMU. Instead social policy has been included in a separate protocol to the Maastricht agreement signed by 11 member states, not including the UK (Commission of the EC, 1992). The Treaty establishes, however, the principle of European citizenship which permits, among other things, free movement and residence in any member state. Free movement of people (along with goods and capital) has been one of the main arguments for European integration (Cecchini, 1988). Formal labour market regulation, high levels of unionisation, and the provision of adequate services, are far removed from the multiple meanings and content that work has for different groups of women in the south. Such arguments also ignore how tied women are to particular places, and therefore downplay or ignore their inability to take advantage of European citizenship by moving freely and claiming the benefits of a Single Market at the point of maximum return.

Women's concentration in forms of work like those discussed in the cases from southern Europe is not a matter of choice. It is, to a great extent, due to the lack of alternatives. It is important to remember that women's unemployment is double that of men in all cases and formal, full-time jobs in unionised workplaces are the minority of the jobs available. It is also due to the lack of accessible and affordable welfare services that would enable women to look for such alternatives. Women's increasing participation in economic activity of any kind has not been matched by a corresponding development and improvement of social infrastructure, as has been the case in northern Europe. Moreover, male identities in the south do not include in their definition caring and domestic labour — which remain "women's work"; yet another set of tasks that are not registered and evaluated as "real work" (see, for example, Brunori, 1991; Carretta, 1990; David and Vicarelli, 1991; CREW et al., 1989; Durán, 1987; Silva, 1983; Vaiou and Stratigaki, 1989).

The fact that women are almost exclusively responsible for looking after homes and families significantly restricts their mobility, in the sense given to the term in EU documents. Constraints are stronger among low-income women who do not have access to private caring services, and live in places where public social infrastructure is inadequate and deteriorating. Education is still based on the assumption that mothers are constantly available to take children to and from school and look after them after (or before) class and during long holidays: schools are open from 8.00 or 9.00 to 13.00 in Italy and Spain and work in shifts in Greece and Portugal (CREW et al., 1989), irrespective of the working hours of offices and factories. Other services operate on the same assumption, while child care for under-fives covers only a small proportion of children in that age group, and usually only for the same short period of time in each day. In this context, there is a need for a full-time housewife in each household.

Such pressures on women are sometimes strongest in rural areas, as examples from Anatoliki Makedonia indicate: schools, health clinics and sometimes shops may be located in a village or town other than their own, public transport is irregular and access to a private car limited. In a different way, however, they are also strong in urban areas, as is the case in Lisboa or Barcelona, where facilities and services are inadequate for the numbers of people they are meant to serve. Some of these pressures are accommodated within (new forms of) extended families, with older women often catering for the services that are poorly supplied or unavailable.

A critical condition for survival in such conditions is the development of informal networks, among relatives, friends and neighbours, so that women can cope with the double burden of work at home and in the workplace. In addition, access to paid work is achieved through such informal networks. The latter develop over a long period of living in a particular place and are, by this token, place-specific. Moving to another place in order to improve working conditions is not therefore a viable possibility, since access to a better (or any) job depends on a whole set of obligations and mutual dependence.

In all the regions discussed in this chapter, when women move they usually follow a male partner at the cost of their own career and employment prospects. They usually have to abandon a job (even an "atypical one") at their place of origin and remain unemployed for an uncertain length of time. A move determined by the job prospects of a male partner does not necessarily mean better chances for women. Local labour markets are themselves segregated along gender lines and women's employment differs between places. Moreover, women lose more than a job, they also have to abandon the whole support network that secures their availability for paid work, especially when they have small children or other dependants to look after. Women who have to combine working hours with the schedules of schools, the opening hours of shops and the timetables of public services can seldom transcend the boundaries of their area of residence in order to look for a job or take part in public life. Their chances and daily lives are further restricted by this kind of attachment to place.

It seems that women of the south will bear the cost of EMU *in situ*, where they are already disadvantaged by the fact that they live in the less developed regions of the Union. European citizenship and the promise of free movement to the places where better chances can be achieved correspond to different patterns of work and responsibilities of everyday life — those of some men in the north, perhaps.

BEYOND MAASTRICHT

The Maastricht Treaty outlines a philosophy of integration and sets rules within which different social agents will be acting in years to come. In many ways it is even more than a constitution for a unified-Europe-to-be, as it fixes the results to be achieved by the Union it "regulates" (see also Lipietz, 1992), thereby leaving little to be negotiated over or fought for by citizens of the EU. For example, EMU not only places the future of the EU firmly in a market economy, but leads back to the market whatever is not already market-based — most notably social and welfare policy, which are held to be creating public deficits that the central banks cannot fund any longer. On the other hand, clauses about a common foreign policy and common defence determine the relationship of the Union to the rest of the world and its preferential alliance with NATO and the USA. Those on collaboration in the domains of justice and internal affairs establish stronger barriers for non-EU citizens and strengthen the role of the police across frontiers.

Proponents of the Treaty emphasise the benefits of strict monetary policies and the advantages of establishing European citizenship that will enable free movement of people within the EU and increase their protection outside of it. There is seldom any reference to the everyday life of Europeans, to the terms of integration of different people and places. There is even less reference to those Europeans who happen to be women and will also bear the cost of European integration.

Critics of the Treaty, on the other hand, concentrate on the "democratic deficit", its neo-liberal orientation, a lack of commitment to environmental issues, and the widening gap between developed and less developed parts of the Union. It is hard to envisage though that these questions apply equally to all people. The meaning and content of democracy, experiences of class, relationship to the environment; these are not the same for women and for men, for minorities, for residents of the south and those of the north, for citizens in large cities and those in the countryside. Important aspects of inequality are thus hidden in a homogenising, albeit critical, analysis.

In the months following the signing of the Treaty in Maastricht, new aspects of European integration became clearer, and in particular the differential terms of integration. The powerful position of Germany became more evident. The Danish "no" to the Treaty (which should have led to its renegotiation) remained a "Danish problem", whereas the French referendum was a "European problem". To paraphrase George Orwell, some countries and regions in the unified Europe are "more equal than others". This chapter has indicated that many regions of the south are among those that are less equal. Women living in those regions are less equal still. Women in southern Europe are so "less equal" that they do not even warrant a mention in the often heated arguments put forward both by proponents and by critics of the Maastricht Treaty.

Problems in and prospects for a unified Europe have received relatively little discussion in the south, mostly confined to parliaments and small groups of better-informed "European citizens". They are left to be felt through the policies derived from the Treaty which will determine women's (and men's) lives for years to come. For women, being excluded from the provisions of that constitution is yet another instance in a story that keeps reproducing itself, albeit in different ways. For the unequal terms of integration of social groups and regions in the European project encapsulated in the Maastricht Treaty, as in many others, are not a matter of "bad" policies that can be "corrected" through Action Programmes or other means of *ad hoc* intervention. Those terms are a structural feature of uneven development, in which winners and losers are mutually determined and continuously reproduced.

Between the lines of debate, it is taken for granted that women in the south will continue to perform the same tasks and contribute to economic development, by bearing the costs and remaining invisible. In the most unfavourable of conditions and with minimal diffusion of information and material means, women are coping, changing and increasingly coming out of the shadows, organising and fighting against marginalisation. Renegotiating the terms of integration may perhaps lead to some different concerns being included in plans and prospects. This, however, cannot be left to the goodwill of "social partners" and the "logic" of the market.

NOTES

1. Regional per capita product, for example, is below 60% of the EU mean in all regions of Greece, Portugal and southern Italy. Only four regions in Spain are above 80% of the mean. If the mean is 100, Anatoliki Makedonia = 56, Attica = 59, Lisboa e vale do Tejo = 70, Alentejo = 46, Andalusia = 58, Catalunya = 84, Calabria = 59, Marche = 106, but Greater London = 164, Hamburg = 183 (Commission of the European Communities, 1991).
2. Material for this chapter is drawn from an EU-funded research project (Vaiou et al., 1991b): Vaiou, Georgiou and Stratigaki in collaboration with Vinay and Melchiorre (Italy), Solsona, Suarez, Trevino and Gonzalez (Spain) and André, Ferreira and Arroz (Portugal).
3. The literature on informal activities in southern Europe is vast as the subject has been on the agenda for quite a while. See (*inter alia*) Barthélemy et al., 1988; Benton, 1986; Bimbi, 1986; CC.OO, 1987; Cocco and Santos, 1984; Council of Europe, 1989; Duran, 1987; Hadjimichalis and Vaiou, 1990a and b; Mingione, 1985; Recio et al., 1988; Sanchis, 1984; Vinay, 1985.
4. "Atypical employment" is a term introduced by Meulders and Plasman (1989) and includes "all those forms of employment which are distinguished from traditional occupations by characteristics as diverse as the number and distribution of hours worked, the organization and localization of production, wage determination and statutory regulations and conventions" (p. 1). "Irregular employment" is used in Barthélemy et al. (1988) with stronger connotations of "informal" or "underground" work or "moonlighting" (*travail au noir*).

REFERENCES

André, I.M., Ferreira, C. and Aroz, M.E. (1991) Regional report: Lisbon and Tagus Valley, in Vaiou et al., (1991b), pp. 247–309.

Barthélemy, P., Miguelez Lobo, F., Mingione, E., Pahl, R. and Wenig, A. (1988) *Underground economy and irregular forms of employment (travail au noir)*, Programme for research and action on the development of the labour market, Commission of the European Communities DG V (V/1799/88-EN), 10 vols, Brussels.

Benton, L. (1986) La informalisación del trabajo en la industria, *Papeles de Economia*, **26**, 43–65.

Bimbi, F. (1986) Lavoro domestico, economia informale, comunità, *Inchiesta*, **74** (Oct.–Dec.), 22–31.

Brunori, A. (1991) Principali aspetti quantitativi dell' evoluzione demografica e della famiglia nelle Marche, *Donne al Lavoro. Atti della Conferenza Regionale sul Lavoro Feminile*, Regione Marche, Osservatorio Regionale sul Mercato del Lavoro, Ancona, Tecnoprint, pp. 82–88.

Carretta, M. (1990) La famiglia, ISTAT *Sintesi della vita sociale italiana*, Rome, pp. 293–344.

CC.OO (1987) *La mujer en la economía sumergida*, Secretaría de la Mujer, Madrid.

Cecchini, P. (1988) *The challenge of 1992*, report on the research programme "The cost of non Europe", Kalofolias, Athens (in Greek).

Centre for Spatial Research (1990) *Skill needs and shortages in the region of Eastern Macedonia and Thrace in Greece*, Commission of the European Communities, Task Force Human Resources, Education, Training and Youth, Brussels.

Cocco, M.R. and Santos, E. (1984) A economia subterrânea: contributos para a sua análisee quantificaçao no caso portugues, *Bolletin Trimestral do Banco de Portugal*, **6**, 1 (March), 67–93.

Commission for Equality and Women's Rights (1991) *Portugal, status of women — 1991*, Lisbon.

Commission of the European Communities (1991) *The regions in the 1990s* (COM/ 90/609), Brussels.

Commission of the European Communities (1992) *The treaty for European unification*, Luxembourg.

Conroy Jackson, P. (1990) *The impact of the completion of the Internal Market on women in the European Community*, working document prepared for DGV, Equal Opportunities Unit, Brussels.

Council of Europe (1989) *The protection of persons working at home*, Strasbourg.

CREW, in collaboration with McLoone, J. and O'Leary, M. (1989) *Infrastructures and women's employment*, Commission of the European Communities, DG V (V/174/ 90-EN), Brussels.

Cruz Villalon, J. (1987) Political and economic change in Spanish agriculture, 1950–1985, *Antipode*, **19**, 2.

David, P. and Vicarelli, G. (1991) Le donne di Ancona. Una ricerca su modelli sociali, doppia presenza, lavori culture, *Politica ed Economia — Studi e Ricerche*, 7–8, CESPE, Rome.

Durán, M.A. (1987) Notas para una critica de textos básicos de economía española, *El Trabajo de las mujeres*, Ministerio de Cultura, Instituto de la Mujer, Madrid, pp. 34–51.

Employment in Europe (1992) Commission of the European Communities, DGV (COM (92) 354), Brussels.

Ferreira, V.M. (1987) *A Cidade de Lisboa: de Capital do Império a Centro da Metrópole*, D. Quixote, Lisbon.

Garcia Ramón, M.D. (1988) Genero y actividad agraria en España: una aproximación a partir del Censo Agrario de 1982, *Documents d'Analisi Geografica*, **13**, UAB, pp. 16–33.

Hadjimichalis, C. and Vaiou, D. (1990a) Flexible labour markets and regional development in Northern Greece, *International Journal of Urban and Regional Research*, **14**, 1.

Hadjimichalis, C. and Vaiou, D. (1990b) Whose flexibility? the politics of informalisation in Southern Europe, *Capital and Class*, **42**, 79–106.

INE (1989) *Employment survey*, Lisbon.

IPA (Institute for Regional Development) (1991) *Presentation of labour market statistics in Greece*, Ministry of Labour, Athens (in Greek).

Lipietz, A. (1992) Contre Maastricht parce que pour l'Europe, *Silence*, **157** (Sept.), 7–9.

Malheiros, J.M. (1990) Le Portugal au sud de l'Europe, entre le Mediterranée et l'Atlantique, *Sociedade e Territorio*, special issue, Lisbon.

Materazzi, R. (1991) Donne e mercato del lavoro nelle Marche: alcune riflessioni, *Donne al Lavoro. Atti della Conferenza Regionale sul Lavoro Feminile*, Regione Marche, ORML, Ancona Tecnoprint, pp. 292–338.

Merelli, R. et al. (1991) La crescita del sistema economico marchigiano: 1980–1987, *Prisma*, **21**, 292–338.

Meulders, D. and Plasman, R. (1989) *Women in atypical employment*, Commission of the European Communities, DG V (V/1426/89-FR), Brussels.

Miguelez Lobo, F. (1988) *Irregular work in Spain*, Programme for research and action on the development of the labour market, Commission of the European Communities, DG V (V/1799/88-EN), Brussels.

Mingione, E. (1985) Social reproduction of the surplus labour force: the case of Southern Italy, in Redclift, N. and Mingione, E. (eds), *Beyond employment*, Basil Blackwell, Oxford, pp. 14–54.

Mingione, E. (1988) *The case of Italy*, Programme for research and action on the development of the labour market, Commission of the European Communities, DGV (V/1799/88-EN), Brussels.

NSS (National Statistical Service) (1987) *Labour force survey*, Athens.

ORML (Osservatorio Regionale sul Mercato del Lavoro) (1989) *Le recenti tendenze del mercato del lavoro nelle Marche*, Bolletini ORML 10, Ancona.

Papayannakis, L., Hadjantonis, D., Hadjimichalis, C., Manolopoulos, N. (1986) *Investment Opportunities in Anatoliki Makedonia and Thraki*, METEK, Athens (in Greek).

Recio, A., Miguelez, F. and Alos, R. (1988) *El Trabajo precario en Catalunya: la industria textil lanera des Vallés Occidental*, Commissión Obrera Nacionál de Catalunya, Barcelona.

Sanchis, E. (1984) *El trabajo a domicilio en el pais Valenciano*, Instituto de la Mujer, Madrid.

Silva, M. (1983) *O emprego das mulheres em Portugal — a 'mao invisivel' na discriminaçao sexual do emprego*, Porto: Afrontamento.

Solsona, M., Suarez, L., Trevino, R. and Gonzalez, M.J. (1991) Regional report: Catalonia, in Vaiou et al. (1991b), pp. 201–246.

Vaiou, D., Georgiou, Z. and Stratigaki, M. (1991a) Regional Report: Anatoliki Makedonia, in Vaiou et al. (1991b), pp. 58–123.

Vaiou, D., Georgiou, Z., Stratigaki, M. et al. (1991b) *Women of the south in European integration: problems and prospects*, Commission of the European Communities, DG V (V/694/92-EN), Brussels.

Vaiou, D. and Stratigaki, M. (guest eds) (1989) Women's work: between two worlds, *Synchrona Themata*, **40** (special issue), 15–40 (in Greek).

Vinay, P. (1985) Family life cycle and the informal economy in Central Italy, *International Journal of Urban and Regional Research*, **9**, 1.

Vinay, P. (1987) Women, family and work. Symptoms of crisis in the informal economy in Central Italy, *Proceedings of Samos Seminar on Changing Labour Processes and New Forms of Urbanisation*, Samos, Greece, pp. 89–96.

Vinay, P. and Melchiorre, G. (1991) Regional report: Marche, in Vaiou et al. (1991b), pp. 124–200.

4 New International Migrations and the "European Fortress"

ENRICO PUGLIESE
University of Naples, Italy

INTRODUCTION

In the course of recent decades, two contemporaneous and interconnected (if apparently contradictory) phenomena have occurred with respect to international migration: an unprecedented volume of laws and regulations produced by national states, and an increase in the number of illegal immigrant workers. There is no causal relationship between the two phenomena, but they are both expressions of the great transformations which are taking place in migratory movements on an international level. This chapter therefore starts by indicating some of the basic dimensions and policies which characterise the present phase of international migration involving European countries.

The first significant development is an extension in the number of nationalities that are participating in contemporary migratory flows. Nationalities which contributed only modestly in the past to great international migrations (mainly African and Asiatic) are now appearing on the scene. Workers from colonial countries have contributed historically to the workforce of certain European powers, but this was to a limited extent and it always occurred within a given colonial relationship. Now international migration to Europe is substantially from the Third World, into practically all countries.

The second noteworthy change is the complex origin and destination pattern of immigration flows. Countries which until 1975–80 could still consider themselves source countries have now become receivers instead. Italy is a particularly significant case, but it is not the only one for the category includes Spain, Greece and even Portugal, which in many ways continues also to be an emigration country (as evidenced by Portuguese migration into France). Consequently there are now on the one hand a greater number of immigration countries — including southern European — and on the other hand a larger number of emigration countries. There are new populations in the migratory scene, and new areas are touched by

Europe at the Margins: New Mosaics of Inequality. Edited by Costis Hadjimichalis and David Sadler
© 1995 European Science Foundation. Published in 1995 by John Wiley & Sons Ltd

migration, bringing people which formerly did not have significant relationships in closer contact. This does not necessarily mean that the number of immigrants has increased, however. The number of countries involved in migration is high, but the specific contribution of each individual nationality is relatively modest.

The third aspect which characterises the present phase is the far greater extent of frontier restriction practised by all receiving countries. They have devoted their legislative efforts to "defending" themselves from new arrivals, and for some time now have stopped encouraging mass immigration. As early as the 1970s, European countries moved from a policy of "flows" to one of "stocks". Even though this terminology — probably borrowed from studies on labour economics — remains current, speaking of stocks of immigrants as if they were merchandise is rather startling, especially if we consider the human and social aspects of immigration. These apparently neutral comments on flows and stocks are in fact an expression of a radical change in orientation and of an intention to close down traditional channels of labour migration. The German *Anwerbenstop* in 1973 was the first significant signal of this reversal of trend. After the Schengen agreements, the homogenisation of restrictive policies appears to be definitive. The "European fortress" might only be a metaphor borrowed from trade theory, but it is certainly a more than adequate one.

It is not just a matter of stopping immigration and not allowing people to search for better job opportunities — or to flee from famine, wars and persecution — in the rich Western countries. Moreover, as we shall see, the "fortress" is never completely closed. The new restrictive measures are a very clear indicator of the lack of solidarity in North–South relationships. A new *limes* — such as the one which was intended to defend the Roman Empire from the barbarian peoples — has been set up in order to defend the "civilised world" from the new potential invaders. This exclusion does not only concern those who are kept out. The ideology of the fortress is based on an increasing division between "us" and "them", even when "they" are already in Europe.

This chapter will devote particular attention to the phenomenon of the closing of frontiers, and will attempt to pinpoint both its causes and its implications and effects. It will emphasise how the growing volume of legislation on immigration implicitly contains a unitary guideline which, in the final analysis, leads to the modification of some of the principles which historically characterised the migratory policies of individual countries. The novel element and the most characteristic one, in all European countries (Martin, 1989), is the (more or less effectively enforced) closing of frontiers to international migrants. The clandestine nature of migration — with all its implications in terms of the marginality of the immigrant population — is an undesirable, but not always dysfunctional, effect of this type of policy. The understanding of these processes and of the position of Third World immigrants in the "European fortress" — since they are present in massive numbers — is easier if we bear in mind the considerable transformations which are occurring in the labour market and producing a new type of labour demand, within the frame of a post-Fordist production model. Therefore the essay will also single out some changes taking place in the structure of the labour market in Europe, and point out the role played by recent waves of immigration of people from Third World countries. It will identify the location of new immigrants in the labour market and in the occupational structure, pointing out the main differences between the present situation and the situation of intra-European migrations, and the reasons why immigrants are in a condition of marginality.

LABOUR MARKET CONDITIONS AND SOCIAL MARGINALITY

Studies on marginality generally include the immigrant population (or at least a large part of it) in their area of research. Immigrants are often considered part of the "new poor", and in fact generally they are. In all European countries a sector of the marginal population is represented by Third World immigrants (see Mingione, Chapter 2 this volume). This is a consequence on the one hand of general processes which account for growing marginality and social cleavage in society, and on the other hand of specific facts concerning the conditions of immigrants in the labour market and the social and welfare policies affecting them.

The occupational structure of Third World immigrants in Europe is very complex. It varies both from country to country and within each country, from region to region. Migration takes place to regions with both low and high official (and real) rates of unemployment, creating additional problems in the analysis of labour market implications. There are also some homogeneous aspects: for example, Third World immigrants are mostly located in secondary jobs both in the traditional areas of immigration in the north European countries and in the new receiving countries of Mediterranean Europe. This is related to the fact that an enlargement of the secondary labour market, together with a general process of casualisation of the labour force, is taking place in all advanced economies.

Changes in the economy and in the labour market directly affect the amount and composition of immigration flows. In the words of Fielding (1993, p. 14):

The most important feature of mass migration under post-fordist forms of production organization is its absence. Mass migration from this perspective can be seen as a corollary of mass production, mass consumption, mass culture and mass society. In so far as flexible specialisation moves away from these, it takes spatial mobility along with it, and leaves behind only small scale and more individualistic forms of inter-regional and international migration.

Even if mass migration, in Fielding's specific and slightly restrictive definition, is no longer in existence, there are large numbers of people, many more than in the past, who tend to move, to migrate, to reach the areas where — with or without flexible specialisation — there are opportunities to make a living (and send something home). Labour instability is, however, the main feature of post-Fordism as far as immigrants are concerned.

In the years of mass immigration driven by the pull factors of Fordist development — that is in the years of *industrial* migration — the demographic composition of migratory flows was characterised by an overwhelming proportion of (mainly young) adult males. Job security coupled with legal status allowed many migrants to settle in ways which often — although not always, as we shall see — implied family reunion and a degree of stability. This does not imply that immigrants had the same labour market position and the same prospect of upward mobility as the local population. In the occupational structure they were at the bottom, with different opportunities of climbing the social and occupational ladder in each of the various countries. They were not structurally confined to marginal jobs, however, because economic growth and increasing demand for primary labour gave occupational opportunities to immigrants, particularly to the first arrivals. Growth and industrial development, in a situation close to full employment, were the basic pull factors.

In the debate among labour economists about migration, two main opposing theses can be singled out (Venturini, 1988). On the one side, proponents of the pull effect are convinced that present-day immigration is caused by an unsatisfied labour demand in receiving countries. On the other side, supporters of the push effect claim that immigration takes place regardless of the situation of labour demand. In the first case the immigrant workforce plays a complementary role with respect to local labour; in the second case there is (supposedly) competition between local and immigrant workers. This was a very important issue at the time of mass migration in industrial societies, when the strength of demand for industrial labour was very important in determining the pull effect. Such a clear-cut division is now, however, unacceptable. The picture is much more complex because of segmentation in the labour market. With the decline of mass industrial production, the picture has completely changed.

There is instead a tendency towards the expansion of demand in jobs with low qualifications offering a low and precarious income. This demand (which might not be satisfied) represents a very important pull factor. Marginal jobs are offered to the new immigrants and this is the structural basis for their social marginality. Their precarious occupational position excludes them from many workplace benefits. In addition, their low and precarious income makes it more difficult to pursue long-term migratory projects. Particularly in the new receiving countries, spatial mobility is one of the most striking aspects of contemporary patterns. A large number of migrants are forced into mobility because of the nature of their work, as they are often agricultural labourers. This is rarely a year-round occupation, and they therefore work also in construction or as street pedlars in the same or in other regions. Even when their jobs do not necessarily imply spatial mobility — as in the case of service workers — they are less stable than in the past.

I shall return to these issues and to changes in the labour market below. For now, I would like to single out an indicator of social marginality which is also related to labour market conditions and spatial instability. In the new immigration countries (such as Spain, Italy or Greece) not only is it impossible to know the exact amount of the immigrant population, owing to the large number of illegal immigrants, but also even the estimates are generally not very reliable. Spatial mobility together with high visibility lead to frequent overestimation of the number of immigrants. Many current "popular" estimates of the magnitude of immigration flows are exaggerated. At the same time, official data on immigration just as frequently underestimate the phenomenon.

Reliable estimates are very difficult to produce. The fact that their existence is unacknowledged expresses in a dramatic way the social marginality of Third World immigrants. Clandestine, unregistered immigrants are truly marginal workers. They cannot benefit from any form of protection, except informal ones. They are very seldom "unemployed" for the simple reason that only by selling their labour power can they survive. They are highly competitive in the labour market because they are forced to accept any kind of working conditions. They are even excluded from welfare and social policies towards immigrants, because their existence is not officially recognised. Nevertheless, they keep coming.

INCREASING "PUSH" EFFECTS AND THE NEW MIGRATORY DESTINATIONS

In the analysis of present-day international migrations, it is necessary to take into account the evolving character (both from a qualitative and a quantitative point of view) of labour demand. On the other hand, the persistent and increasing strength of the push effect has also to be considered as a key issue. A fruitful way of approaching the problem is to analyse the various determinants of the push as well as of the pull effect, paying special attention to recent trends and to the population groups involved. In this section I shall first deal with the causes of expulsion (push) from Third World countries, and then comment on the reasons why part of the flow which originates in the Third World ends up in Europe.

As far as the push effect is concerned, the causes of its growing significance are various. There are demographic factors; it is well known that the rate of population increase in most Third World countries is such that local resources cannot satisfy the needs of an increasing population (Zollberg, 1989). In all countries which make up the present migratory flow to Europe, an impressive amount of new jobs would have to be created just to maintain unemployment and underemployment at present rates (which are extremely high). On the other hand the demographic approach to the problem does not take sufficiently into account the social and economic factors that cause a radical disequilibrium between population and resources, that is to say the fundamental causes of the impoverishment of these regions.

I do not mean by this that the demographic problems of Third World countries are not relevant. Overemphasising them is, however, misleading and it contributes to an interpretation of the phenomenon as a natural catastrophe. One of the factors behind the siege mentality which is spreading rapidly within the "European fortress" is the idea of the "demographic bomb". I think it is more important to take a look at the ratio between population and resources, and at the factors which modify that ratio. In all the Third World countries there is an ongoing structural crisis in peasant agriculture which is considerably reducing their autonomy where food production is concerned. The immigrants who arrive in Europe do not come so much from the countryside directly but from cities, because it is there that the population driven out from the countryside is concentrated. This also helps to explain, among other things, the social structure of the new migrations.

Increasing poverty is not the only cause strengthening the push effect. There are others, including the inability of the local economy to absorb a labour force with high levels of education (which explains the frequency of immigrants with high educational levels found in menial jobs in Europe). Finally, there are also cultural factors (which of course cannot be seen independently from the pull effect) which contribute to the decision to migrate. For the young people who have attended school and for those with higher expectations, the urge to emigrate involves the objective of fulfilling a life plan which would be destined to be frustrated in their country of origin. The diffusion of the means of mass communication stimulates expectations of consumer goods which are far from irrelevant among younger immigrants.

The new arrivals in Europe are only a small part of the enormous population movement originating in the Third World. Besides the South–North migratory flows, we should remember the internal South–South ones. What is seen in Europe is in fact only the tip of the iceberg. When Eritreans represented one of the most significant components of immigration into Italy, and it was considered a mass phenomenon, there were several dozen Eritreans in Sudan for every Eritrean who had taken refuge in Italy.

This case also highlights the growing significance of populations which have been displaced as a result of wars or persecution. The increase in applications for refugee status is real, even though it must be stressed that in all European countries the percentage of those who actually obtain refugee status is very modest. Though it varies from country to country (with minimum rates in Italy for example) it rarely exceeds 10%. This component of the new immigration is typically in an even more precarious position.

Present migratory flows are made up of people coming from almost all Third World countries, and they are directed to various European countries, according to very peculiar trajectories which cannot be explained only on the basis of labour market characteristics. Some main flows can be singled out originating from a few main areas and leading to one or more developed countries (Salt, 1989). Income (or wage) differentials are only able to highlight the obvious fact that people move to countries where wages are 10 or 20 times higher. They are not able to explain why, for example, migrants from the Philippines come in massive numbers to Italy. There are a series of historical, cultural, religious and geographic factors which account for any given particular flow.

In some cases pre-existing colonial relationships explain why some nationalities and ethnic groups are present in a given country. In others, geographical proximity is the most important factor. In addition, the role of some "connecting agencies" which create specific trajectories should be considered. This is the case, for instance, of Catholic organisations as far as the connection between the Philippines and Italy is concerned. An important reason which explains the presence of immigrants in some countries is the simple fact that they have not been allowed into others (Calvanese, 1983). This is certainly relevant for part of the first wave of immigration to Italy. The migratory flow to other richer European destinations has been diverted to Italy because of stricter immigration policies elsewhere.

Where the destination of flows is concerned, it is necesssary to distinguish phase from structure. The example of Italy indicates how the less rigid closing of frontiers turned it into a privileged goal of immigration — not only from the Mediterranean countries — over the period up to 1990. In recent years Spain too favoured a policy which could be defined as at least tolerant of immigration. This "diversion of flow" due to the opening of frontiers explains the phase element: that is, the great influx towards Italy, Spain and Greece in the 1980s. The thrust towards these countries is continuing in spite of the end of this "opening" phase. Now, especially where Spain is concerned, there are cases of the shipwrecking of would-be immigrants, who end up with their boats destroyed, as corpses on the beach facing Morocco. The push from countries on the southern shore of the Mediterranean is strong, and southern Europe is a significant goal for this new wave. The overall picture of flows within Europe has certainly changed drastically. The old flow from the South has been replaced by a pattern with varied points of departure, and which reaches different areas in Europe depending on the precise combinations of the push effect and immigration and frontier policies (including the social services offered to immigrants) which distinguish the host countries.

So the "European fortress" is penetrated through a variety of small passages, each of which is affected by the specific conditions of arrival. Thus in Germany, after the restrictions of the 1970s, new and distant nationalities (Vietnamese, Cambodians, Eritreans) have arrived as refugees, or rather as aspiring refugees. The traditional policy of acceptance established by the constitution has been under discussion and now a constitutional amendment has reduced the possibility to aspire to refugee status. Before that though, many Third World people entered the country each year in the late 1980s and in the early 1990s.

The other novelty is the intensification of the flow within the Mediterranean area between the southern-shore countries and the northern-shore countries. The improvement of living conditions in countries like Spain and Italy — together with the extension of their welfare systems — has certainly reduced the willingness of the local labour force to accept certain kinds of precarious occupation (such as, for example, agricultural labour). The most significant explanation, however, for increased trans-Mediterranean migration has to do with geographical proximity and with less rigid frontier policies (at least until the last decade). Among the great present-day international flows, that across the Mediterranean is one of the most significant and novel. At present, departures from southern Europe are limited (even though we ought not to undervalue the persistence of a certain turnover) while there has been a strong incoming flow — legal and semi-legal as well as illegal.

Some groups such as the Algerians, who were absolutely irrelevant outside of France until a few years ago, are now an important component of the Mediterranean flow towards Spain and Italy. This is a very recent development, and it is mostly illegal precisely because it began during the period in which the Mediterranean countries enacted restrictive policies. This highlights the fact that mere demographic pressure is not sufficient to explain the outflow from an emigration country: this migration was unleashed when demographic and economic aspects (in fact their combined effect) were summed with elements of political and social crisis.

Within the Mediterranean basin, the countries of the southern shore (the North African countries) had a rather modest role in the mass migration of post-war decades, while an important flow originating from the northern shore was directed towards central and northern European destinations. Spain, Italy and also Greece are now receiving countries, but the flow was also more northward. It is difficult to estimate the outcome of this powerful push effect. According to Sture Oberg (1993, p. 210),

South of the Mediterranean in Morocco, Algeria, Tunisia and Egypt, the relative increase of the workforce is five to ten times as rapid as it is in France, Italy or Greece. . . . Demographic differences — such as a young rapidly increasing population south of the Mediterranean and an ageing population north of it — will, together with differences in living standards (per capita GNP is five times higher in France than in Algeria), create a scenario for potential mass migration. Thus both push and pull factors will contribute to future immigration into Europe, from neighbouring and more distant countries. The big difference is that whereas in the past the main force was the pull of industry needing cheap labour, now the main force is a demographic push from the south. Future migration streams cannot be estimated with any degree of scientific rigour because of the way they are affected by a large number of unforeseen factors such as political changes, wars and ethnic tensions. It is common, instead, to make "educated guesses" and assume certain immigration levels based on expected political scenarios.

The literature on Mediterranean migrations suggests that the push factors will be more and more active and that there will be a migration flow from these regions (Montanari and Cortese, 1993).

More complex is the picture as far as potential flows from eastern European countries are concerned. Here the degree of scientific information is even lower and therefore guesses — often "non-educated guesses" — are the basis for analyses and comments. Journalists' reports are the source of widely shared convictions about an "eastern invasion" (Nava, 1993). The potential migration from the east is generally exaggerated, but it is relevant and many economic and political factors may contribute to activate and mobilise it.

FROM INDUSTRIAL TO POST-FORDIST IMMIGRATION

Greater significance of push factors is hence the main difference between present-day migrations and the mass migration of past decades. There is, however, another aspect, closely related, which concerns the occupational destination of immigrants, which in turn is a reflection of the prevailing occupational structure in society. The migratory experience of the 1950s and of the 1960s has been extensively illustrated in studies which are now classic (Boehning, 1984; Castles and Kosack, 1973). Immigrants in this period largely entered the working class of the host countries, although in different ways and with many contradictions. The process was very complex and various scholars have singled out different stages in the evolution of the condition of the immigrants in these countries (Boehning, 1984; Piore, 1979). Industrial development in the core countries was the motor behind labour demand and migratory inflows. The labour requirement of manufacturing industry (as well as mining and construction) was the factor initiating population movements. This does not mean of course that all immigrants entered industrial employment. Italian ice-cream parlours as well as Greek restaurants have a long history in France and in the UK. For the majority of intra-European migrants, though, industrial employment was certainly the main destination.

Immigration to an industrial society does not only mean entrance in a society where industrial employment is prevailing or important. It entails entering a world where industrial development, and the corresponding social relations of production, impress a distinctive mark to society in general and to its main social and political institutions; where factory life, the working class and industrial conflict are the most significant elements of everyday existence. This was the case in most developed European countries.

Immigration was industrial immigration because industry was the economic and productive basis of society. Of course there were differences in the specific conditions of immigrants in the various countries, related to their quantitative incidence in the total national population and labour force, and to their occupational structure. Other differences were the effect of migratory policies in terms both of degree of restrictiveness, and social policies towards immigrants. Nevertheless some common features in this industrial migratory flow could be singled out.

In Europe it was a migration from poorer rural regions to richer industrial regions. It changed the occupational and class position of millions of people. Migrants who had been farm-workers, peasants or small local artisans, became part of the working class of the host countries. Immigration was a powerful contributory factor in the development of industrial capitalism (Castles and Kosack, 1973) in these countries, but at the same time it caused an enlargement and an internal modification of the working class. People of different nationalities and cultures were attracted to urban–industrial areas. At times divisions within the working class related to ethnic conflicts took place in various immigrant countries. These differences — and the consequent divisions and contradictions — were, in a certain way, counteracted by a homogenising element: the fact of having a similar position in the industrial relations of production. The Taylorist model in industry fostered this character. The international mass worker became an important social actor in industrial conflict in some countries, as evidenced for example by the active role of Turkish and Italian workers in the car industry in Germany in the 1970s.

This was of course only one dimension in the complex human and social experience of migration. Other aspects of the phenomenon led to different and contrasting results. Only a part of the immigrants in the industrial capitalist countries considered immigration a definitive experience leading to settlement in the new country. The policies of host countries influenced the temporary character of immigration. Taking Germany as an example, the fact that the country always defined itself as "a non immigration country" (Kammerer, 1975) is not irrelevant. It is not by chance that the number of Italian workers who spent some time in Germany is several times higher than the number of those who chose (and who were able) to remain there. In other countries, at the time of industrial expansion, immigration policy was less restrictive and return migrations were less favoured. A notable proportion of the total migrants settled in the host countries through complex processes, which have been the object of a series of studies. The processes whereby these immigrants became integrated — and related difficulties — are also well known, and many scholars have pointed out the problems of the second generation (Piore, 1979; Mehrländer, 1990; Kreidler and Pugliese, 1983). Crucially, however, relatively stable employment and consequently a degree of territorial stability characterised intra-European migrations in the "golden age" of the welfare state.

Things are quite different now. Even a superficial view of present-day immigration to Europe shows a noticeable change in the occupational destination of the majority of migrants, with the prevailing role of tertiary employment. The crisis of the Fordist model of production has serious consequences for labour demand and consequently on the occupational structure, and also on the social structure. With the transition from this model to a new one based on flexible specialisation, decentralised production in small units tends to take the place of large workplaces. The general process of deindustrialisation is accompanied by a reduction of employment in large-scale industries. From the point of view of the social structure, such changes imply a reduction in size of the industrial working class. The implication for international migration is that new immigrants have a different, and more marginal, class position.

A related aspect — very important for the occupational location of immigrants — is a decrease in the amount of regular, steady, year-round employment (which was the employment pattern that characterised the Fordist model of capitalist accumulation up to the 1970s). Precarious employment tends to characterise many of the new jobs in industry and, above all, in the service sector. Casualisation of the labour force is one of the most powerful trends in the labour market. Many scholars (Calvanese, 1983; Dell'Aringa and Neri, 1987; Sassen, 1988) have also emphasised a relationship between migratory status and working conditions. The existence of a causal relation between the facts may be debatable. Nevertheless, the occupational location of Third World immigrants (that is of migrants of the present wave) both in the new destination countries and in the old ones shows a general pattern of precarious, unprotected and unsteady jobs.

This also explains why migrants are located both in regions which are not particularly affected by unemployment and in regions where unemployment rates are high. Reference to basic elements of labour market segmentation theory (Piore, 1979) helps in understanding this seemingly paradoxical situation. Labour demand is more dynamic in those jobs and in those occupations which are less attractive for workers, particularly in those areas where unemployment mostly involves young people and there is a large supply of highly educated labour. On the other hand, an oversimplistic application of this theory would lead to an overestimation of the rigidity of the local labour force and consequently to an overestimation of the demand for jobs in the secondary labour market, supposedly rejected by the local workforce.

It is evident that the majority of immigrants are located in the secondary labour market, and this is more and more true now than in the past. On the other hand, the lack of preference of the local and national labour force for this type of job does not imply their capability to reject it. The presence of an immigrant workforce cannot be taken as an indicator of unsatisfied labour demand, even in the secondary labour market. In Italy some ideological interpretations of the situation take immigration as demonstration of the fallacy of national unemployment data or as proof of the voluntary character of youth unemployment.

This process of enlargement of the secondary labour market can also be understood as — and actually it corresponds to — the process of development of what is generally referred to as the informal economy (Mingione and Redclift, 1986). More specifically, Mingione (1985) points out that three processes, strictly interwoven, cause changes in labour demand with strong implications for the demand for immigrant workers. These processes are technological development, tertiarisation of the occupational structure, and development of the informal economy.

The first process aggravates the dualism between those sectors where technological innovations are possible — and therefore productivity may increase so that higher labour costs (and labour rigidity) can be afforded — and those sectors where the degree of technological innovation is more modest. As the less innovative sectors (including state-provided services) expand, they require a cheaper and less demanding labour force. The process of informalisation tends to satisfy this requirement. At the same time international migrations, and in particular immigration from Third World countries, provide on a massive scale a labour force ready to accept low productivity and low-paid jobs in the informal sector, or more generally in the secondary labour market. The illegal status of a sizeable part of the migrant population facilitates their ghettoisation in the labour market.

While analysing migrations in the age of industrial development, I have focused on intra-European flows; but migration from southern Europe was only one component (albeit a predominant one) of post-1945 migratory flows (King, 1993). In the same period, in the case for instance of the UK, citizens from ex-colonies made up almost all the migratory inflow. In

France immigrants from Algeria, Morocco and Tunisia played the same role. The impact on the labour market was the same. They all took part in the mass migration process at the time of mass production. Gordon (1991) provides evidence on the declining employment of foreign and minority workers in manufacturing jobs across Europe, following trends affecting the national labour force. The over-representation of migrant workers in the secondary labour market is stronger now. In the past immigrants in some countries also entered primary labour market jobs (although the less skilled ones) in core industries. The situation has changed because the overall balance of employment has shifted, with many of the primary jobs in heavy industry being casualties of industrial restructuring.

Many misunderstandings concerning the situation of Third World migrants in the new destination countries such as Italy (Macioti and Pugliese, 1991) have been caused by the fact that analytical schemes developed in the context of intra-European industrial migrations of previous decades have been applied to present-day flows. On the basis of the argument so far, the differences between the two situations should be clear. They do not, however, only involve the labour market and labour demand. Restrictive policies force people into irregular conditions and make them more available for irregular jobs.

THE ROLE OF MIGRATORY POLICIES

Present-day Third World migrations are taking place in a context of restrictions. Such policies are an old tradition in countries such as the USA, while they are relatively new in Europe. This is not to say that frontiers have always been open, but the 1970s witnessed a real innovation in the nature of migratory policies. Consequently we should make a more detailed analysis of these in order to evaluate their implications for the immigrants' situation.

The models of migration into different European countries have varied greatly in the past. It was a known fact, for example, that France practised a welcoming policy because of demographic problems. A combination of welcome and assimilation has historically characterised the migratory policy of the French state. In the course of different phases, and with different geographical and professional situations, countless nationalities have contributed to the flow towards this country, starting with Italians in the last century, Poles and other eastern Europeans in the first half of this century, and, especially in recent decades, people from the colonies and later the ex-colonies. It was not even particularly difficult to gain French citizenship, within a rigorous assimilation process directed towards all immigrants "sans distinction de race".

At the opposite extreme was Germany's migratory, or rather anti-migratory, policy. At the height of the inward flow of workers Germany liked to define itself as being not an immigration country, but a country for prolonged and temporary sojourn for foreign workers. The object of this was rotation. From this point of view we should note, among other things, a significant (and in a way perverse) identity of intentions between the Italian emigrants to Germany and this state's migratory policy. The former, as is often the case with first-generation migrants, considered their sojourn a temporary one with a view to putting aside consistent savings to invest in some productive activity when they returned to Italy. The fact that for a long time both Italian and Spanish immigration into Germany consisted mainly of workforces without dependent families was not accidental. In this migratory project the immigrants were perfectly coherent with the objectives of the German government. The prolonged sojourn became for many a "definitive emigration with characteristics of transience" (Mottura and Pugliese, 1975). While many Italians who emigrated to Germany returned, some — a more modest though certainly still quite consistent number — moved definitively, bringing their families with them; but the process was complex and not organic. The decision to transfer their families was rarely a part of the initial migratory plan and this caused significant problems in placing the young second-generation migrants in education and work. These problems are still on the agenda now, but they are much more difficult for Third World migrants, particularly in the new political climate.

England filled a particular place within the framework of migratory and frontier policies. This country, which was the centre of a colonial empire and was linked by a complex history to Ireland, directed its immigration policies towards Ireland and the Commonwealth countries. During the period of great expansion of labour demand in the golden age of the welfare state (the 1950s and 1960s) entry conditions were less restrictive. Finally, Mediterranean countries such as Spain and Italy were traditionally emigration countries and their migratory policy certainly did not concern entry but rather the exit of the population and help for workers abroad.

At present the most evident trend concerning migratory policies is a process of homogenisation towards greater restriction. In France, a country in which entry restrictions have been applied for some years now, the policy of citizenship itself is under discussion. The restrictions called for by right-wing movements go far beyond greater rigour in frontier policy, as they are asking for a reduction of integration policies as well as the separation of foreigners. In Germany, modification of the articles of the constitution concerning refugees is the best indicator of the new situation. In Italy — to give an example of a country new to immigration — policy has become restrictive and its present objective appears to be one of greater frontier control and reduction in the possibility of applying amnesties which in the recent past allowed many immigrants to move from a clandestine to a regular status.

The policy of the EU is very clear on this subject. On the one hand it is pursuing the process of integration within Europe, which also guarantees mobility of the population and labour forces in the common market, and on the other this "internal opening" of the EU corresponds to greater restrictions on outsiders. The Schengen agreements will lead to a reduction in the possible available spaces for migration to individual EU member states. The policy of restriction is supranational: the "European fortress" is officially quite closed. It is now extremely difficult — if not quite yet impossible — for people from the Third World to enter the EU legally for work. Such policies have a double effect. They do actually reduce the number of people who enter the country; they also tend to modify the character of the immigrant population, extending significantly the percentage of illegal workers.

At the time of mass migration in the age of industrial growth, the amount of legislation in the field of immigration policy was much more modest than it is now. According to Calvanese (1983) "the time of politics in immigration" characterises our age. The volume of migratory legislation has been very substantial in all countries. Measures have a twofold objective: both to regulate (that is, limit) new entrances, and to meet social needs of immigrant groups. More restrictive immigration policies do not necessarily mean more discriminatory social policies towards immigrants. The situation is much more complex. Some countries such as Italy have progressive immigration policies as far as general principles are concerned, but these are nullified by the fact that many immigrants are forcefully kept in an illegal status.

This is not just an Italian problem. When the policy of stocks overtook the policy of flows in the traditional destination countries, many initiatives were taken concerning the settlement of a part of the immigrant population. The declared purpose was to facilitate and support by appropriate social measures (concerning housing, educational opportunities for children and a certain amount of political citizenship) a limited stock of immigrant population. Such benevolent attitudes were, however, largely contradicted by the other basic principle, which set a halt to any new (official) entrance. A set of measures encouraging return migration was adopted at the same time, in order to reduce the quota of those aspiring to definitive settlement in the destination country, but there is general agreement on the lack of efficacy of these policies (Calvanese, 1983).

SUMMARY AND CONCLUSIONS

The analysis in this chapter has focused on the causes of the growing marginality of immigrants in Europe. Migrants are more and more marginal in the labour market and in society. The worsening condition of immigrants is an effect of general changes in the economic structure and in the labour market, and of more restrictive migratory policies both in terms of entry and of granting status through social policies. Closely interwoven with these two aspects is the changing attitude of native populations towards migrants, with a mounting xenophobic wave (sometimes with overtly racist tones). This makes it more and more difficult to carry on progressive migratory policies, and at the same time is often taken as a justification for the restrictive policies that almost all European governments are now carrying out.

European frontiers, as we have seen, are closed; but the external pressure is still strong, although it is not so powerful as to justify the "siege syndrome" which is fostered by the mass media, and which in turn is exploited in order to carry on restrictive state policies. The first part of this chapter singled out the reasons why the push effect is greater than in the past — or, better, why the push factors now have an increasing relevance over the pull factors. The worsening of the economic conditions of Third World countries, together with the economic crisis and, on the other hand, the freedom to migrate from the countries of the former socialist bloc: all these indications of growing disparities between Western industrialised countries and the rest of the world are the basic reasons for the potential migratory flow.

"Economic immigration" is now banned in Europe. The pull factors which accounted for the mass intra-European migration from the 1950s to the 1970s are not as strong as in the past. The assumption of contemporary European policy is that such pressures do not exist any more. In these circumstances migrants in search of work (that is to say the majority) can enter only in an illegal or semi-legal way. Their precarious migratory status corresponds to their occupational position; as they are clandestine, they may only work informally. In other words, the confinement of these immigrants to the secondary labour market is strengthened by their legal situation, which leads to marginal employment and acceptance of worsening work and pay conditions, and to social marginality.

All these factors make it more difficult to develop a process of integration in the host societies. Informal work relations make their organisation in the workplace more difficult. As a general consequence, the role of traditional forms of horizontal solidarity, such as those expressed by the labour union, is weakened. This problem does not only concern immigrants. The post-Fordist model of production is characterised among other things by a reduction of the scale of productive units and by a decreasing role for the industrial working class. The working class and its organisations are weaker. The core working class is less extended and it is more and more difficult for migrants to become part of it. The qualitative and quantitative changes in labour demand — the tertiarisation of the economy, the increasing role of service activities, with low productivity and low wages — imply also a change in the structure and the conditions of the labour force, which can aptly be defined as casualisation.

Immigrant work — in the old, as well as in the new destination countries — is casual work. It is not only a matter of discrimination. Primary labour market jobs are less prevalent for local as well as for immigrant workers; precarious working conditions are there for both. In these circumstances not only are chances of upward work mobility extremely limited (and almost impossible for illegal immigrants), but also defence against overexploitation and poor working conditions is more difficult. Although there are differences from country to country, immigrants (in particular new immigrants) are, however, discriminated against and marginalised. Labour market tendencies lead to fragmentation and segregation, and policies are not able, or do not intend, to counteract them. Law and order considerations rather than solidarity are at the basis of recent migratory policies; and an increasing amount of legislation is "correcting" the more progressive policies of the past in those countries where working-class organisations and parties of the left had secured citizenship rights for migrants. In these conditions the gap between the local and the immigrant population widens, and forms of solidarity based on universalistic principles of the working class decline. As a consequence immigrants develop different forms of solidarity — based mostly on ethnic or community ties (Cordeiro, 1990) — and look for new forms of organisation which are less based on their identity as workers and more on other elements. This process is a result of fragmentation, and these new forms of organisation live in a more and more hostile environment.

The "new helots" was a definition given by Robin Cohen (1987) to immigrants and Third World workers, in order to underline the forms of discrimination and overexploitation that they suffered. In the time of mass industrial migration, a process of partial emancipation was apparently taking place. With new economic trends, the ideology of the "European fortress", and the clandestinisation of immigrants, a reverse process is happening in most European countries. Increasing marginalisation is what we can observe today.

REFERENCES

Bastenier, A. and Dassetto, F. (1984) L'Islam Transplante, APO/AVO.
Boehning, R.W. (1984) Studies in international labour migrations, Macmillan, London.
Calvanese, F. (1983) Emigrazione e politica migratoria negli anni '70: l'esperienza italiana ed europea, Laveglia.
Calvanese, F. (ed.) (1990) Emigrazione e politica migratoria negli anni ottanta, Dipartimento di Sociologia e Scienza Politica, Università degli studi di Salerno, Salerno.
Calvanese, F. and Pugliese, E. (1990) La presenza straniera in Italia: il caso della Campania, Franco Angeli, Milan.

Castles, S. and Kosack, G. (1973) *Immigrant workers and the class structure in Western Europe*, Oxford University Press.

Cohen, R. (1987, first published 1966) *The new helots*, Gower, Aldershot.

Collectivo IOE (1987) *Los immigrantes en Espana*, no. 66 de Documentacion Social, Madrid.

Cordeiro, A. (1990) Da immigrati a cittadini non nazionali nella società francese e nell'Europa del 1993, in Calvanese (1990), pp. 195–214.

Dell'Aringa, C. and Neri, F. (1987) Illegal immigrants and the informal economy in Italy, *Labour*, 2, 102–126.

De Prada, M. (1990) La Spagna da paese di emigrazione a paesi di immigrazione, in Calvanese (1990), pp. 146–152.

Fielding, A. (1993) Mass migration and economic restructuring, in King, R. (ed.), *Mass migration in Europe: the legacy and the future*, Belhaven, London.

Gordon, I. (1991) The impact of economic change on minorities and migrants in Western Europe, in JCPS (ed.), *Poverty, inequality and the crisis of social policy. Western states and the new order*, Sage, New York.

Kammerer, P. (1975) *L'immigrazione Italiana della RFT*, Mazzotta, Milan.

King, R. (1993) European international migration: 1945–1990, in King, R. (ed.), *Mass migration in Europe: the legacy and the future*, Belhaven, London, pp. 19–39.

Kreidler, S. and Pugliese, E. (1983) Problemi della seconda generazione degli immigrati nella RFT, *Inchiesta*, 62, 24–36.

Macioti, M.I. and Pugliese, E. (1991) *Gli immigrati stranieri in Italia*, Laterza, Bari.

Martin, D. (1989) Effects of international law on migration policy and practice: the uses of hypocrisy, *International Migration Review*, 3, special silver anniversary issue, 547–578.

Mehrländer, U. (1990) Emigrazione e politiche migratorie nella RFT, in Calvanese (1990).

Mingione, E. (1985) Marginale e povero: il nuovo immigrato in Italia, *Politica ed Economia*, 6, 61–64.

Mingione, E. and Redclift, N. (1986) *Beyond employment*, Basil Blackwell, Oxford.

Montanari A. and Cortese, A. (1993) South to North migration in a Mediterranean perspective, in King, R. (ed.), *Mass migration in Europe: the legacy and the future*, Belhaven, London, pp. 212–213.

Nava M. (1993) *Carovane d'Europa*, Rusconi, Milan.

Oberg S. (1993) Europe in the context of world population trends, in King, R. (ed.). *Mass migration in Europe: the legacy and the future*, Belhaven, London, pp. 195–211.

Piore, M. (1979) *Birds of passage*, Cambridge University Press, Cambridge.

Salt, J. (1989) A comparative overview of international trends and types, *International Migration Review*, no. 3.

Sassen, S. (1988) *The mobility of labour and capital*, Cambridge University Press.

Venturini, A. (1988) An interpretation of Mediterranean migrations, *Labour*, 2, 125–154.

Zollberg, A. (1989) The next waves: migration theory for a changing world, *International Migration Review*, no. 3, 403–430.

5 The Creation of Socio-spatial Marginalisation in Brussels: a Tale of Flexibility, Geographical Competition and Guestworker Neighbourhoods

CHRISTIAN KESTELOOT
Catholic University of Leuven, Belgium

INTRODUCTION

Since the second half of the 1980s a vast amount of literature has documented the socio-spatial restructuring of American and European cities in terms of the global restructuring of capitalism, dualisation of the economy, and fragmentation of Fordist growth models (see among others Castells, 1989; Sassen, 1991; Fainstein et al., 1991; Mingione, 1991; Herbert and Smith, 1989). Tendencies towards a polarised social structure can be traced back to additional causes and processes, dating from the crisis of the 1970s. These include deindustrialisation, economic growth without employment creation due to increases in labour productivity (especially in services), flexibility going hand in hand with subcontracting, informalisation and deskilling, and last but not least growing competition in the labour market, giving a strong impetus to discrimination especially against youth, women and ethnic groups. Nevertheless, the results appear as one huge problem of growing marginalisation, which has its spatial dimension in the city.

Brussels has not escaped these tendencies, and its status of European capital has in fact amplified them. More and more, the second and third generations of immigrant workers appear to be the main victims, and the guestworker neighbourhoods the places where problems are concentrated and interact in a negative spiral. This chapter deals with the formation of these marginal neighbourhoods. In a first part the rise of guestworker neighbourhoods in the 1960s and 1970s is described. The second part unravels the processes at work in Brussels that generate new forms of marginality. Flexibility and geographical competition are seen as their main

Europe at the Margins: New Mosaics of Inequality. Edited by Costis Hadjimichalis and David Sadler
© 1995 European Science Foundation. Published in 1995 by John Wiley & Sons Ltd

components. The last part considers the impact of these on the guestworker neighbourhoods.

THE RISE AND CONSOLIDATION OF GUESTWORKER NEIGHBOURHOODS IN BRUSSELS

Brussels has a high proportion of foreigners in its population (over 28% of 954 000 inhabitants in 1992).[1] Approximately half of these foreigners are guestworkers and their second- and third-generation descendants. The main nationalities are Moroccan, Italian, Spanish and Turkish. Their residential location corresponds clearly to a general pattern with four main characteristics: spatial concentration; different degrees of concentration according to nationality (the most recently arriving groups of Turks and Moroccans being more clustered); some ethnic mixing between different nationalities and Belgians, meaning an absence of ghettos *sensu stricto*; and poor residential conditions, mostly low-grade private rental housing in poorly equipped nineteenth-century inner-city neighbourhoods (Kesteloot, 1987).

One has to start with the mass suburbanisation of the post-war period in order to understand this spatial pattern. Indeed, suburbanisation was quite a strong social and spatial process in the 1960s and the first half of the 1970s, linked to economic growth and a general upward social mobility of the Belgian population in terms of education and income. Relative job security and continuous wage improvements drove the middle class to home-ownership. The absence of any restrictive planning regulation together with incentives to owner-occupation channelled this movement into private house building on cheap land in the urban periphery.[2]

Guestworkers came from the second half of the 1960s onwards, to fill in both the socio-economic and spatial gaps left by the suburban population. As an inexpensive and unskilled labour force, they took over jobs in the construction and transportation industry and in the low-paid, labour-intensive services like hotels, catering and cleaning. They concentrated in the inner-city nineteenth-century neighbourhoods, abandoned by the Belgian population. Although there are some ethnic elements playing a role in maintaining the concentration of foreigners in guestworker neighbour-hoods (such as the presence of a strong ethnic infrastructure or the resistance of Belgian landlords in adjacent neighbourhoods), the fundamental reason for spatial concentration of these groups in the inner area lies in the combination of their socio-economic position and the structure of the housing market.

In Brussels, as in most other Belgian towns, there is very little social housing (8% of the stock). Therefore access to the social sector is rather selective (partly because households with high income security are preferred, partly because most of the sector is under the control of the local political class and foreigners are disadvantaged since they have no voting rights). Guestworkers concentrate in what can be called the residual rental sector — the private rental sector offering cheap housing in old buildings. The sector is residual in the sense that it lies at the bottom of the quality range and in the sense that one applies for accommodation in this sector when all other possibilities appear to be inaccessible. One could equate this with a marginal housing sector. However, the residual sector is not marginal at all in quantitative terms since it represents about 20% of the whole housing market. It is spatially limited to the nineteenth-century neighbourhoods of the city, except the central and eastern zones where the Central Business District (CBD) developed. Moroccans are the largest group (with 77 000 persons) and they can be found in the whole zone, while Turks (21 000) are concentrated in the northern part. Spanish (26 000) and Italians (32 000) are much more dispersed. Nevertheless, their original guestworker concentrations were in the southern part of the zone and these are still visible today.

With the economic crisis, unemployment has grown among the guest-workers, even if there was a stop to immigration in 1974 as in most other west European countries.[3] In relative terms, unemployment among foreigners is even more important than among the Belgian population because they were employed in the most vulnerable sectors. In this position the guestworkers still fulfil one of their functions on the labour market, that of depressing wage rises. They do not do this now as a cheap labour force, but rather as a labour reserve army. In 1984, the year of highest unemployment, there were nearly 68 000 unemployed foreigners in the country, who represented 13.2% of the unemployed. In 1992 the overall unemployment rate was lower, but the proportion of foreigners in that total had grown to 16.1%. Today, in Brussels, 40% of the nearly 55 000 (registered) unemployed are foreign, and the figure is as high as 46% among men.[4]

The general consequence is that the purchasing power of guestworkers relative to the rest of the population drops, and their housing situation deteriorates, within the confines of guestworker neighbourhoods. Indeed, any change in residential location would entail higher housing costs, loss of access to the ethnic infrastructure or abandonment of the local labour market.[5] There is at the same time a relatively important increase in owner-occupation among the same group. Many of these owner occupiers are "emergency buyers" — guestworkers who purchase derelict houses because they can no longer afford the rent of relatively better housing. They hope to find the necessary funds to renew their dwelling and sometimes let out one or more floors of it. These houses are none the less located in the same neighbourhoods, so that the spatial concentration of guestworkers in the inner city is maintained.[6]

In summary, one can say that the guestworker neighbourhoods have been consolidated as a result of the economic crisis. It prevented upward social mobility and a gradual deconcentration of these groups out of their original neighbourhoods, while many Belgian households were restrained from suburbanising, which barred any possibility for a filtering-down process. Indeed, the crisis has kept many middle-class households — which would have moved to the suburbs otherwise — in the city. Some of these people tend to remain in their urban neighbourhoods through buying and renewing low-cost housing. A similar effect on the inner-city housing market results from demographic developments. The increase in single households and in couples without children more than compensates for the overall loss of population, in terms of number of households.

These processes have deepened the socio-spatial contrasts between centre and periphery in the urban region (Figure 5.1). This is very clear between the 19 municipalities of the Brussels Capital Region and the rest of the (geographical) urban region. In the Capital Region, a concentric pattern is still visible, but it is somewhat blurred by an additional NW–SE contrast and the fact that some municipalities extend from the nineteenth-century inner city to the limits of the region. Only two municipalities have their whole territory limited to the nineteenth-century zone (Sint-Joost-ten-Node and Sint-Gillis). They show the lowest mean income per person in the whole of Belgium (see Figure 5.2), and also the highest share of foreigners in their population. In contrast, the richest municipality of the country lies in the south-eastern periphery of the Brussels urban region. While this urban duality has to be attributed to the economic crisis, recovery since the mid-1980s has not reversed the trend, but paradoxically deepened socio-spatial opposition, albeit in contradictory ways.

URBAN REVIVAL, FLEXIBILITY, AND GEOGRAPHICAL COMPETITION

In the second half of the 1980s, economic restructuring started to yield a certain coherence. This can be summarised with the term "urban revival". Its spatial implications can be contrasted with the "golden 1960s" era of suburbanisation. Certainly, this is rather a simplistic conception of a complex process. Nevertheless, the essentials of two aspects of the new growth strategy are particularly relevant for urban revival: flexibility and geographical competition.

Flexibility and dualisation

Instead of establishing growth by creating an outlet for mass production, the new strategy turns this relation upside down: production is following demand. This means the abandonment of uniform mass goods in favour of

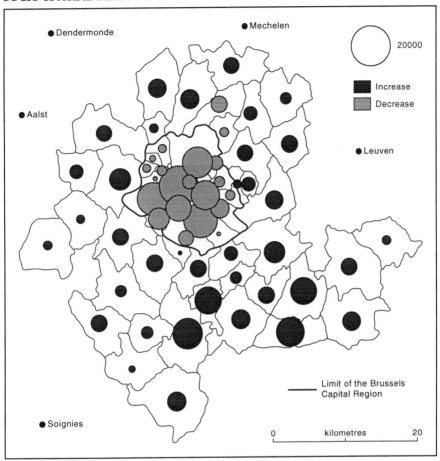

Figure 5.1. Population change in the Brussels urban region, 1976–90

small batches, that can be switched very rapidly to new products whenever a shift in demand is detected. Every possibility of diversifying and changing the structure of demand is exploited in order to create new products which have their pre-established outlet in the consumer market. The overproduction problem is, at least temporarily, resolved. Such a strategy is only possible with a very flexible organisation of production. Thanks to new computer technologies and associated developments in telecommunications, this flexibility is achieved with productivity gains. Besides the opening of new markets, the new production system eliminates the need for large buffer stocks. As a result capital circulates more quickly, and less capital remains unproductive for long periods. Profit rates are restored and economic growth is resumed (Swyngedouw, 1986). So

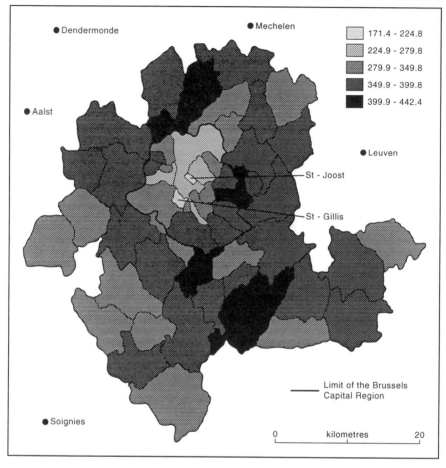

Figure 5.2. Mean income per capita in the Brussels urban region, BFr 1000s, 1990

flexibility does not only concern labour, but also diversified consumption norms, rapid investment shifts, and finally reorganisation of the spatial structures of production and consumption.

Flexibility does not only necessitate the introduction of new technologies, but also the transfer of labour-intensive and marginal activities (that could hinder profitability in innovating firms) to subcontractors and suppliers. In turn these firms can only secure their survival through low wages, flexible employment through temporary and part-time contracts, overtime work, poor conditions and the maximum involvement of unskilled labour. This development creates an informal economy producing the same goods and services for innovating firms, without the burden of social contributions and taxes. In Marxist economic terminology, one could speak about the return of absolute surplus value, or the creation of an internal Third World or low-wage sector.

This trend is manifest in Brussels through a series of important changes. The first (although only partly the result of flexibility) is the loss of industrial employment in the city, because transportation and communication are key functions of flexible production, which are better realised in the urban periphery. Between 1980 and 1991, Brussels lost more than 25 000 industrial jobs (a reduction of 23% — less severe than in the 1970s, when deindustrialisation was at stake). The change is less marked in terms of manual work (down 7.8%). Significantly, however, this type of job opportunity is growing in the urban periphery (+7.6% in the district Halle-Vilvoorde). Non-manual work is also growing faster in the periphery than in the centre (+37% in the Halle-Vilvoorde district, against 6.7% in Brussels). A related development is the polarised growth in service industries as a result of vertical disintegration and subcontracting: on the one hand are activities like cleaning, security, catering, and transportation and courier services; on the other, specialised and highly qualified services like marketing, advertising, headhunting, auditing and lobbying consultants. While this is difficult to measure, services to enterprises (including real estate) show an increase in employment of 57% between 1974 and 1991. The new services (classified as not elsewhere specified) nearly tripled in employment terms (representing more than 20 000 jobs in 1991). Cleaning firms on the other hand, after stagnation in the first half of the 1980s, provided an employment increase of 18% between 1984 and 1991 (see also Allen and Henry, Chapter 10 this volume, for similar evidence from the UK).

Thus, flexibility goes hand in hand with dualisation. On the one hand, it creates new social groups, which find their job opportunities in the innovative firms and institutions and in new urban activities. These groups have a tendency to dwell in the inner city, partly because of a new urban culture which results from consumption diversification, but also because this is the best location for their business. Urban revival is therefore largely a result of the way in which these groups wish to transform their new living places. On the other hand, they are confronted in the same urban space with the low-skilled, low-paid and irregular workers who bear the physical burden of flexibility. While in many west European cities these groups are not predominantly located in the inner areas (be it because of a later urban industrial take-off, huge state intervention in cheap housing in the urban periphery, or large post-war rural–urban migration) the Belgian case has more in common with the North American pattern. The inner cities were left by the well-to-do as early as the second half of the nineteenth century. This was a process of socio-spatial distanciation from a growing "dangerous" working class. During the "golden 1960s" this urban working class was replaced by an expanding middle class which had nothing to run from, but searched for a location to fulfil its consumption dreams and opened the inner city for guestworkers.

However, the future of these inner-city neighbourhoods is not only threatened by the claims of other social groups, but also by a second general process linked to the new form of economic growth, that of geographical competition.

Geographical competition

The flexible economy presupposes a dramatic increase in capital mobility. The greater this mobility, the more regions and places have to compete with each other to maintain or attract investment. The selling of one's city or region, and "urban marketing" are the new keywords in this competition. This process has been echoed by the rather awkward term "glocalization". Since the theatre of economic activities and location choices has expanded to a global scale, the sensitivity to local distinctiveness has grown (Swyngedouw, 1989).

Geographical competition can play a positive role, since it represents a mechanism that would yield the best location choice. Moreover, as in standard market competition, the economic actors of regions and cities are spurred to innovate. Even local authorities are driven to develop new attractive economic, social and cultural policies. The dark side of this process, however, is that from the point of view of local communities, competition forces them to pay for cutting the costs of footloose investors. In order to attract these investors, they have to bear larger financial burdens than competing regions in the form of more and better infra-structures, tax holidays or reductions, investment and employment subsidies, and maybe also less stringent environmental regulations. Cities have to develop their social, cultural and scientific image to create an attractive investment climate.

Not every local community can be a winner in this game. Losers reveal another negative consequence of geographical competition. Across western Europe, cities and regions are building hotels, modernising and expanding airports, constructing high-speed railways, erecting new conference and exhibition halls, extending office floorspace or creating golf courses or waterfront developments. These amenities do not correspond to real needs — certainly not in cities who fail in the competition. They do, however, benefit the developers, who are paid through the financial efforts of local communities, at the expense of other individual or collective consumption. A further negative effect of geographical competition concerns even "winning" localities, and brings us back to flexibility and dualism. The endowment of cities with every attribute of geographical competition requires not only money but also space. Many of these attributes need a central location. The consequence is, as with gentrification, a repulsion of weaker social groups from central urban spaces.

The concrete manifestations of urban competition and their location rationale can be divided into four fields (according to Harvey, 1985). The attraction of production, be it in terms of investment or employment, is the first of these. At the urban scale, one thinks of high-technology industries — or more broadly activities having a competitive edge because of their high productivity and research content. If such industries can be attracted and maintained, they offer good prospects of economic development for the region. The location factors of these industries are known: in as far as they concern research and development and not routine production of high-tech goods, they include links with the scientific world, international communication and transport channels, state subsidies, potential outlets and an attractive environment (physically, socially and culturally) to help retain highly skilled personnel. In Brussels this field of urban competition mainly concerns the periphery, where the Regional Development Corporation (GOMB) created four science parks, all of them co-managed by the universities. Three of these are located in the immediate vicinity of university hospitals and are intended to develop activities linked to medical research and practice (computer science, pharmaceuticals, biotechnology, scientific instruments, precision robotics). The last one is located on the connection between the city and the airport, near the NATO headquarters and a series of computer firms which form what is sometimes called the "Brussels Silicon Valley", although these firms are more involved in distribution and marketing than research and development.

Since flexible production is tuned to rapidly changing demand, cities do not only compete for investment in production, but also for consumption. Indeed, the concentration of purchasing power creates in turn an attractive investment climate. Urban renewal is an important means of attracting new inhabitants and their incomes. The neighbourhoods with old but culturally interesting buildings attract new groups, who obtain state subsidies to buy up and renew these buildings. In other neighbourhoods companies buy old mansions and transform them into offices or expensive flats. Neighbourhoods of this sort can be found in the central and the nineteenth-century parts of the city, but they are also concentrated on the eastern side of the canal (the western side being traditionally more industrial).

It is not only new inhabitants that enhance consumption in the city. Every activity that temporarily brings consumers is also encouraged. One can interpret in this way the boom of hotel construction in the city. The logic of flexible growth fits very well into activities where production and consumption fall together in one event. Many cultural and sporting events are such cases. The concept of urban spectacle corresponds to the tremendous increase of such activities in recent years. In Brussels one can find a whole series of them. The revival of the Opera House (Théâtre de la Monnaie) is probably the best known internationally. There are numerous other new cultural centres, film, theatre and music festivals, exhibitions, fairs and conferences. The revival of Flemish culture right in the centre of the city is most striking in this context.

The new urban mode of living has also created new shopping and entertainment areas. Diverse ethnic shops and restaurants are now part of Brussels life. Other central places have undergone dramatic changes, commodifying their environment. The new young Flemish community that activates the Flemish cultural revival in the central city is also the founder of a real "yuppie" centre with exclusive fashion shops. The traditionally marginal neighbourhood of the city (the Marolles in the south-east part of the old town) with its typical cafés, second-hand shops and flea market has been gradually transformed into a socially exotic antiquarian centre and exclusive eating place. Last, but not least, plans are being made for a Brussels waterfront development along the canal. The first private sector impetus to the project was given by one of the banks, which decided to shift 2000 employees from the centre to a new office block along the water.

In large part, these new consumption centres are focused on the new urban groups who are developing a new urban way of living. Some developments though are aimed at a much broader public of consumers. These are located outside the centre. Along the Heizel a huge entertainment centre, Bruparck, has been developed with the largest European cinema centre (25 halls with 7000 seats). It is not only linked to the central city by a new underground line, but also to a large catchment area through the ring road and the motorway network around the city. A similar locational logic could be applied to a new sports infrastructure in the south-west, where the former mayor once dreamed of holding the 1992 Olympic Games. It now contains the only golf courses within the city region and there are strong pressures to link it to the underground.

A third field in which competition between cities and regions takes place is economic and political power. Once such decision-making is linked to the city, many positive consequences can be expected. To attract this power, the instruments and infrastructure necessary to exercise it have to be available. The production and collection of information, and transportation and communication channels are central in this respect. On the national level Brussels has a winning card as the national capital. State reform has created a new issue, however. While the Walloon region chose to locate its capital in its region, the Flemish region and the Flemish and the French communities located in Brussels. A new axis of public administration offices is developing on the north side of the old town. As a result a series of private companies are trying to locate their headquarters near this new axis, particularly the financial sector and companies that depend on government orders.

The same logic applies at a higher level to the attraction of the European institutions.[7] The installation of the European Parliament in Brussels in the purpose-built International Conference Centre has attracted embassies, banks, headquarters of firms and organisations, lobbies, catering firms and journalists to Brussels. New housing and offices have been necessary. Today, Brussels has nearly 8 m² of office space per inhabitant, probably a world record. Most of these new developments lie on the eastern side of the canal, with a pole around the North station (where the administration of the Brussels Region will be concentrated) and the Leopold quarter where the European institutions are located, and several axes all leading in the direction of the airport.

In order to attract investors, consumers and decision-makers, cities must find the means to adapt their infrastructure, activities and image. The struggle for these financial means is the fourth and last field of competition between places. Distribution rules for public finance are on the agenda of European, national and regional authorities. Financing of the European infrastructure in Brussels, recognition of the city as a full third region in the nation, redistribution of tax incomes from the national level to the regional level, intervention of the national level for the financial reconstruction of the large cities and new ways of spending municipal financial means are all at stake.

All these tendencies in the economic and spatial organisation of Brussels (which are nothing other than the refurbishing of the city for flexibility and geographical competition) are taking place in the eastern part of the city. They form a district where decision-making and innovation centres and the means of communication and transportation are located. Regional, national and European governmental and administrative institutions, NATO, the universities (and the big Catholic universities of Leuven and Louvain-la-Neuve are reached in less than half an hour in the directions of Leuven and Namur), the airport and "Brussels Silicon Valley", the four most important railway stations of the city and the future terminus of the TGV are all located to the east of the canal, which appears as a physical separation dividing the inner city into a socially and economically expanding eastern part and a relatively declining western part. This division line is a traditional one in Brussels: high city and low city, merchants and nobility, workers and bourgeois were broadly separated by the same frontier.

One should be cautious about an explanation in terms of spatial inertia, however. The content and the social meaning of this divide were different in each period. As the development of marginalisation in the guestworker neighbourhoods shows, the present-day process entails more a rupture than a deepening of this socio-spatial structure.

THE FUTURE OF ETHNIC NEIGHBOURHOODS: FROM
SURVIVAL STRATEGIES AND THE INFORMAL ECONOMY TO
MARGINALISATION

The ethnic neighbourhoods are places where survival strategies have gradually developed since the economic crisis of the 1970s. The reason for this lies in the first place in the incapacity of the formal economic and social system to provide the guestworkers and some other social groups with a decent standard of living. As a consequence, survival strategies developed at the household and neighbourhood level in order to cut back costs or to make an additional income through the informal production of goods and services which corresponded to local needs (Mingione, 1983; Pahl, 1985). Ethnic infrastructure plays an important role in this process. Such neighbourhoods have many ethnic shops, which are substantially cheaper than others. Ethnic entrepreneurship is a convenient way to escape unemployment, but resulting conditions entail low investment in the premises, long working days, and the mobilisation of family members. The number of foreign self-employed in Brussels rose from 7170 in 1981 to an estimated 10 000–12 000 in 1992, and their share in the total of self-employed passed from 13 to 21% (see Vanhoren, 1992; Kesteloot et al., 1992). One can also discover parallel circuits of hairdressing, tailoring, painting and decorating, and car maintenance.

Survival strategies are not always expressed as an increase in more or less informal and/or household activities. Difficulties in making a living can also mean that the ownership of a series of consumer durable goods is impossible, yet these are necessary to household survival. Where essential needs are concerned, such people have to turn to collective consumption. In this sense, the crisis can bring about a formalisation of informal (household) activities. Self-service laundries, cheap neighbourhood restaurants and telephone shops, are examples of how the private sector is reacting to these developments.

Survival strategies are also designed to produce secondary income sources. The circuits of cleaning women and handymen who serve outside the neighbourhoods fall into this category, as do the children helping their parents in running shops or restaurants. In addition a whole set of activities within the local formal economy plays the same role. As an example, restaurants which formerly looked to local groups for custom have modified their outlook and their menus to attract external customers. This shows how the existing formal and informal neighbourhood economy, while having mainly a local servicing character, can be extended to the production of goods and services for the whole urban economy and fitted into the needs of subcontracting and dualisation of the flexible economy. As this tendency develops, the immigrant population, in its marginal social position, concentrated in neighbourhoods where the networks of informal work are already well structured, and aspiring for economic betterment, becomes a human resource for the flexible economy. Their neighbourhoods provide cheap labour reproduction and low-cost labour-intensive service industries for the formal urban economy.[8]

Some visible changes in the guestworker neighbourhoods illustrate their new economic role. Brussels being a tertiary city (85% of employment is in this sector), subcontracting is geared towards office work. Italian, Portuguese, Spanish and Moroccan cleaning firms are found in the guestworker neighbourhoods. Restaurants and snackbars shifting from local customers to Brussels employees are located there too, near the city centre. They offer quite cheap meals and have the advantage of being open almost the whole day long. Subcontracting is also growing in printing and copying, mailing services, and security and surveillance, although there is little evidence about the specific location of these services in the neighbourhoods.

The tendency to flexibility and the role of guestworkers in this process can also be traced in the changes in employment of foreigners between 1970 and 1981 (data combining activity and nationality are not yet available for the 1991 census). The decrease in employment of foreigners in traditional industrial sectors follows the general pattern of deindustrialisation (Figure 5.3); but the strong increase in the trade sector, which comprises catering, maintenance and repair activities, is striking. The relatively strong increase in the financial sector may be due to the internationalisation of financial activities and thus concern foreigners other than guestworkers, but the sector also comprises services to enterprises, where flexible employment is of great importance. The "other services" concern the civil service — from which foreigners are excluded in Belgium — but also cleaning and personal and domestic services. In this context the shift from secondary to tertiary employment becomes an important indicator of the installation of a flexible service economy.

All this indicates that the guestworkers and their descendants are captured in their neighbourhoods because these are the places where they can develop survival strategies. Moreover, such places are functional to the development of the formal and informal circuits of subcontracting and supply, mainly for the tertiary sector in Brussels. This interrelation reinforces the spatial concentration of economic activities. The flexible workforce also has to be located near its place of employment, because of its low spatial mobility combined with rapidly changing job opportunities. Thus new economic developments confine the guestworkers to their neighbourhoods, which are located close to the main activity centres. Dispersion of immigrants, sometimes seen as a possible solution to ethnic and racial problems in the city, appears as quite dysfunctional in this context.

Contemporary manifestations of urban revival are, however, threatening the future of these neighbourhoods. The reason for this lies in the fact that

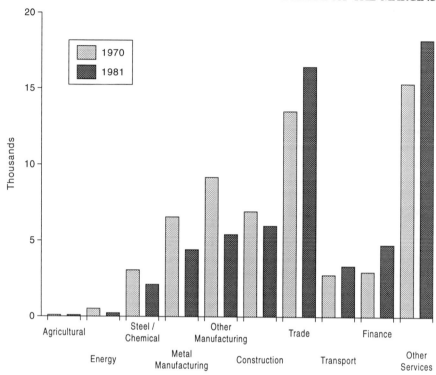

Figure 5.3. Foreign employment by activity sector, 1970–81

guestworkers and the poorest Belgians are presently living in all the residential nineteenth-century parts of the city. There is strong competition between the lower- and middle-income groups for housing in the eastern inner-city neighbourhoods. Firms and institutions, and tourism and entertainment activities, are also looking for more floor space at the inner edge of the same districts. If one adds the effects of land speculation (housing prices have doubled since 1988), housing is under pressure, especially in this eastern part. As a result, guestworkers are being pushed out of their neighbourhoods, losing the social networks and material infrastructures for their informal economic activities. Recent population figures by nationality show a tendency for foreigners, especially Moroccans and Turks, to be pushed out of the eastern city.[9] Their only way out is the western inner city, where this process is causing overcrowding and a general decline of living conditions.

The riots of May 1991 took place in this part of the city, reflecting the consciousness of social marginalisation in these neighbourhoods, particularly within the second generation of Moroccans.[10] This was further strengthened by the confrontation of guestworkers and their second- and third-generation descendants with the new urban social groups (which are at both ends of the dualisation process) and the fact that the city centre is regaining importance as an innovation place nurturing flexibility, especially in terms of consumption. Among other factors, the riots were triggered by a clash between rich suburban youths and those of guestworker origin around a former swimming pool, transformed into a trendy dancing hall to which local coloured and poor are not admitted.

Repulsion of weak social groups from the inner cities is not a problem common to all European cities. In southern Europe and even in many French cities, the centre remained in the hands of higher classes, due to later industrialisation, greater demographic pressures in the cities in the post-war period than before, and a smaller suburbanising middle class. The effects of dualisation on the lower classes are more (although not exclusively) a problem of banlieues, while those of geographical competition affect primarily the inner cities as in north-west Europe. The Belgian case appears to be the most severe in terms of superimposition of dualism and competition in the inner city, due to strong indirect state support for individual suburbanisation of the middle class and low control of the housing market. The share of social housing is not enough to influence the global socio-spatial structure of the cities and the private rental sector dominates in the inner cities, resulting in a stronger concentration of the lower class in these inner areas. In Brussels, urban revival and social repulsion are even more strongly associated, since it is the largest urban region of the country and since the administrative boundaries of the region are limited to the urban area under pressure. Gradual confirmation of Brussels as capital of Europe, together with the increasing role of the European institutions in the context of a unified market, give an additional impetus to the city's strategy in geographical competition, thus reinforcing the dialectic of revival and marginalisation.

While hundreds of billions are invested in Brussels, profit rates are being restored and land speculation has never been as profitable,[11] the guestworkers and other weak social groups are chased out of the neighbourhoods where they had developed their own social and economic life. This situation is leading to territorial conflicts, in the same vein as those created in the nineteenth century by the Haussmannisation of the city (when the workers' slums were cleared and replaced by wide boulevards and bourgeois housing), or those created in the late 1960s when working-class neighbourhoods were transformed into office zones. The expulsion of guestworkers from the inner city can generate resistance because these groups have no other place to go. It can also be dysfunctional since it thwarts the locational logic of the labour force in a flexible urban economy.

NOTES

1. Brussels refers to the Brussels Capital Region, which includes 19 municipalities.
2. This process was particularly important in Belgium, in contrast to other European countries (see Cortie and Kesteloot, 1992).
3. However, family reunification was still allowed. This, together with the high fertility of the guestworkers, explains their further increase.
4. The figures are for June 1993. Foreigners represent about 22% of the active population in Brussels (based on a sample survey in 1990).
5. Intercity movements have been reported, but mainly from industrial regions hit by the crisis towards Brussels, rather than away from the city. On the other hand, the fiscal crisis of the Brussels municipalities has undermined their welfare provision and induced some people to move to other cities like Charleroi or Mons. Permanent residence on campsites in the countryside has also been reported, but this generally concerns low-income Belgians.
6. Between 1970 and 1981 the percentage of owner-occupiers among Moroccans and Turks rose respectively from 3 to 9.5% and from 3 to 12%. The 1991 census figures are not yet available, but a survey in a sample neighbourhood yielded figures of 20 and 16% respectively in 1991.
7. European unification is part of the logic of economic revival. Free mobility of persons, goods and services is crucial to the organisation of flexibility on a large scale. The opening of national markets to other European producers gives them access to a more diversified demand structure and at the same time to a more diversified supply of production goods and labour force. In the absence of a stringent social programme, opportunities for subcontracting and shedding less profitable tasks have multiplied dramatically. The significance of national economic policies and of national frontiers fades away, and this unleashes the competitive struggle between regions and cities for investment, consumers and decision-making power.
8. However, some recent signs show that clandestine refugees are undermining this employment niche of the guestworkers. Polish temporary clandestine workers are active in light construction (renewal), textiles and cleaning. Another example is a concentration of second-hand car import/export firms, employing more and more Ghanaian refugees instead of local Moroccans.
9. This movement is also resulting from the efforts of most of the central municipalities to get rid of the Turks and Moroccans (and today also of the political and economic refugees) and to replace them by middle-class people (see Kesteloot and De Decker, 1992).
10. For an account of these riots and a discussion about their significance, see Rea and Brion (1992) and Rea (1992).
11. Between 1985 and 1990, 365 billion Belgian francs were invested in property development (see Timmerman, 1991, who gives a vivid account of some of these projects and of land speculation and political involvement).

REFERENCES

Castells, M. (1989) *The informational city: information technology, economic restructuring and the urban–regional process*, Blackwell, Oxford.
Cortie, C. and Kesteloot, C. (1992) Political systems and the formation of urban regions: Amsterdam and Brussels, in van der Wusten, H. (ed.), *The urban political arena: geographies of public administration*, Nederlandse Geografische Studies, Amsterdam, Vol. 140, pp. 165–184.

Fainstein, S., Gordon, I. and Harloe, M. (1991) *Divided cities: New York and London in the contemporary world*, Blackwell, Oxford.

Harvey, D. (1985) *The urbanisation of capital*, Blackwell, Oxford.

Herbert, D.T. and Smith, D.M. (eds.) (1989) *Social problems and the city*, Oxford University Press, Oxford.

Kesteloot, C. (1987) The residential location of immigrant workers in Belgian cities: an ethnic or socio-economic phenomenon?, in O'Loughlin, J. and Glebe, G. (eds), *Foreign minorities in European cities*, Steiner Verlag, Wiesbaden, pp. 223–239.

Kesteloot, C. and De Decker, P. (1992) Territoria en migraties als geografische factoren van racisme, in Desle, E. and Martens, A. (eds), *Gezichten van het hedendaags racisme*, VUB-Press, Brussels, pp. 69–108.

Kesteloot, C. and Meert, H. (1993) Informele economie: sociaal-economische functies en geografische dimensie van een dubbelzinnig verschijnsel, *Ruimtelijke Planning*, A, 53–90.

Kesteloot, C., Meert, H., Savenberg, S. and van der Haegen, H. (1992) *Informele economie en etnisch ondernemerschap: een literatuurstudie*, De geografische dimensie van de dualisering in de maatschappij, deelrapport I, Instituut voor Sociale en Economische Geografie, K.U. Leuven, Leuven.

Mingione, E. (1983) Informalisation, restructuring and the survival strategies of the working class, *International Journal of Urban and Regional Research*, 7, 311–339.

Mingione, E. (1991) *Fragmented societies: a sociology of economic life beyond the market paradigm*, Blackwell, Oxford.

Pahl, R. (1985) The restructuring of capital, the local political economy and household work strategies, in Gregory, D. and Urry, J. (eds), *Social relations and spatial structures*, Macmillan, Basingstoke, pp. 242–264.

Rea, A. (1992) Ethnicisation de la pauvreté ou pauvreté de l'ethnicisation?, *Revue Nouvelle*, 11, 62–68.

Rea, A. and Brion, F. (1992) La construction médiatique et politique des émeutes urbaines, *L'année sociale 1991*, Editions de l'ULB, Brussels, pp. 282–305.

Sassen, S. (1991) *The global city: New York, London, Tokyo*, Princeton University Press.

Swyngedouw, E. (1986) *The socio-spatial implications of innovations in industrial organisation*, Working Paper 20, Johns Hopkins European Center for Regional Planning and Research, Lille.

Swyngedouw, E. (1989) The heart of the place: the resurrection of locality in an age of hyperspace, *Geografiska Annaler* 71, B, 31–42.

Timmerman, G. (1991) *In Brussel mag alles; geld, macht, beton*, EPO, Antwerp.

Vanhoren, I. (1992) *Etnisch ondernemerschap in het Brussels Hoofdstedelijk Gewest*, Hoger Instituut voor de Arbeid, K.U. Leuven, Leuven.

6 Culture and Marginality in the New Europe

KEVIN ROBINS
University of Newcastle, UK

ASU AKSOY
Istanbul, Turkey

A group is a collection of people who are resolved to keep quiet about the same thing. . . . This "point of silence" holds the group together, sustains it, and even structures it. Daniel Sibony (1993)

It was suddenly clear that Europe hadn't learnt its lesson, that history always repeats itself and that someone is always a Jew. Once the concept of "otherness" takes root, the unimaginable becomes possible. Slavenka Drakulic (1993)

FROM "1992" TO 1989

A recent report from the Crédit Suisse First Boston financial group takes up the question of core and periphery for economic development in the new Europe. As one of its major recommendations, it argues that the European Union must come to terms with the "Eastern periphery" that has emerged as a consequence of the events of 1989. The stark simplicity of its proposal is that, to deal with this new Eastern question, Europe's politicians should "allow *more* imports (especially food, steel and textiles) but *fewer* immigrants from Eastern Europe, the CIS, Turkey and the Maghreb". "Ultimately", it claims, "the EC must choose between imports and immigrants" (Shepley and Wilmot, 1992, pp. 8, 4).

We shall not occupy ourselves here with the narrowly economic sense or non-sense of this proposal (except to ask why there has to be such a choice, and why choice is presented in such simplistic terms: *either* imports *or* immigrants). What concern us far more are the *cultural* implications and assumptions that inform this, and a great many other, blueprints for a new Europe. Who can claim to be at the heart of Europe? And who will be consigned to the peripheries, margins and hinterlands of the new Europe? The Crédit Suisse First Boston report is straightforward about these matters of distinction, and we cite it because it is transparent where others are

Europe at the Margins: New Mosaics of Inequality. Edited by Costis Hadjimichalis and David Sadler
© 1995 European Science Foundation. Published in 1995 by John Wiley & Sons Ltd

more circumspect. From it we can gather who are the marginals in the new European order. Those on the eastern periphery, the Turks, the Arabs, the Muslims, the gypsies, the immigrants, the migrant workers, the asylum-seekers, the poor — these are the extra-communitarians.

In this chapter, we aim to look at how issues of culture and identity are being mobilised in the construction of the European Union of "1992" and Maastricht. What concerns us particularly is the relationship between changing cultural geographies and psycho-geographies. Questions of culture and identity must be considered, we shall argue, in the context of the risks and dangers, real or imagined, associated with the changing world order of the 1990s. The construction of cultural community necessarily involves principles and processes of inclusion and exclusion. The aim is to differentiate and separate "us" (Europeans) from "them" (non-Europeans). But all too easily this can become a matter of insulating and protecting us against them. What seems to be at work is what Cornelius Castoriadis (1990, p. 29) describes as "the apparent incapacity to constitute oneself as oneself without excluding the other — and the apparent inability to exclude the other without devaluing and, ultimately, hating him". Constituted in this way, cultural identity is exposed to feelings of anxiety and vulnerability. The coherence and integrity of "our" community is always under threat from the "others": "Because their mere existence puts our values into question" (Grass, 1992, p. 107).

It is clear to us all that there is now something very troubled at the heart of European culture and identity. The mood of optimism that was mobilised by the "1992" project has been invaded by the forces of gloom and pessimism. The exultant sense of triumphant liberalism that followed the events of 1989 — the end of history, the end of ideologies — has been rapidly dissipated. In 1992, under the headline "Europe in pieces", *Newsweek* magazine declared that "millions of Britons and Germans and Spaniards and Danes are far from ready to submerge their identities and their interests for the sake of some unproven entity stretching from the Mediterranean to the Baltic". "While Europe may be a community", it went on, "it isn't yet a state of mind" (*Newsweek*, 28 September 1992, pp. 10–11). "Down in the dumps" is how *Newsweek* described the European mood in 1993. The continent has seen an abrupt shift, it observed, from "the epochal collapse of communism in 1989, seen at first as a lavish gift from history and a unique opportunity to re-launch Europe as a world power", to a situation now in which "Europe remains disunited, mired in recession, threatened by massive emigration from the south and east" (*Newsweek*, 12 April 1993, p. 10). Europe is caught in a mood of depression and anxiety; it is experiencing what must be seen as an identity crisis.

The collapse of an old world order, with the end of the cold war, has clearly been fundamental to these processes, and is increasingly perceived as such. It was the cold war equilibrium that had held everything in place, and it is the shattering of that equilibrium that is now creating a sense of instability and disorder. In the case of Italy, to take just one example, Lucia Annunziata (1993, pp. 444–445) describes the present upheavals as being a consequence of the erosion of Italy's role in the confrontation between the superpowers: "What is now crumbling in Italy is, in effect, the political system created there almost single-handedly by the United States government at the end of World War II. The Italian crisis is nothing less than the symbolic equivalent of the fall of the Berlin Wall." The Berlin Wall is a potent symbol for all the old partitions that are collapsing in the European continent. According to Dominique David (1992, pp. 10–11), the disappearance of the Soviet Union has undermined and destabilised the whole "European architecture"; with the demise of the Soviet "Other", Europe is now compelled "to redefine itself, to discover around which space, according to which values, in line with which project, it now wants to define its collective life". In its moment of triumph, the old continent finds itself disorientated, exposed, caught up in an identity panic.

It may even be that this period of disruption is more than just the end of the cold war era, however. Immanuel Wallerstein has put forward the argument that what is actually in crisis is the ideology of liberalism that, over two centuries, had been shared by conservatives and socialists alike:

> The world revolution of 1848 set in motion an historical process that led to the triumph of liberalism as an ideology and the integration of the working classes. . . . The world revolution of 1968 unravelled the ideological consensus and the 20 years that followed saw the undoing of the credibility of liberalism, of which the collapse of Communism in 1989 was the culmination (Wallerstein, 1992, p. 32).

With the crisis of liberal ideology and polity, Wallerstein (1992) argues, "not progressive change, but social disintegration is now coming to be seen as normal". As they experience this predicament people look for protection, and whereas once they "turned to the State to secure change, they are now turning to group solidarities (all kinds of groups) to provide protection" (1992). The crisis of liberalism is a crisis of the political, which then seems to license the resort to more "primordial" attachments.

The nation states of western Europe are in disarray, and their project for an enlarged community in distress. Europe is now caught between two countervailing forces: "the logic of economics and interdependence that spells community, and the logic of ethnicity and nationality that demands separation" (Joffe, 1993, p. 43). What it lacks, between economics and identity, is political resolution and direction. As national states, and sovereignties, have become weakened, they have been replaced by an administrative and bureaucratic pseudo-state. This political emptiness has been disastrous and damaging as the European Union has sought to navigate a path through the events of 1989. Confronted with the requests and demands from eastern Europe and the Balkans, the Twelve found it impossible to conceive a political project that would encompass the whole of the old continent (Riche, 1993).

The events in Bosnia, in particular, have cruelly exposed the inability of western European interests to coalesce around a unified political principle and purpose. Later in our discussion we shall focus on the "Eastern periphery", and particularly on the Balkans, for it is here that what Europe means and stands for is presently most exposed. Paul Thibaud (1992, p. 113) invokes the possibility of "a new Europe where the 'little nations' would find a way to recreate themselves and to participate actively in a history from which they have been separated for forty years". Such a Europe would, he concludes, "have little in common with the Europe which is now taking shape in the West, levelled as it is by the combined forces of market and technocracy". We think that this is indeed the case. Our inclination, then, is to shift the agenda from one of concern about the "Eastern question" to one of reflection on what must be seen as the Western question.

As political agency seems to prove itself unable to deal with the Balkan problem, so the mechanisms of cultural defence and identity protection come to take precedence, and sometimes to take over. That for which there is no political solution comes to be feared as a threat. All that is possible, it seems, is to insulate "our" community against the threat of madness and fragmentation that "they" represent. What motivates European identity is the desire "to exclude non-Europeans, those intruders who are not from European stock, those strangers without entitlement or worth, who are brutes compared to the civilised and democratic refinement which is proper to Europe" (Gallissot, 1992, p. 5).

What we are seeing now is a small Europe trying to rediscover and redefine itself in the light of the threats it perceives from both the East and the South. As Philip Schlesinger (1992, p. 19) argues, "it seems that the new geopolitical lines of Europe could broadly follow those of the Great Schism of 1054 between Rome and Constantinople". The criteria of inclusion and exclusion would once again be religious, and both Orthodoxy and Islam would constitute that Other that cannot belong to the essential Europe.

Old walls are coming down, but new ones are being erected to replace them. New frontiers, new territories, new maps, and that means new communities, new insiders and new outsiders — new marginalities. What we must address are the emotional and psychic energies that suffuse this geopolitical ordering and reordering. Julia Kristeva (1992a) suggests that Europe is presently suffering from depression, which often expresses itself through manic defences:

I don't know who I am, but I'm holding on to a self-aggrandising image that keeps me on my feet and also designates a foreign scapegoat I can fight. The depressed subject puts on a kind of armour by drawing on archaic identity values: land, race, the cult of language, everything that is most closely connected with the family, the maternal and with warmth.

In what has been called the new world disorder, the question that confronts us is how, or whether, these archaic sentiments can be contained and civilised through new forms of political life and expression. Can Europe assume the new continental responsibilities that have fallen to it with the end of the cold war? Can the citizens of Europe deal with the psycho-cultural drives that create scapegoats, aliens and marginal figures?

CULTURE AND IDENTITY IN EUROPE

Jacques Derrida (1992, pp. 8–9) refers to an occasion when François Mitterrand suggested that Europe "is returning to its history and geography like one who is returning home". "What does this mean?" Derrida asks, "Is it possible? Desirable? Is it really this that announces itself today?" These seem to us to be vital questions in thinking about the parameters of identity in the changing continent.

Europe is returning to its history and geography in apparently different ways. The most expansive involves the construction, or reconstruction, of a united and unified European cultural space; the ideal of belonging to a "common European home". It was this sense of enlarged community that the "1992" campaign sought to promote and popularise. What it might have invoked were the universalist aspirations of the continental Enlightenment, the principles of Kant's cosmopolis, the appeal to human rights, democracy and citizenship made by political modernity. What was mobilised instead was what T.S. Eliot celebrated as the "spiritual organism of Europe", the narrative of a supposedly common European descent rooted in Greece and Rome and 2000 years of Christianity. Within this perspective, the idea of Europe has been reduced to tradition and heritage. As Cornelius Castoriadis reminds us, "what was proper to the Greco-western tradition . . . was the questioning of all established significations, institutions and representations". If Europe no longer exercises an emancipatory influence in the world, it is because this dynamism and creativity no longer exist there; it is because all that now seems possible is the formulaic repetition of old truths and values.

Another, and probably a more meaningful, homeland is that provided by the national community and culture — which, over the last 200 years or so, has anyway existed, more or less easily, in compromise with the idea of Europe. There is a sense in which when we speak of European culture we mean the plurality and variety of national cultures that make it up. This draws upon the Romantic conception of culture developed by Herder, and articulated more recently by Isaiah Berlin: "To be human mean[s] to be able to feel at home somewhere, with your own kind . . . Like Herder, I regard cosmopolitanism as empty. People can't develop unless they belong to a culture" (Gardels, 1991, pp. 19, 22). In the aftermath of 1989, this spirit has been reanimated across the space of Europe, and we are seeing how strong are claims to the difference and distinctiveness of national cultures. If there was, for a moment, the belief that "1992" symbolised the beginning of the end for the nation state in Europe, what has become increasingly clear is that state nationalism remains a very powerful way of belonging (Hassner, 1991). Even within the EU, we are seeing the reassertion of national differences, sovereignties and interests. And what we are seeing, too, are deeply worrying tendencies in this resurgent nationalism. In the German case, Jürgen Habermas (1993, p. 66) makes the accusation that the Kohl government has "relied on imputing the diffuse morality of a nation based on ethnicity and deliberately passed over a nation based on citizenship". Ethno-nationalism has also reasserted itself in France where Le Pen's National Front Party has been working towards the "re-ethnicisation" of national identity, aiming "to reinvent the authentic national community and to oppose it to the open society, which is stigmatised as globalised and 'cosmopolitan'" (Taguieff, 1992, p. 35). In this case, national difference demands the purity of national culture and identity.

A third kind of allegiance in the new Europe is to small and local cultures and identities. We might see it as the same particularism that was being invoked in Eliot's ideal of a regional "constellation of cultures" in Europe. In this idealised form, it finds expression in the regionalism and small nationalism that is gathering force, and in the invocation of a "Europe of the regions" (Baier, 1991/92). The appeal of a Europe of the Heimats — Basque, Lombard, Catalan, Breton, or whatever — is to a more authentic way of belonging. In its opposition to the abstract and universalising forces of globalisation, it represents a return to, or development of, Herder's cultural community. The rich pluralism of regional traditions, languages, dialects and ways of life is held up as the basis for a more rooted experience of community. But it is possible to see this new localism and separatism in quite another light. According to Enzo Mingione (1993, p. 305), what it in fact reflects is the extent to which European societies are being subjected to processes of fragmentation, with the consequence that "localism, regionalism, ethnic and sub-national attachments are challenging the social order everywhere". These developments have been described in less favourable terms as marking the emergence of new kinds of "tribal" behaviour. What should be emphasised, Mingione argues, is that tribal belonging "gives rise simultaneously to strong forms of solidarity towards the members of the in-group and equally strong forms of discrimination against outsiders" (p. 309). Being "with your own kind" is likely to find its most intense expression in the neo-regionalist movements.

These various identities appear to offer different ways of responding to the forces of change that are now sweeping across Europe. We should not see them simply as alternatives, however. To be European now is to be implicated in all three — continental, national, regional — and being European must be about negotiating some compromise between these different scales of identity. Anthony D. Smith (1992, p. 67) develops a perspective in which it is a question of managing identities in terms of "concentric circles of allegiance": we must recognise, he argues, that "human beings have multiple identities, that they can move between them according to context and situation, and that such identities may be concentric rather than conflictual". There is something reassuring in this benign image of nested identities. But that reassurance is sustained through disavowal or denial of the real tensions and contradictions at work in European identity choices. Rather than coherence and continuity across identities, what seems to us to exist is in fact a condition of suspension between identities; a condition in which none of the alternatives seems entirely adequate.

Thus, for many people, the idea of a unified and united Europe has great appeal, promising to fulfil their aspirations for a more cosmopolitan and ecumenical way of belonging. But, if at one moment being within an integrated Europe seems desirable, then at another it is associated with anxieties that something about who we are is being lost or damaged in the process. There is also the sense that European identity is lacking in substance. As Geoffrey Barraclough (1963, p. 41) argues, when it comes to defining what constitutes Europe, it has always proved far easier "to formulate a negative, exclusive notion of European identity directed against some allegedly non-European or anti-European power or movement, than to find some pan-European objective to which all could adhere". Against the abstraction of European identity, the alternative of cultural nationalism or regionalism may then reassert itself as a way of hanging on to that something. Particularly in times of uncertainty and upheaval, Miroslav Hroch (1993, p. 15) observes, "people characteristically tend to over-value the protective comfort of their own national group . . . people will regard their nation — that is, themselves — as a single body in a more than metaphorical sense". But if attachment to particularistic identities remains a powerful force, there is also considerable awareness of its limitations and of the need for positioning in the European context.

Europe is caught, then, in a kind of suspended state between integration and fragmentation. And it seems as if it is in the discomfort of this tension-filled condition that it is most itself. The question that must be asked is whether Europeans can live with their identity desires in ways that are less ambivalent and stressful. In addressing this question, it seems to us that choice — *which* identity — is not the fundamental issue: more significant is the nature of identification, *what kind of* identity is being mobilised. With all identities — European, national, regional — what must concern us is the *mode* of belonging, the motivations and dispositions that inform attachment and belonging.

COMMUNITY AND MARGINALITY

Ways of belonging in Europe have been powerfully shaped by the experience of nation states. The principle, or the aspiration, at work in the formation of national communities has been that of homogeneity — ethnic, religious, linguistic, cultural, territorial. Monolithic and inward-looking, the unitary nation state has seemed to be the realisation of a desire for coherence and integrity (though we might suspect that, rather than being the realisation of this desire, it was the *realpolitik* of nation-building that created the conditions of possibility for such a desire, or such a kind of desire, to be imagined). And, in so far as it has sought to eliminate difference and complexity, the formation of a national community and culture has involved the extrusion or marginalisation of elements that have seemed to compromise the "clarity" of national being. As Zygmunt Bauman (1992, p. 683) argues, the "promotion of homogeneity had to be complemented by the effort to brand, segregate and evict the 'aliens'". As such, this kind of nationalist identity "is perpetually under conditions of a besieged fortress. . . . Identity stands and falls by the security of its borders, and the borders are ineffective unless guarded" (pp. 678–679). Whatever coherence and integrity is achieved, it is at the cost of a perpetual vigilance in maintaining the boundary between "natives" and "strangers". It is this identitarian logic, with its anxious, self-enclosed way of being and of belonging that has come to seem the natural and unavoidable mode of identification in modern times.

It is this kind of identity-thinking that, at a higher order, is now shaping the present attempts to construct a sense of European community. It is the promotion of homogeneity at this higher level that seems to fulfil our expectations of community, culture and identity. What is being created, then, through the transference or the aggregation of nationalist sentiments, is the unity of a unitary continent. The language of official Euro-culture is significant: it is the language of cohesion, integration, unity, community and security. The new European order is being constructed in terms of an idealised wholeness and plenitude, and European identity is conceived in terms of boundedness and containment. At this higher level, what still seems to be needed is the clear distinction between natives and aliens. Imagined in this sense, of course, it is likely to be as precarious and fearful as the national communities described by Bauman. Its desired coherence and integrity will always have to be sustained and defended against the forces of disintegration and dissolution at work in the world.

In the new European Union, the matter of territorial coherence and integrity is paramount. As economic frontiers have been lifted within the

EU to create the Single Market, the security of Europe's external borders has become, all the more, a fundamental issue. If, for most of this century, the "communist bloc" defined a "natural" boundary to the east, the end of the cold war has brought this convenient state of affairs to an end. Once again the Eastern question is on the agenda; along its eastern and south-eastern edges, Europe is now seeking to renegotiate its territorial limits as an economic and political entity. As J.G.A. Pocock (1991, p. 10) argues, "Europe is again an empire concerned for the security of its *limites*". It finds itself in a position where "it must decide whether to extend or refuse its political power over violent and unstable cultures along its borders but not yet within its system: Serbs and Croats, if one chances to be an Austrian, Kurds and Iraqis if Turkey is admitted to be part of 'Europe'". Who can be assimilated? Who is destined to be excluded? Pocock suggests that it is those populations "who do not achieve the sophistication without which the global market has little for them and less need of them" that are fated to become the "new barbarians".

But it is not simply a matter of economic or even political criteria for inclusion and exclusion. What is happening along these eastern and southern margins is also about the culture and identity of Europe. As Lord Owen observed in an interview with *Newsweek* (6 August 1990, p. 54): "You have to have clarity about where the boundaries of Europe are and the boundaries of Europe are not on the Turkish–Iran border." This desire for clarity, this need to be sure about where Europe ends, is about the construction of a symbolic geography that will separate the insiders from the outsiders, those who belong to the community from the strangers that threaten its unity. Through the same process by which it is creating itself, this small white and western European community is also creating the aliens that will always seem to haunt its hopes and ideals. Already we see how fears are turning to resentment against immigrants, refugees, terrorists, drug-dealers, asylum-seekers — all those who do not seem respectful of Europe's frontiers. And we see, too, how defences are increasingly being mobilised against these intruders and marginal figures. As Jonathan Eyal (1993) argues, western Europe is building up "a set of defences, often imperceptible but much more efficient than the Berlin Wall. From an airline clerk to a Hungarian border guard, everyone is working to prevent people coming to the West."

The nature and scale of transformation across the continent are such, however, that "the east's problems will move west, regardless of what subterfuge western governments concoct" (Eyal, 1993). Those who are considered to be aliens and strangers — the "new barbarians" — will be increasingly in the midst of the European Union. Europeans will not be able to avoid them, but it seems that they do not have the resources to live with them. If they are to find the means to do so, then they will have to struggle towards some better accommodation between their own needs and desires to belong and the obligation they surely have to be open to the needs of others. They will have to find some way of bridging national and cosmopolitan values.

First, this will entail a reconsideration of the nature of community at the European level. The question is whether it will be possible to imagine the European space as anything more than a scaled-up nation state. We must remember that, at certain times and in certain places, Europe has been more than this, and we should recall that it has, in its past, required more complexity and a greater openness from its citizens than the present EU seems to expect. While he counsels against nostalgia, Claudio Magris (1992, p. 54) for example, observes that the Austro-Hungarian Empire was a "rather satisfying example of how different elements can be brought together". Georges Corm suggests that the identity of populations in the Ottoman Empire was rich because of the complex circulations and permutations of ethnic, religious and linguistic groups across large geographical regions. "Not that it was idyllic or perfect", Corm (1989, p. 50) observes, "but at least, where it prevailed, difference was never experienced as a scandal or as a defect of identity." Pluralism and complexity of identity were a resource and a source of enrichment.

The point is not to celebrate fallen empires, but to suggest that identity has been, and can be, experienced in ways that are richer than those offered by the nation state. There have been cosmopolitan populations in Europe, populations that have transcended national boundaries and engaged with difference. But we do not have to look to the past. There is a population of 8 million people in Europe now that is both transnational and non-territorial. "They could teach us how meaningless frontiers are", writes Günter Grass (1992, p. 108) "careless of boundaries, Romanies and Sinti are at home all over Europe. They are what we claim to be: born Europeans!"

This has a Utopian ring, however. We should not forget or ignore cosmopolitan traditions in Europe, but we must be pragmatic. In this spirit, there is a second issue that must be reconsidered: we must think seriously about the nature of nationalist and regionalist attachments and recognise the needs they are presently responding to. Tom Nairn (1993, p. 6) poses the key question for our times: "Why has the End of History carried us forward into a more nationalist world?" In posing this question, Nairn argues, "we must avoid demonising nationalism as some kind of irrational and atavistic way of belonging". We would not go so far as Nairn in recognising the positive aspects of nationalist sentiments. None the less, we do recognise that nationalism is here to stay for the foreseeable future, and that we must therefore work with it, rather than throwing our arms up in horror. Julia Kristeva (1993, pp. 7, 46) has forcefully argued that it is important "not to reject the idea of the nation in a gesture of wilful universalism but to modulate its less repressive aspects. . . . The time has perhaps come for pursuing a critique of the national tradition without selling off its assets." In her interrogation of the national idea, Kristeva draws on the psychoanalytical concept of the transitional object:

I imagine the national as a sort of transitional object, an identity aid that provides us with security and at the same time acts as a relay towards others. It would be a question of thinking out and organising a series of bonds reaching out to others without entirely eliminating the archaic one, in this case that of nationhood (Kristeva, 1992a; cf. Kristeva, 1993, pp. 40–43).

Kristeva puts forward this transitional conception as an alternative to the romantic and integrating conception of the nation that recent events have shaken back to life. The transitional nation provides the security and stability necessary to sustain an openness to others beyond its confines. What is necessary, Kristeva (1993, p. 52) is arguing, is that we should work towards "the insertion of the national entities inherited from the past into higher political and economic wholes".

EUROPE AND ITS MARGINS — WHY BOSNIA MATTERS

The present events in the Balkans, and particularly in the former Yugo-slavia, provide a critical and disturbing example of what is problematical in the European Union project. Here we can see clearly how the logic of marginalisation works, and how it is working to protect European civilisation against the "tribes" on and around its margins. In this geopolitical region, the collapse of the Soviet Union has had a particularly devastating impact, reactivating old political agendas in which the nation states of western Europe are deeply implicated (the Paris Conference, the Yalta Agreement). The Balkans matter because they are now a touchstone for whatever new order, or disorder, is to come in the continent (Yerasimos, 1992). It is difficult to see how the European Union could continue in the way it was before 1989.

Bosnia, for its part, matters because it has "continued to evolve a culture which expresses the plural and tolerant side of the Ottoman tradition," and because it has struggled over the past years to defend "the values of multi-cultural long-evolved and mutually fruitful cohabitation" (Hitchens, 1992, pp. 240–241). What was achieved through a long and complex historical process is now being destroyed, to be replaced by a series of purified national communities. Most shockingly, this has involved the devastating assault on a population which can only be compared to that carried out by the Nazis against the Jews. And this, once again, in Europe. Branka Magas (1992, p. 110) says what must be said: "The genocide being conducted today against the Moslem population of Bosnia-Herzegovina, and the destruction of a unique society based on the centuries-long co-existence of different nations and religions, amount to a crime against humanity." "How", she asks, "could this be allowed to happen in peacetime Europe?" How could it now seem that Bosnia does not matter to Europe?

Taking up this European question, we must consider what is at issue in the European Union's ambivalent position between engagement and disengagement. What are we to think of this position that combines involvement with what appears to be an absence of commitment and responsibility? Europe seems to have been stricken by a moral and political paralysis with respect to the Yugoslav crisis. But perhaps it only looks like paralysis. Perhaps there is a certain coherence and logic — albeit one that is denied or disavowed — in Europe's fatal strategies.

The European powers were quick to recognise the resurgent nationalisms in the former Yugoslavia and, in so doing, they affected the course of events. "Through its insistence on an essentialist treatment of ethnicity", observes Cornelia Sorabji (1993, p. 35), "in which Serbs, Croats and Muslims have immutable identities, Europe has played a part in legitimating nationalist leaders, highlighting the ethnic boundaries, and creating the sort of ethnic war (one based on mutual and compelling hatred and fear) which, so it claims, has been there all along." Perhaps such recognition seemed justified in so far as nationalism is seen as the desirable, and inevitable, form of association for all peoples. Perhaps nationalist aspirations seemed "natural" assertions of freedom by those who had been imprisoned in the monolithic culture of the Soviet Empire. But perhaps there were less than altruistic motivations at work. Observing this tendency to essentialise religious and ethnic differences whenever they manifest themselves outside the "civilised" world, Georges Corm (1992, p. 19) suggests that it reveals "the emotion, the passions, the exoticism and the mythologies [that are mobilised] whenever it comes to analysing developments outside western Europe". What it reflects is the persistence of the colonial and Great Power mentality.

Within this mentality, recognition is not given to these new Balkan states and other centrally-planned states in order to acknowledge that their nationalist aspirations are like those of western European states. On the contrary, what are emphasised are the differences between Balkan and European nationalisms. Balkan nations are recognised, but in recognising them "for what they are", what is then emphasised is how much "they" are unlike "us". Western European nations are organised around civilised values and traditions, while Balkan nationalisms are rooted in primordial loyalties and driven by ethnic and tribal hatreds. In acknowledging the "true nature" of these atavistic allegiances and inspirations, Europe may be seen as gaining clarity about what is incompatible with, and therefore cannot be admitted into, its Union. As the Croatian writer, Slavenka Drakulic (1993, pp. 2–3), puts it:

In this way the West tells us, "You are not Europeans. You are Balkans, mythological, wild, dangerous Balkans. Kill yourselves, if that is your pleasure. We don't understand what is going on there, nor do we have clear political interests to protect. The myth of Europe, of our belonging to the European family and culture, even as poor relations, is gone.

What becomes clear is where Europe ends.

And what then seems to become clear is the threat that Balkan nationalism presents to Europe. The Evil Empire is replaced in Western demonology by the Balkan tribes. Paula Franklin Lytle (1992) observes how this resurgent nationalism has come to be seen through the imagery of infection and virus, with all its associations of latency, contamination and mutation. As with the threat of AIDS, there is the fear that this new tribalism will affect us all. Of course, "labelling nationalism as a pathology places it beyond human control"; "the language used to discuss the war is consistent with seeing Yugoslavia as a body infected by nationalism, rather than as a war possibly amenable to any form of mediation or intervention" (pp. 304, 316). Nationalism of this kind is virulent and threatens to spread with disastrous consequences. As Jacques Delors expressed it in an interview, "it is like a contagious disease that is spreading everywhere in Europe" (*Time*, 28 December 1992, p. 21). From a European perspective, what becomes necessary is to make sure that those already infected are kept isolated and quarantined. A *cordon sanitaire* must be put up as protection around the healthy body of the European Union.

As it struggles to disengage itself and to secure its eastern frontiers against the perceived threat from the Balkans, the European Union has made crucial distinctions between the different parties. In general, it has bowed to Serbian pressure and given tacit acceptance to Serbian expansionism. It has been as if we were still in the cold war era, only now the other side has ceased to be the communist bloc and has become the Slav nation (Sibony, 1993). This has produced an accommodation to the project for a Greater Serbia, and an anticipation that Slav nationalism may provide the stabilising force in the region that was once provided by the Soviet Union. This process has been associated with an inability either to understand or to respond to Bosnian and Muslim aspirations (which have not been grounded in ethnic identities). The rejection of Bosnia's claims has now created a situation in which "a path is paved for Muslims to reconstruct the nature of 'Europe' in less positive terms and the meaning of their own Europeanness in more radical terms" (Sorabji, 1993, p. 35). But it has also created the feeling among many that Europe is conspiring with the Serbs and Croats to eliminate Islam from Europe. There is the sense that a new wall is being built to divide Europe from, and to insulate it against, the Islamic threat. For Europe, it seems, the overriding imperative is to resolve its Eastern question.

Writing at the time of the Greco-Turkish War, Arnold Toynbee (1923) made some important observations on that earlier period of Balkan conflict. He describes how the way of life of the Ottoman Empire was expelled from European culture because it was considered to be radically alien to Western civilisation. And he goes on to give an account of how nationalism — "this fatal Western idea" — was imposed on the geographically mixed populations of the region with disastrous consequences, arguing that "the principle of nationality offers no more than a partial solution to the problems of South-Eastern Europe" (p. 26). Toynbee is moved to anger by what he sees as the indifference and callousness of European attitudes to the region — "this conjunction of great effect on other people's lives with little interest in or intention with regard to them" (p. 2). His judgement is that "this combination of maximum actual effect with minimum consciousness and interest has made the Western factor in the Near and Middle East on the whole an anarchic and destructive force" (p. 5).

What is thought to be the Eastern question would better be seen as the Western question. This is the spirit of what Slavoj Zizek (1992) has to say about the present crisis. It is difficult, he writes, "not to recall Hegel's dictum that true evil does not reside in the object perceived as bad, but in the innocent gaze which perceives evil all round. The main obstacle to peace in ex-Yugoslavia is not 'archaic ethnic passions', but the gaze of Europe fascinated by the spectacle of these passions." The Western factor continues to be a potent and destructive force in Balkan politics.

WESTERN QUESTIONS

In considering the question of culture and marginality in contemporary Europe, what is at issue is the way in which the construction of a European Union is at the same time constructing the marginality and peripherality of those who are excluded from the EU. The idea of Europe, as it is presently imagined, is structured around the fatal division between those who are natives and those — the strangers inside its frontiers as well as those beyond them — who are aliens. The mythification of origins, the xenophobia and the racism that have been characteristic of nationalist sentiments are being transposed to the European level and to a Union that looks to distinguish those of "European stock" from non-Europeans. And the more it works towards the creation of a new Europe, the more it becomes alert to those, within and without, whose very existence seems a constant threat to the European ideal. In 1938, the French writer, Jean Giraudoux, wrote: "Our land has become a land of invasion. The invasion unfolds in exactly the same way it did in the Roman Empire, not by armies, but through continuous infiltration by the barbarians." These words are quoted by Alain Gresh (1993, p. 3), who notes that some months later the Nazis made their decisive move.

In the 1990s, in the context of the emerging new world order or disorder, Europe is faced with enormous and daunting problems. It would be foolish to deny the scale of the difficulties presented to Europe by the collapse of the Soviet Union or by the wave of migration from East and South. What we are arguing is that those difficulties, which have to be faced in one way or another, are exacerbated by the mentality of the European Union itself. It is a certain idea and ideal of Europe that now stands in the way of the broader geopolitical and geocultural changes that are called for. It is with Europe as an imaginary institution that we shall have to come to terms.

In trying to overcome the reflex to closure in order to construct a more ecumenical and open cultural space, there are resources that can be drawn on. There is the cosmopolitan tradition of both Christian and Enlightenment philosophy. There is, as we have already suggested, the experience of heterogeneity and mixture that characterised the Ottoman and Austro-Hungarian empires, and which still has at least a residual presence in certain areas; in his book, *Danube*, Claudio Magris (1989, p. 292) tells of an old poet who said in an interview that he had "learnt to think with the mentality of several peoples". There is a body of work in sociology (for example, Park, 1928; Wood, 1935; Schutz, 1944), and more recently in cultural theory (particularly Kristeva, 1991), that has spoken eloquently about the positive contribution of "the stranger" to modern societies. "Only strangeness is universal", writes Julia Kristeva (1993, p. 21). For Elie Wiesel (1991), "we are all foreigners. . . . When I look at a foreigner it's easy to see that like him, I am a foreigner in someone else's eyes." Within European culture, there are traditions of respect and compassion for strangers and outsiders, and there are traditions within which difference is regarded as the basis for an enriched and expanded cultural life. Clearly, then, there are intellectual and moral resources from which we might begin to construct a more complex and open cultural space.

But we are a long way from achieving that. In these times of change and upheaval, cultures and identities — European, national and regional — tend towards closure and security, and difference is more likely to provoke fear, resentment or hatred. Cosmopolitan values are an inspiration and an ideal, but we must begin with the cultural attachments and identities that seem now to exert a stronger force. Julia Kristeva (1992b, pp. 105–106) describes the "violence of identity desires" and the "psychic violence" that adheres to the idea of the nation; "so the great moral work which grapples with the problem of identity", she argues, "also grapples with this contemporary experience of death, violence, and hate". The immediate priority must be to moderate these defensive, and at their worst manic, forms of identification. This cannot be done simply through the principled appeal to more tolerant and cosmopolitan values. It requires the acknowledgement and accommodation of particularistic sentiments and attachments. For the foreseeable future, we shall have to live with nations and nationalisms; the objective, then, must be to find more flexible — what Kristeva calls transitive or transitional — ways of relating to the nation-object. For "there is no way for an identity to go beyond itself without first asserting itself in a satisfactory fashion" (Kristeva, 1993, p. 59).

But if it can assert itself in a satisfactory fashion, we must then expect that it should go beyond itself. What makes this difficult, however, is precisely the way in which it is questions of culture and identity — the "self" of a community — that have come to seem paramount. The problem we face is that the discourse of identity and community has displaced the discourse of politics:

> The "new" racism is the hatred of the other that comes forth when the political procedures of social polemics collapse. The political culture of conflict may have had disappointing outlets. But it was also a way of coming to terms with something that lies before and beneath politics: the question of the other as a figure of identification for the object of fear . . . I would say that identity is first about fear: the fear of the other, the fear of nothing, which finds on the body of the other its object. And the polemical culture of emancipation . . . was a way of civilizing that fear (Rancière, 1992, pp. 63–64).

In the realm of culture and identity, what is affirmed is the "self" of a community and its difference from other communities. What is not dealt with is the relationship between the selves of different cultural communities (with the obvious danger that the unconscious processes — the fear and the anxiety — take precedence). If national identity is to go beyond itself — that is to say, if it is to recognise the right of other identities also to assert themselves — the discourse of culture must be subordinated to that of politics. It is on the terrain of politics that it becomes possible to raise the moral issue of what responsibilities and obligations a national community has towards those — beyond and within — who are not, or are not seen as, its members.

This is also the fundamental issue at the European level. It will be on the terrain of politics that the project to build a European Union will succeed or fail. In the case of those beyond its present frontiers, there is the question as to whether it can replace cultural mythologisation with a political programme for the whole of this geopolitical region. "What is Europe dreaming of?" asks André Glucksmann (1993, p. 8) in the context of events in ex-Yugoslavia, "will it ever realise that it is not trapped in a past of atavistic warfare; that, rather, it is struggling with a post-communist present, and is tripping up over wars of the future?" In the case of the "non-members" within its frontiers — migrants, marginals, minorities, aliens — what must be addressed is the question of citizenship. As Étienne Balibar (1992) argues, this should be a matter, not of "citizenship for Europeans", but of "citizenship in Europe", of the rights to political expression for all those within the European space.

Will Europe simply assert itself? Or does it have the commitment and resolve to go beyond itself? Can it develop a political life that is strong enough to overcome the cultural logic of exclusion and marginalisation?

REFERENCES

Annunziata, L. (1993) The fall of the cold war order, *The Nation*, 5 April, 444–445.
Baier, L. (1991/92) Farewell to regionalism, *Telos*, **90**, 82–88.
Balibar, É. (1992) Le citoyen aujourd'hui?, *Raison Présente*, **103**, 27–44.
Barraclough, G. (1963) *European unity in thought and action*, Basil Blackwell, Oxford.
Bauman, Z. (1992) Soil, blood and identity, *Sociological Review*, **40**, 4, 675–701.
Castoriadis, C. (1990) *Le Monde Morcelé*, Seuil, Paris.
Castoriadis, C. (1992) Le délabrement de l'occident, *Esprit*, December, 36–54.
Corm, G. (1989) *L'Europe et l'Orient: de la Balkanisation à la Libanisation — histoire d'une modernité inaccomplie*, La Découverte, Paris.
Corm, G. (1992) L'Occident saisie par la violence des replis identitaires, *Le Monde Diplomatique*, May, 18–19.
David, D. (1992) Le continent européen en danger de décomposition, *Le Monde Diplomatique*, December, 10–11.
Derrida, J. (1992) *The other heading: reflections on today's Europe*, Indiana University Press, Bloomington.
Drakulic, S. (1993) *Balkan express*, Hutchinson, London.
Eyal, J. (1993) All subterfuge, no refuge, *The Guardian*, 15 February.
Gallissot, R. (1992) Dépasser le nationalisme sinon les nationalismes nous dépassent, *L'Homme et la Société*, **103**, 3–13.
Gardels, N. (1991) Two concepts of nationalism: an interview with Isaiah Berlin, *New York Review of Books*, 21 November, 19–23.
Glucksmann, A. (1993) Stop the crocodile tears and start fixing the bayonets, *The European*, 22–25 April, 8.
Grass, G. (1992) Losses, *Granta*, **42**, 97–108.
Gresh, A. (1993) Ces immigrés si coupables, si vulnerables..., *Le Monde Diplomatique*, May, 3.
Habermas, J. (1993) The second life fiction of the Federal Republic: we have become "normal" again, *New Left Review*, **197**, 58–66.
Hassner, P. (1991) L'Europe et le spectre des nationalismes, *Esprit*, October, 5–22.
Hitchens, C. (1992) Appointment in Sarajevo, *The Nation*, 14 September, 236–241.
Hroch, M. (1993) From national movement to the fully-formed nation: the nation-building process in Europe, *New Left Review*, **198**, 3–20.
Joffe, J. (1993) The new Europe: yesterday's ghosts, *Foreign Affairs*, **72**, 1, 29–43.
Kristeva, J. (1991) *Strangers to ourselves*, Harvester Wheatsheaf, New York.
Kristeva, J. (1992a) Le temps de la dépression, *Le Monde des Débats*, October.
Kristeva, J. (1992b) Strangers to ourselves: the hope of the singular, in Kearney, R. (ed.), *Visions of Europe*, Wolfhound Press, Dublin, pp. 99–106.
Kristeva, J. (1993) *Nations without nationalism*, Columbia University Press, New York.
Lytle, P.F. (1992) U.S. policy toward the demise of Yugoslavia: the "virus of nationalism", *East European Politics and Societies*, **6**, 3, 303–318.
Magas, B. (1992) The destruction of Bosnia-Herzegovina, *New Left Review*, **196**, 102–112.
Magris, C. (1989) *Danube*, Collins Harvill, London.
Magris, C. (1992) L'histoire, vue de Trieste, *Esprit*, July, 50–61.

Malcolmson, S. (1991) Heart of whiteness, *Voice Literary Supplement*, March, 10–14.

Mingione, E. (1993) Italy: the resurgence of regionalism, *International Affairs*, **69**, 2, 305–318.

Nairn, T. (1993) Demonising nationalism, *London Review of Books*, 25 February, 3–6.

Park, R.W. (1928) Human migration and the marginal man, *American Journal of Sociology*, **33**, 6, 881–893.

Pocock, J.G.A. (1991) Deconstructing Europe, *London Review of Books*, 19 December, 6–10.

Rancière, J. (1992) Politics, identification and subjectivization, *October*, **61**, 58–64.

Riche, A. (1993) L'élargissement de la Communauté en question, *Le Monde Diplomatique*, June, 3–4.

Schlesinger, P. (1992) "Europeanness" — a new cultural battlefield?, *Innovation*, **5**, 1, 11–23.

Schutz, A. (1944) The stranger: an essay in social psychology, *American Journal of Sociology*, **49**, 6, 499–507.

Shepley, S. and Wilmot, J. (1992) *Europe: core vs periphery*, Crédit Suisse First Boston, London.

Sibony, D. (1993) Bosnie: le point de silence, *Libération*, 7 June, 6.

Smith, A.D. (1992) National identity and the idea of European unity, *International Affairs*, **68**, 1, 55–76.

Sorabji, C. (1993) Ethnic war in Bosnia?, *Radical Philosopy*, **63**, 33–35.

Taguieff, P-A. (1992) Nationalisme, réactions identitaires et communauté imaginée, *Hommes et Migrations*, **1154**, 31–41.

Thibaud, P. (1992) Westernism and the eastern left, *Thesis Eleven*, **32**, 108–113.

Toynbee, A.J. (1923) *The western question in Greece and Turkey*, 2nd edn, Constable, London.

Wallerstein, I. (1992) Liberalism and the legitimation of nation-states: an historical interpretation, *Social Justice*, **19**, 1, 22–33.

Wiesel, E. (1991) Welcome, stranger, *The Guardian*, 14 June.

Wood, M.W. (1935) *The stranger: a study in social relationships*, Columbia University Press, New York.

Yerasimos, S. (1992) Quelle politique pour les Balkans?, *Hérodote*, **67**, 61–63.

Zizek, S. (1992) Ethnic dance macabre, *The Guardian*, 28 August.

Part III

CAPITAL, LABOUR, STATE
POLICIES

7 Remote Rural Areas: Villages on the Northern Margin

JUKKA OKSA

University of Joensuu, Finland

INTRODUCTION

This is a story about villages in North Karelia in Finland, a remote north-eastern corner of western Europe. It is a tale about different ways of coping with new forms of marginality. The term "marginality" refers here to a situation where a group of people has been excluded, or is on the brink of being left out, from the main development stream of society. Life in a small and remote village entails special obstacles, which hinder social participation. The fundamental question of local and especially rural development is, how can limited resources be mobilised to exploit general paths of social change? In this chapter I link together two levels of analysis — national policy projects (and their different mechanisms for integrating rural areas), and village actions to create connections with emerging social development streams and to fight against marginalisation. Even in a remote village, life is not outside the sphere of national politics. On the contrary, the history of these villages can be seen as one of coping with central policies, made either in Stockholm, St Petersburg, Helsinki, or in future in Brussels.

Enzo Mingione points out in Chapter 2 in this volume that different forms of welfare capitalism have given rise to alternative kinds of marginality. This means that policies aiming at integration should follow different paths, taking account of this diversity. The villages discussed here have been coping in the context of a "Scandinavian model" of society, in which the role of the state has been central in guaranteeing social welfare, providing services and also regulating regional development and sectoral restructuring of relatively small, open national economies. The public service system has helped to diminish the significance of the family as a source of social security. This has in turn produced a high rate of women participating in the service sector labour force as full-time salaried workers. The end-product is a kind of state-supported individualism, with high social and geographical mobility and loosening economic significance

Europe at the Margins: New Mosaics of Inequality. Edited by Costis Hadjimichalis and David Sadler
© 1995 European Science Foundation. Published in 1995 by John Wiley & Sons Ltd

attached to kinship. The family is shrinking into a small nuclear unit or a one- or two-person household.

Marginalisation in this system means being left without resources for social mobility (through lack of training, skills or work experience), pushed out of the labour force (by unemployment), cut off from meaningful social contacts (isolation), or excluded from policy-making processes (powerlessness). Remote and rural location has strengthened all these mechanisms, and local people have tried to find ways to cope with them.

Finland's specificity compared to other Nordic welfare states is in the relatively strong position of the forestry sector and a forest-owning peasantry. This has also been the basis for strong peasant representation in the arena of politics and interest bargaining. In turn, this had some impact on welfare state measures, extending them to the farming population (with paid holidays for farmers and relatively good provision of services in rural areas), and bringing welfare state ethics into agricultural policies (for example direct financial support for small farmers; see Granberg, 1989). Although farming has been modernised, it has, however, maintained its family character. In agriculture the family is still a production unit (in spite of its shrinking towards a one-generation nuclear family), although in other sectors Finland has not seen similarly strong traditions. If there is a farmer in the family, the farm has, until recent decades, served as a kind of social buffer and also as a meeting place.

I use a very rough division of Finnish history into three main policy projects, or modes of regulation, each of which links to the villages in specific ways. These successive policy projects are construction of a nation from the late nineteenth century to 1945; creation of an industrial welfare state from the 1950s until the 1980s; and the phase of European integration starting in the 1990s. I briefly characterise these projects, defining in this way the main waves of social development, in relation to which marginality was defined, and to which rural localities had to respond. First, however, we need to set the scene.

SETTING THE SCENE

North Karelia in eastern Finland (see Figure 7.1) is a province of forests and lakes, where winter is dark and harsh, and summer is light and short. Keeping a family house warm throughout the year costs 25% more than in southern Finland. It is sparsely populated, with about 10 persons per square kilometre. It is a border district, where central political decisions have changed the location and significance of the boundary. Its people have paid taxes to the Swedish Crown, the Russian Emperor and the Finnish Republic. Its major resources are forestry (the foundation of Finland's timber-based multinationals), and people, whose ancestors moved there because they were promised farming land of their own.

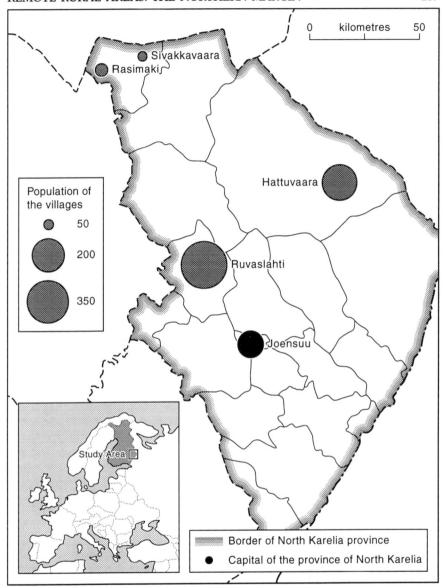

Figure 7.1. Location of the four study villages in North Karelia, Finland

When North Karelia got its present status as a province in 1960, the population was at a peak of 207 000. During the 1960s and the 1970s (the "great move" of Finns to industrial towns), the population declined to 177 000. Compared to other provinces in Finland during that period, North

Karelia endured the greatest population loss, its per capita income was the lowest, and its unemployment rate one of the highest. It had the highest percentage of population working in primary production (family farming and forestry) and the lowest in manufacturing.

During the late 1970s and the 1980s these tendencies levelled out somewhat. Population continued to concentrate in the provincial capital Joensuu, a university town of 50 000 inhabitants, and also in municipal service and administrative centres. There are considerable income differences between urban and rural areas. Joensuu has about the same per capita income as the whole of Finland, but in smaller rural communes incomes can be below 60% of the national average. If we compare North Karelia's local per capita incomes with EU averages, Joensuu would be almost at the level of Denmark, and the rural municipalities a little below Ireland, but above Portugal. The outflow of people from remote villages has continued (with a few exceptions, some of which I shall discuss in this chapter). Remote villages seem to be losing their functions. Farming is becoming concentrated in a few locations, forest work is being further mechanised with a new generation of harvesters, and pensioners get better care in larger centres. The only relevant issue for many of the villages seems to be the timetable for their final desolation.

Research material is drawn from four places (see Figure 7.1). The family farming village of Ruvaslahti has 350 inhabitants, and is trying to adapt to the age of information technology with one of the first telecottages in Finland, which was founded in 1986. Rasimaki is a new farming community of about 70 inhabitants that was cleared from the forest after 1945, for relocated families who lost their farms in those parts of Karelia that were annexed to the USSR. Sivakkavaara is an old forest workers' village of around 50 inhabitants, which had its best years during the labour-intensive period of forestry in the 1950s. Hattuvaara is a modern forestry workers' settlement of about 200 inhabitants (on the outskirts of the town of Lieksa) which thrives in the new period of mechanised, large-scale forestry.

CONSTRUCTION OF A NATION

The early Finnish state (see Table 7.1) has sometimes been characterised as "a peasant state". Finnish nationalism at the end of the nineteenth century was a coalition of cultural intelligentsia and peasants, united by the language question (one language, one nation). The central social divide in this emerging nation was landownership. The most important marginal group was the landless population of rural labour. Upward social mobility meant acquiring land, that could one day be bequeathed. Land was an important mobiliser of political movements. Following independence in 1917, the first central question became the healing of memories from the

Table 7.1. Construction of a Finnish nation, 1850–1940

Core objective of the project	Construction of independent nation state
International economic orientation	Export of forestry products ("green gold")
Main tensions	Class conflicts and rural poverty
National hegemonic bloc	Forest sector coalition of landowning peasants and forest industries
Mechanism of regulation in relation to countryside	Land reforms and settlement policies
Mode of marginalisation	Being left without land
Rural response mode	Land clearing, demands for land, protection of peasant landownership, local community based on landowning peasants

violent class war of 1918. A central mechanism for creating social coherence was land reform, giving land to rural workers. Private landownership was the cement of rural coherence in the 1920s. Settlement programmes and the creation of new farms were also used in a similar way after 1945. National coherence was built on compromise between two wings of the forest sector élite, private owners (peasants) and forest-based industries. These both benefited from the export of forestry products, which defined the role of Finland from 1918 to 1939 in an international division of labour. Because of this political structure, Finland has also been characterised as a "forest sector society" (see Koskinen, 1985).

During this construction of a nation phase, our case villages grew through difficult but optimistic times. A form of local economy developed based on large-scale forestry and a combination of smallholder farming and forest work, providing a seasonal labour force for the timber forestry.

THE INDUSTRIAL WELFARE STATE

In the 1950s Finnish state policies started to emphasise industrialisation. In the early 1960s there was a sharp turn of orientation, towards industrial growth and adapting the nation's economy to a new international division of labour, first in co-operation with EFTA, and later with the EEC (see Table 7.2). At the same time, profound centralising changes took place in the organisational framework of both farming and forestry. In agricultural policies there was a move away from subsidising small farms towards structural policies, emphasising productivity, specialisation and mechanisation. The forest industries and state forest agencies campaigned for more intensive production, providing more raw material for board, pulp and

Table 7.2. Industrial welfare state, 1950-80

Core objective of the project	Economic growth
International economic orientation	Trade agreements to east and west
Main tensions	Distribution of growing wealth
National hegemonic bloc	Export industries, farmers' lobby and labour unions
Mechanism of regulation in relation to countryside	Central agreements guaranteeing average income and welfare services for family farmers, regional policies, regional and local planning
Mode of marginalisation	Being forgotten by reform makers, "forsaken people"
Rural response mode	Local political protest and demands to state

paper exporters. This brought pressures to cut down the cost of round-wood. New forms of organisation and new technologies were introduced to forestry work, with dramatic impacts on the fabric of rural communities depending more on forestry than agriculture.

The industrial growth project turned into a forceful structural change during 1965-75, the so-called "great move". In a decade almost one generation of Finns moved from the countryside to industrial centres in the south. The violence of this change brought about counter-forces, including populist political protest from the "forsaken" rural people and growing sympathy for the periphery among radical students and youth. Partly in response, welfare state reforms in the later 1970s included regional policies for rural industrialisation and welfare services in rural areas. Investments in both capital-intensive forest industries (pulp, chipboard, sawmills) and labour-intensive light manufacturing (wood manufacturing, metal pro-ducts, clothing) were subsidised by the state. In the 1980s such regional industrialisation policies were found to be ineffective, and new regional policy measures were geared to supporting the establishment of smaller firms and the rationalisation of existing enterprises (through product development and improved marketing).

The core management mechanism of the welfare state was a so-called income policy agreement. This triangular compromise of labour organis-ations, employers' associations, and the government regulated what share of national economic growth was used to build a public system of basic social services. In Finland the strong role of the rural bloc (particularly a strong farmers' lobby) managed through political struggle to give its own character to the welfare system, guaranteeing basic services (including a national pension plan, equal childrens' allowance, health services, and holidays) to the farming population. The expansion of Finnish welfare state services had a balancing effect on regional differences in the 1970s and 1980s. Several reforms (in the school system, in health and social services) added to the functions of municipal administration. In rural areas these new jobs (often opening new possibilities of employment to the female labour force) were located in service centres. Thus some places in rural areas grew rapidly, even though the total population of these districts declined. Rural service centres captured part of the migration outflow from remoter villages. The industrialisation policy also meant rationalisation of farming into bigger production units. The strength of the peasant lobby geared state policy to support a model of modernised family farms producing raw material (in eastern Finland milk and meat) for food processing industries.

For our case study communities the industrial welfare state period meant social differentiation, both inside villages and between them. In Rasimaki there were two waves of internal polarisation. The first began in the late 1960s. Some of the farms dropped out of production (mainly because they were too small) with the help of a state programme of "field packaging". In the mid-1970s came a second wave, when one-third of the 33 active farms changed to the new type of "industrial" (mechanised, specialised, capital-intensive) farming. Those who went through this transformation had a higher income than those who kept on the former way of farming. About 10 farms went out of production and about the same number doubled their arable field area from 12 to 22 ha.

The new organisation of mechanised forest work meant an end to the old combination of small farms and forestry work. New salaried forest workers replaced the old seasonal lumberjack. In the 1950s Finnish forestry used labour amounting to 150 000 worker-years, but by the 1980s it needed only 30 000. The whole form of the local rural economy was crushed in 10 years. Smaller family farms and part-time farms were forced to seek new sources of income or go out of production. The village of Sivakkavaara was transformed from a rural forest workers' centre into a retreat for pensioners and the unemployed. Its farms were too small for more intensive agriculture. In 1970 there were still 20 persons working in forestry, but 10 years later only four. The elementary school, which had about 60 pupils in the 1960s, closed in 1982. In 1988 only 7 of 52 inhabitants were working.

The inhabitants of villages such as these felt increasingly that society was forgetting them. They reacted by giving their political support to rural protest expressed by the Finnish Rural Party SMP, previously known as the Smallholders' Party. In the parliamentary elections of 1970 and 1972 this movement surprised all political analysts by getting 18 members (out of 200) elected to the Finnish Parliament, the greatest loser being the Centre Party (formerly the Agrarian League). This protest gave impetus to new reforms regarding regional and employment policies and rural services.

THE TELEVISION EVENING OF THE SMALLFARMERS' WIVES

One winter night in 1975, the inhabitants of the farming village of Rasimaki and the old forest workers' village of Sivakkavaara performed in a nationwide television programme *The Evening of the Smallfarmers' Wives*. In front of the whole nation they put questions about the fate of rural villages to members of the government, including the Ministers of Agriculture and of Social Affairs. The villagers had also prepared their own cultural programme, with sketches, poems and songs. The programme brought the women of these two villages into the limelight as representatives of rural people. The women of the family farming village Rasimaki were active in formulating sharp and sometimes angry questions about agricultural and social policies. They formulated their position in terms of politics. The women of the traditional forestry workers' village Sivakkavaara took a different role. They were active in the cultural and entertainment part of the show, reading poems of their own, singing, and acting in sketches. Their strategy was to provide a representation which described the endless toil of the farmer's wife, and the lifelong succession of hard working days. Other themes were the burden of taxes, difficulties in repaying debts, youth moving away from the village, and frustration with decision-makers. Folklorist Seppo Knuuttila interpreted this strategy for dealing with publicity as one of the "poverty culture", one feature of which is the lack of a plan in life (see Knuuttila, 1989).

The television show instigated strong public debate. It was attacked by both major ruling political groups. The Social Democratic newspapers did not like villagers criticising the rural impacts of industrialisation policies and claimed that the programme served the propaganda needs of the Centre. The Centre Party newspapers wrote that Social Democratic leaders did not have the courage to answer the questions put to them, and did not like the accusation that the agricultural co-operatives had no interest in the lot of smallholders. Two researchers participating in the show (this author being one of them) were condemned for "rioting with their statistics".

The political ardour of the villagers had been sharpened during the nationwide rural protest of the early 1970s. In the 1960s our farmers' village (Rasimaki) had been a stronghold of the Agrarian League, which took 70% of the votes cast there in 1966, but in the early 1970s about half of the voters protested by opting for the SMP. Our traditional forestry workers' village, Sivakkavaara, had been a stronghold of "backwoods socialism" (81% of votes went to the two leftist parties in 1966). Here the SMP protest vote got 30% support in the early 1970s. However, in the 1983 election, when the economically active population had almost vanished, the SMP vote grew to 46%. The pensioners and unemployed of the village felt that they had been forsaken by the welfare state.

NEW RURAL COHERENCE AND VILLAGE COMMITTEES

During the "great move" villages were polarised economically, socially and politically. After the mid-1970s, however, a new rural coherence started to emerge. New investment in some farms put village agricultural production on a firmer footing. Some activists modernised their farming, and returned to the Centre Party. The new forestry workers were organised as a profession and tended to support the Social Democrats. Local alliances or blocs were created in the form of village committees, and many activists from the political protest period became central figures in these.

The modern village has a population consisting of several professional groups. It is a localised miniature of industrial welfare society. The village committee co-ordinates organisations such as the Foresters' Union, the Agricultural Producers' Association, local shopkeepers, and the Hunting Association. Its typical activities include maintaining the sports ground and cleaning the village beach, organising festivals and skiing and fishing competitions, and preparing initiatives for the commune to get services such as electric lighting on the village road.

MODERNISED FORESTRY VILLAGES

Although the rationalisation of forestry sounded the death knell for many villages dependent on a mix of small farming and seasonal forest work, a few (three in North Karelia, to be exact) found a new function as housing and service centres for modern, full-time forest workers. Hattuvaara is a base for timber operations in a radius of 40–50 km around the village. Collective transportation to the felling sites is organised by the employer, the State Forestry Board, which has also built 10 rental apartments for its workers. The municipality has strengthened the village by building a few apartments for families and the elderly (see Rannikko, 1987). The core of 30 state forestry workers has been enough to maintain basic public services (school, post office, meeting hall, shops) and even acquire new ones (a pub serving beer, a bank, and taxi-drivers).

Hattuvaara's success might turn out to be only temporary, however, as a new wave of mechanisation is restructuring the industry once more. One new harvester replaces 10 workers. Unemployment among forest workers is increasing, and new environmental issues may put limits on forest use.

NEW CONFLICTS OVER THE FOREST ENVIRONMENT

One day in 1985 the forest workers of Hattuvaara joined inhabitants of other villages from state forestry districts. In the centre of the small municipality of Ilomantsi there was a demonstration march of 1000 people. This local protest was against a giant paper mill investment plan, that regional political organisations had been arguing for over several years. Enso Gutzeit, a state majority stock company and one of the biggest forest industry firms in Finland, owned a cellulose plant that had become obsolete. Saving the plant through modernising investment was vital for the municipality and especially for the community around the plant. Enso Gutzeit proposed to build a paper mill, if all the major sawmills of the district were organised into one new corporation and if the state supported the project by giving 100 000 ha of state-owned forests to the new company. This project was opposed by a local social movement. The local inhabitants felt that the company plan would mean a loss of forestry jobs and restrictions on rights to use forest areas for recreation.

This movement represented a new type of social response. It ignored the boundaries of older organisations and caused a rift inside almost all the political parties. Groups participating in the movement formed a new coalition of various interests: some were fighting for jobs, some were marching for hunting and fishing rights (their hobbies), some were defending environmental values, some felt that the foundation of local communities and the municipality was threatened. This kind of coalition was far from typical in the traditional countryside. It expressed a new complexity of rural interests, which was also reflected in events after the protest rally. The idea of giving state forests to the new company was buried. In spite of these "successes" the coalition disintegrated and the movement died out. Later, however, the municipality got its pulp and paper mill, when Enso Gutzeit invested in a new project, relying instead on roundwood supplies from Russia.

Concern about environmental values is usually connected with city people, longing for the natural, wishing for the idyllic rural life or wilderness. These views are also shared by the new inhabitants of the countryside, who see nature as an environment for living and leisure and not as an object of work from which to win a living. Through these social groups the urban system is reaching into the countryside. These changing values also affect national policies, creating new challenges for rural professions to establish links into the urban-centred system.

THE PROJECT OF EUROPEAN INTEGRATION

We are now once again in a transitional period from one mode of regulation to another. The central issue around which a new coalition is building is that of European integration (see Table 7.3). Groups that see their future prospects connected with global markets are mobilising for Finland's membership of the EU. The collapse of the Soviet bloc has given Finland more political leeway to re-evaluate its neutrality-based foreign policy. The new pro-European integration coalition is trying to finance structural change by cutting down the welfare state. The question of

Table 7.3. European integration, 1990–

Core objective of the project	European Union membership
International economic orientation	Global markets
Main tensions	Management of decline, struggles over consumption of goods, services and forest resources
National hegemonic bloc	Forest cluster, new export industries, service class
Mechanism of regulation in relation to countryside	Attempts at a new rural policy supporting: • housing and commuting • new pluriactive profiles for farms • quality food products for targeted consumer groups • rural experience products • specialised production in networks (new technologies, teleworking)
Mode of marginalisation	Being left out of labour or commodity markets, "non-competitiveness"
Rural response mode	Competitive strategies for localities and regions (coalitions of enterprises, service class and public agencies)

forsaken or marginalised people is coming on the political agenda again alongside the issue of European integration, but the form of the mode of regulation is still being struggled over. In this ongoing transition some elements of the welfare state are being carried across to the new order. Which they are will depend on the balance of political forces.

The connection of rural communities into this new social project takes place through several shifts of emphasis:

• from agricultural rurality to housing rurality (rural living environment)
• cutting the cost of the welfare state and transferring the burden of public services to the local level
• rechannelling state rural development funds into new rural industries (new rural policy)
• integration of villagers into new information technology networks

Rural communities find it hard to see positive prospects in the new integration project. It has meant problems for small industries producing for local markets, it threatens to halve the income of agriculture, to cut down public service budgets, and decrease all transfers that have been beneficial to rural areas. New market-oriented ways to avoid marginalisation are harder to find.

Besides struggles over the welfare state, there is another element. Local rural coherence is changing on the basis of increasing recognition of the new market-based rules of marginalisation: you are marginalised by being pushed or left out of labour or commodity markets. New local coalitions are emerging, based around issues to do with industrial development, the environment, tourism and leisure. Their responses are new competitive strategies for villages, municipalities and regions. These strategies are not just coping and surviving mechanisms for individuals and households. Various rural organisations and agencies are preparing strategic plans, training their members and personnel and rethinking their activity in terms of competitiveness.

The key common feature of these local development blocs is their orientation towards new forms of rural–urban interaction. They try to fight exclusion from the market by finding new ways of controlling their exchange with the towns. These pursuits correspond quite well with new national-level developments, such as Finland's new comprehensive rural policy outlined in the 1991 National Rural Programme. The same tendencies are also encouraged by international recommendations for rural policies in Western industrialised countries, like the European Commission report *The future of rural society* (1988) and the OECD rural policy report *What future for our countryside?* (1993). These view the countryside as something to be integrated in town-run markets. Finland's new rural policy was recently cited by the head of the OECD's rural development programme as a pilot test-case for OECD policy recommendations.

Finland's National Rural Programme aims at reallocation of public resources to support all sectors of the rural economy, instead of agriculture and forestry alone. It puts the burden of detailed planning and implementation on local municipalities. The main aims are creation of rural networks; rural competitiveness; focusing resources on expanding rural industries; reorganisation of rural service provision; and more pluriactive farming. The plan strongly emphasises networking and places a lot of hope in possibilities derived from new information technologies. They are represented as a new device for the countryside to fight against isolation, to get information-age jobs and new sources of income, to attract educated people from the towns, and to sell rural services, products and labour.

The development of such information technology (IT) initiatives can be illustrated by the case of one village. In November 1985 about 80 inhabitants of Ruvaslahti gathered to hear a new summer inhabitant's lecture on "Work and Housing in Information Society". The speaker worked at the University of Copenhagen and had moved to a summer house nearby. She had a doctorate in technology and business economics.

During the discussion there arose an idea to start IT courses in the disused village school. A decision was made to contact the rector of the municipal adult training institute. He reacted positively. The provincial governor's office and the Ministry of Education were identified as possible sources of financing. The governor's regional planning office accepted the notion of North Karelia as an experimental area for rural IT, as one part of its development policy. The governor's office had just financed another experiment of IT training in primary schools. The Ministry of Education was interested in the rural training experiment. Computer training courses started in the autumn of 1986, and soon the activity took the form of a telecottage, a rural IT community centre (Cronberg, 1991).

In the beginning, during introductory training, the enthusiasm of participants was high. However, looking for computer applications suitable and beneficial for local farmers brought disappointments. The goal of creating new rural jobs (telework) has not brought the expected results, although the telecottage has kept itself running and maintained two permanent jobs. After an initial subsidised period the telecottage had to finance itself independently. Finding clients willing to pay for the services has been difficult. Although the project was a rural IT experiment, the impact was partly evident in new social processes. The people of the village could identify themselves as a community capable of meeting modern challenges. Getting rid of the stigma of backwardness was a task met with enthusiasm.

The present role of the telecottage is twofold. One aspect is as "village secretary", connecting the telecottage intimately to the village community and giving it a social (moral and political) justification. The telecottage helps in the routines of village organisation: text processing, accounts, membership register, producing and mailing of bulletins, computer service for results of a winter fishing contest, or the register of landowners leasing out hunting grounds. Staff expertise in writing official letters and petitions is also utilised. The telecottage premises are important for the village community. They are used for village events and several courses of the adult training institute are held there.

The second role of the telecottage is to get jobs (telework) into the village. Ruvaslahti has produced a bibliography of rural research, a report on distance working and a regional database of rural experts, and organised a village development seminar. The biggest contract involved entering part of the national agricultural census data from 1990 into a database (five part-time jobs for two months). In 1993 Ruvaslahti telecottage made an agreement with the Central Association of Finnish Municipalities to act as its national village service centre. Telework has been based partly on available part-time female labour in the village (farmers' wives with, for example, commercial school training), and on hardware and software bought with public funding (see Oksa, 1993).

Although Ruvaslahti telecottage has received plenty of favourable publicity, the municipality of Polvijärvi has not used it for marketing the district. This is very apparent when Polvijärvi is compared to another North Karelian telecottage municipality, Kontiolahti, which has a high IT profile and well-demonstrated image-making skills. An explanation could be that in Polvijärvi municipal strategy was formulated by the industrialisation (manufacturing) bloc, but in Kontiolahti by an IT bloc. In its own municipality Ruvaslahti village is an exception, that links to IT by bypassing municipal development policy. Kontiolahti has had a longer-term, consistent IT strategy. This has been constructed and supported by a coalition, a bloc consisting of three groups: rural developers, a rural service class, and rural entrepreneurs.

The rural developers are well-trained professionals, whose work or activism is connected with defining and expressing "rural interests". These people can be politicians, planners, activists in rural organisations, or development project workers. The rural service class could also be called "new rural residents" or "rural yuppies". They are middle-class people living in the countryside, often working in urban professions. They want to combine the best qualities of urban and rural life, to live in the natural environment, and to bring up their children in small communities. They want to have a successful career and utilise urban services, culture and information networks. For them IT gives a vision of uniting urban life and rural surroundings. Rural entrepreneurs may need better communications to develop their production and trading. They want to solve their practical problems with new technology. They want reliable technology that is easy to manage. If it is available for a reasonable price, they employ it.

These three groups form the classic coalition promoting rural IT projects. If they are strong and able to join forces on a municipality level, as in Kontiolahti, the result can be a long-term local development strategy that includes IT projects.

CONCLUSION: CHANGING PICTURES OF THE RURAL SCENE

Changes in the countryside can be illustrated by the different experiences of three generations living today. The generation of the grandfather grew up in a world where the hero was a hard-working peasant, clearing new lands and fighting against nature. Political struggles against social marginalisation were about the land. The next generation grew up building the welfare state, fighting to get the reforms that also benefited a farming population. The heroes of that generation were leaders of political movements and interest organisations. Reforms also protected farmers against the calamities of markets. Now these heroes seem to be fighting hopeless battles with rising problems of overproduction, increasing concern over the environment, and decreasing benefits from the welfare state.

Today's emerging heroes — or role models — are not pioneers conquering nature, nor are they organisers of movements or parliamentary orators. Rather they are inventors and producers of new products with rural qualities demanded by urban consumers. These products might, for example, be ecologically grown foodstuffs, naturally coloured textiles, or other designs and creations of country style. These people simultaneously work "away from it all" and interact constantly with urban life. They are aware of the new rules of marginalisation, and they are also supporters of the new national project.

What elements of the earlier project are most likely to be transferred to the next? More likely to continue are those parts where the stronger points of the old and the new period meet, or to put it in terms of political forces, where stronger groups of the old bloc can compromise with the new (or eventually even join the new bloc). This is in much the same way that an earlier peasant state rationale was able to flavour the welfare state, especially its agricultural policy, social security and social services.

In the emerging policy project rural places are drawn in new ways into an urban-led production and consumption system. The new rural heroes are grandchildren of the peasant age. For urbanised grandchildren rurality becomes a special feature of the past, of reminiscence, part of identity, and a quality of cultural artifacts. It becomes a commodity, something to be consumed. The groups forming new rural development blocs, like telematic development coalitions, are fighting rural marginalisation with increased urban–rural interaction. Even when they express solely rural interests, their most important resource is the urban connection. Take three groups forming the rural IT bloc. Rural developers connect to the centres of finance and link their communities to national and international development programmes. Members of the rural service class link to urban consumption styles and their relevant professional organisations. Rural entrepreneurs act in internationalising markets. This intensification of interaction with the urban system brings about a paradoxical situation. It improves the expression of rural interest (by these groups), but it also helps to annihilate the distinction between the rural and urban, and to destroy the specificity of the rural in their interests.

REFERENCES

CEC (1988) *The future of rural society*, Brussels.
Cronberg, T. (1991) Final project report on Ruvaslahti computer training project, Unpublished MS.
Granberg, L. (1989) *Valtio maataloustulojen tasaajana ja takaajana* ("The state as a leveller and guarantor of agricultural income"), Societas Scientiarum Fennica 138, Helsinki.

Knuuttila, S. (1989) What Sivakkavaara people tell about themselves: a research experiment in folk history, in Siikala, A-L. (ed.), *Studies in oral narrative*, Studia Fennica 33, pp. 111–126.

Koskinen, T. (1985) Finland — a forest sector society? Sociological approaches, conclusions and challenges, in Lilja, Kari, Räsänen, Keijo and Tainio, Risto (eds), *Problems in the redescription of business enterprises*, Helsinki School of Economics, Studies B-73, pp. 45–52.

OECD (1993) *What future for our countryside? A rural development policy*, Paris.

Oksa, J. (1993) *Case report on Ruvaslahti telecottage*, Danish TeleConsult International, EC/ORA/ANAGO project.

Rannikko, P. (1987) *Metsätalous ja kylä. Suurmetsätalouden vaikutus maaseudun asutusrakenteeseen 1900-luvulla* ("Forestry and village. The impact of large-scale forestry on rural settlement structure in the twentieth century") University of Joensuu, Publications of the Karelian Institute 81.

8 New Forms of Transport and Communication, New Patterns of Disadvantage

JORGE GASPAR

University of Lisbon, Portugal

The urban and regional restructuring that has been occurring in Europe since the end of the 1960s has an important component which concerns accessibility. This is a decisive factor in relation to strategic objectives and as an instrument for increasing competitiveness. Thus the Commission of the EU has launched policy instruments which aim to reduce physical barriers to the circulation of people, commodities and information. These are being developed even further as a part of the search for economic and monetary union. This process has been assisted by important innovations, especially in the field of telecommunications but also with respect to rail, road and maritime transport (with changes such as containerisation and the introduction of high-speed trains). In the field of energy too, new networks of transport for natural gas and electricity have begun to develop.

Through specific policies (of which STAR — Special Telecommunications Action for Regional Development — is one example) the EU has supported programmes which have the aim of improving infrastructure in the less developed regions of the Union. Recently, the question of accessibility has been seen in a broader context, particularly after the transformations which have occurred in eastern Europe. Proposals for Trans-European Networks have appeared, to be financed partly by the Cohesion Fund set up under the Maastricht Treaty. Analysis of similar processes in other geographical and historical contexts (the best known case being the North American Inter-State Highway system at the end of the 1950s, which gave form to the restructuring of the settlement system of the USA) shows that with enlargement of scale, the most favoured areas are the main nodes of the network and their adjacent areas, at the expense of the rest of the territory (Garrison et al., 1985). Some preliminary evaluations of the impact of accessibility improvement programmes in the less developed regions of the EU indicate that the main winners are likely to be the principal urban

Europe at the Margins: New Mosaics of Inequality. Edited by Costis Hadjimichalis and David Sadler
© 1995 European Science Foundation. Published in 1995 by John Wiley & Sons Ltd

agglomerations, which will experience both relative and absolute improvements to their competitiveness, while minor centres marginal to the new infrastructures will suffer.

At the start of a "new age" of telecommunications, the idea that new information technology will favour regions and smaller settlements which are physically peripheral has grown in popularity. The "global village", it is argued, will be the same for all and peripheral areas can participate in economic and social integration. The new reality which is being configured in European space, however, shows that we are currently involved in a process of concentration which is revealed at different spatial scales (Goddard, 1991; Gillespie and Robins, 1989; Hepworth, 1989).

TRANS-EUROPEAN NETWORKS

The design of these networks suggests that the objective of making the more peripheral regions accessible to the centre is to reinforce rather than counterbalance the celebrated pattern. The high-speed train and the natural gas network constitute two examples of an infrastructure whose impact manifests itself fundamentally in the reinforcement of the relative position of the most urbanised and industrial zones of Europe. In the centre of Europe, the high-speed train will provide fast reliable services, adequate for business purposes as much as for journey-to-work trips, for which there is considerable demand. In this way, an existing urban network which is very dense and highly interconnected will reinforce its position and more easily attain a critical (European) mass (Figure 8.1). The heart of Europe will also benefit environmentally and with respect to air traffic congestion as the high-speed train will partially substitute for aeroplane and automobile transport.

The Paris–Lyon TGV, which has run in its entirety since 1984 and partially since 1981, is the most studied of all of the new high-speed rail lines (Plassard et al., 1986). Significant changes have been observed in travel patterns, including an increase in business journeys and commuting, a decrease in the importance of air travel from Paris to Lyon, and greater tourist travel. Nevertheless, the effects are not yet so clear as to generate a consensus (Brotchie et al., 1991). It is not possible to affirm that locational patterns have been transformed or that there has been a change in the organisational practices of firms. Nor is information available on the fears generated by opening of the service with regard to possible reinforcement of the position of Paris in the economy of France.

In the regional context of the Iberian peninsula, such changes are clearly to the disadvantage of Portugal relative to Spain. The high-speed train is certainly advantageous for Barcelona, joining it to the central region of Europe and improving its attraction over poles such as Madrid and Valencia. It may well have some advantages for Madrid, in particular

Figure 8.1. European high-speed rail network, 1991 and 2010

reinforcement of its centrality relative to Portugal (particularly Lisbon and Porto), but for more peripheral regions, its efficiency with respect to the development process is questionable.

In the case of Spain and Portugal there is an additional burden, that of the different gauge between the Iberian peninsula and Europe beyond the Pyrenees. The Spanish solution of introducing the European standard on the stretch of high-speed track between Madrid and Seville, means that the peninsula will in future have two different networks. The likely development of a system of European gauge high-speed trains in the Iberian peninsula will create a limited number of nodes, mainly the principal cities with connections beyond the Pyrenees. If this network has a capacity to promote interaction, the consequence will be greater differentiation, favouring the main centres and generating a new pattern of disadvantage for the extensive poorer regions in the west and north-west. Additionally, areas in gaps within the network will remain poorly served. This new

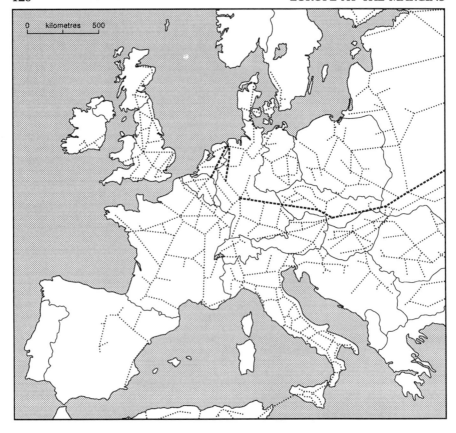

Figure 8.2. European gas transmission network, 1988

infrastructure therefore reinforces a developing scenario. In general, the Iberian peninsula shows tendencies to strongest growth in the north-east, despite the presence of Madrid in the centre and Lisbon in the west.

In the case of natural gas, it is not only a question of territorial design reinforcing existing disequilibria, but there is also a temporal dimension which augments asymmetries (Figure 8.2). Portugal will be integrated into the European network very late, first receiving natural gas from Spain, to supply the most urbanised coastal zone between Setubal and Braga. The country will have to cope for some time with a situation of higher energy costs relative to Spain. Thus, Portugal has already lost and continues to lose opportunities in sectors where potentially it would have comparative advantages, due to the availability of qualified and cheap labour. Ceramics and some metallurgical products are cases where it has become very difficult to maintain competitiveness with relative increases in energy costs. Agriculture provides a further example: the Portuguese market has recently been invaded by imports of fresh Mediterranean products — both inside and outside the natural growing season — from the Netherlands, where they have been produced in greenhouses with very low energy costs, made possible by the availability of natural gas and a public policy of support to agriculture (Carrière, 1989).

In the field of telecommunications, there has been faster integration, resulting in an accelerated rate of diffusion of innovations. Nevertheless, great regional differences in the quality of telecommunications infrastructure and access to advanced services exist. These inequalities have cumulative effects in the sense of accentuating the disadvantage of peripheral regions, provoking increased marginalisation. The most densely populated regions are the most developed in this respect. This contributes to rapid modernisation of their economic base and to enhanced relative competitiveness there. In more developed countries, the intermediate regions, located between major urban centres, have also benefited from progress in telecommunications. Their economic performance has contributed to the idea that telecommunication has a positive role to play in the decentralisation of economic activity, although the results of empirical analysis tend to be inconclusive in this respect (Bakis, 1988). The difficulties which rural areas face in profiting from the potential of telematics are well known, and also the potential to revitalise their economies and especially to avoid depopulation and increasing marginalisation (see Oksa, Chapter 7 this volume). Awareness of these questions prompted the European Commission to develop infrastructure development programmes. In addition, the Commission has launched a large number of studies aiming to evaluate the role which telematics might have in rural areas (the ORA programme).

AN INTRA-NATIONAL CONTEXT: PORTUGAL

After a period of general infrastructural improvement which started in the mid-1970s and lasted until the end of the 1980s, which had the objective of satisfying basic needs throughout the national territory (though including some elements of agglomeration) we can now see the contours of a different policy. Public investments are becoming more selective, in the sense that they are primarily benefiting stronger regions and centres with a global orientation, in order to give Portugal greater competitiveness in an international context. This new direction is clearly observable in the geography of networks of communication and transport, but can also be seen in specific infrastructures for the support of production (such as industrial and science parks, and centres of excellence and quality control).

One aspect which manifested itself in the 1980s, and which will probably be one of the important questions of the 1990s, is related to processes of relatively late urbanisation. This characterises most of Portugal, particularly the centre and north of the country, extending towards Galicia. Urbanisation is taking place in a period dominated by a paradigm of state non-intervention, coincident with a weakening of the welfare state. This is contrary to the urbanisation process of the 1950s and 1960s in more developed countries, which was accompanied by strong public intervention (by both central and local state) with respect to housing and provision of social infrastructures. Therefore there is a lack of co-ordination between the policy response to economic restructuring, and measures related to settlement and urban systems. Local powers subsidise the productive sector at the cost of competing interests in the sphere of reproduction and particularly in the area of housing.

The continuation of such policies and the implementation of the Community Support Framework for Portugal will probably lead to a decrease in the relative weight of social transfers in the family income structure. This can cause problems, especially in peripheral rural regions. Income transfers (both private and public) from the central regions to the periphery are not only a factor of social stability, but also contribute to a reduction of regional inequalities, creating employment in the service sector. Orientation of this support almost exclusively to assist production — as has been established in many municipalities — can have a lesser impact on local development than a policy more orientated towards social infrastructure development.

A consequence of this policy shift is that lower income rural groups have only two alternatives: remain in their village, as long as the distance to their place of work is acceptable, or emigrate further and further away, where they can get a higher salary and better housing. Those who do not follow either of these two options become marginalised or migrant workers in the building industry, living on the premises during the week and returning home at the weekend.

There has been a fundamental change in municipal budgets. Housing is the sector most affected, with a smaller proportion of social or supported housing. A paradox is therefore generated when the public sector promotes or supports a process of urbanisation and concentration (through hierarchical developments in transport, supporting infrastructural development related to productive investment, and direct incentives for production) and simultaneously leaves almost exclusively to the market the resolution of housing problems. Thus regional policy has difficulties in affirming itself outside a conflict with sectoral policies, which will create situations of compromise and a crisis of identity. In both theory and practice, the principles of equilibrium and of endogenous development are losing ground, as convergence occurs with sectoral policies which are ruled by principles of efficiency maximisation, in the sense of increasing national competitiveness.

With respect to transport and communication infrastructure, there have been important improvements in Portugal in roads and telecommunications, giving rise to general increases in interregional accessibility, though this did not occur at the intraregional and local levels. Therefore, in the metropolitan areas, and in particular in the suburbs, the situation is bad and there seems to be little possibility of improvement. In the more remote areas, even if infrastructure has improved, there has been a tendency for deterioration of transport services. The same phenomenon can be observed in relation to telecommunications. The density of the telephone network in terms of capacity of transmission as well as number of telephones increased substantially and the quality of services improved, but the areas with lower population densities experienced a worsening in relative terms.

These observations broadly correlate with general tendencies of Portuguese regional development during the 1980s. Population continued to decline in the poorer and more peripheral regions, with the exception of Algarve (see Figure 8.3). There was, however, a modest reduction in interregional inequalities in terms of employment and gross value added. The joint weight of the two metropolitan areas of Lisbon and Porto decreased in relation to the rest of the country, and the other coastal subregions grew relatively strongly.

There was a difference with respect to the evolution of the settlement system, however, compared to earlier periods. Small settlements immediately outside the main cities, benefiting less from increased accessibility, lost importance. In all subregions, centres with less than 2000 inhabitants lost population, while settlements with more than 5000 inhabitants increased their relative importance. Inside each subregion and especially inside each municipality, increased asymmetries can therefore be observed. The new pattern of advantage and disadvantage is particularly clear at local and subregional levels in the new configuration of the settlement system. There is a reinforcement of the urban network with advantages of polarisation accruing to the main town of the municipality (Gaspar and Jensen-Butler, 1992).

The principal town of the municipality is a basic unit in the process of urbanisation and redistribution, as it is here that local administration and public and private services are concentrated. Even in the poorest subregions there is convergence of important financial resources resulting from public transfers (administration, services, pensions and intermunicipal equalisation grants) and private sources (emigrant remittances and interest). This has prompted in many cases a marked local take-off at the same time as an agricultural crisis. In some cases we can talk of cities without territory.

It is at the local level where the primary resistance to these tendencies occurs and the arguments for more even development are to be found. In many municipalities in more peripheral regions we can, however, detect a

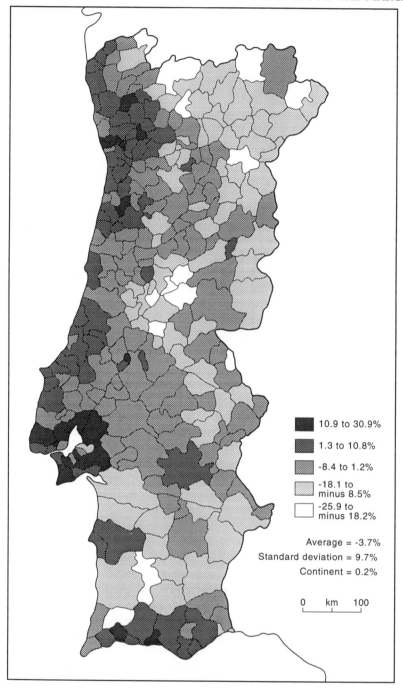

Legend:

- 10.9 to 30.9%
- 1.3 to 10.8%
- -8.4 to 1.2%
- -18.1 to minus 8.5%
- -25.9 to minus 18.2%

Average = -3.7%
Standard deviation = 9.7%
Continent = 0.2%

0   km   100

Figure 8.3. Population change in Portugal, 1981–91

position which is increasingly like the national one: reinforcement of the most efficient pole(s) of the municipality. The final outcome is to promote concentration of infrastructural investment and to increase the value of connections to the exterior which will support the attraction of external investment, to the detriment of endogenus development. Such tendencies will disadvantage many areas that have been economically active and marginalise much of the rural and semi-rural population.

CONCLUSIONS

The profound transformations presently occurring across Europe are creating new patterns of disadvantage. Infrastructural development is increasingly directed towards improving competitiveness. In this way, new forms of agglomeration economy are promoted. Trans-European Networks simultaneously improve performance of the whole economic system and increase the disadvantage of traditionally peripheral regions as well as generating new situations of marginality. The most peripheral regions of Europe, in Ireland, Greece, the Iberian peninsula and southern Italy, have tended to maintain their relative deficit in transport and communication infrastructures. At present, such networks seem to be an important instrument for generation of regional inequality, giving considerable advantages to the most central regions in Europe.

The pipeline network for natural gas is one case in point. In Portugal, delays in the introduction of natural gas created a disadvantageous situation for agriculture and industry. With respect to telecommunications in countries such as Portugal, a substantial improvement has occurred, both through an expansion of the network and through introduction of new services. This also tends to accentuate previously established patterns of inequality. The main beneficiaries are the principal urban areas and the intermediate regions located between these areas and their axes of communication. On the other hand, other areas are experiencing growing difficulties in gaining access to new telecommunications services.

Portugal initiated a process of industrialisation very late, in the 1950s, and modernisation of the productive base was further delayed by a long and bitter colonial war (1961–74). It was only after accession to the EC in 1986 that Portugal even began to overcome its accumulated deficiencies. One consequence of this process was reinforcement of the major urban centres which had the greatest potential for interaction. This process converged with various strategies of infrastructural and communications development: roads, railways, telecommunications and energy. In the "new Europe", it is still — indeed even more than ever — necessary to evaluate the implications of infrastructural programmes for patterns and processes of regional development.

REFERENCES

Bakis, H. (1988) *Entreprise, espace, télécommunications*, Paradigme, Caen.
Brotchie, J. et al. (eds) (1991) *Cities of the 21st century*, Longman, Harlow.
Carrière, J.P. (1989) *Les transformations agraires au Portugal: crise, réformes et financement de l'agriculture*, Economica, Paris.
Garrison, W.L., Berry, J.L., Nysteran, J.D. and Morrill, R.L. (1985) *Studies of highway development and geographic change*, Univ. of Washington, Seattle.
Gaspar, J. and Jensen-Butler, C. (1992) Social, economic and cultural transformations in the Portuguese urban system, *International Journal of Urban and Regional Research*, **16**, 3, 442–461.
Gillespie, A.E. and Robins, K. (1989) Geographical inequalities: the spatial bias of the new communications technologies, *Journal of Communications*, **39**, 3, 7–18.
Goddard, J. (1991) New technology and the geography of the UK information economy, in Brotchie et al. (1991), pp. 191–213.
Hepworth, M. (1989) *Geography of the information economy*, Belhaven Press, London.
Plassard, F. et al. (1986) *Les effets socioéconomiques du TGV en Bourgogne et Rhône-Alpes. Document de synthèse*, DATAR/OEST/SNCF, Paris.

9 Old Industrial Places and Regions: the Limits to Reindustrialisation

DAVID SADLER
University of Durham, UK

INTRODUCTION

The impacts of global competition — the ebb and flow of capital around the world — were felt particularly severely during the 1970s and 1980s in some of those places in western Europe which historically depended for their existence upon one or a limited number of industries, such as coal-mining, iron and steel production, shipbuilding and textiles. Regions like north-east England, northern and eastern France, and the Ruhr, experienced a period of almost continuous decline in the staple employment bases around which they had been physically constructed almost a century previously. In that sense these areas were dramatically affected by the broader global restructuring described by Mingione (Chapter 2 this volume).

One consequence was that processes of social and economic transformation were initiated, partly encouraged by government policies of reindustrialisation. These aimed to re-create the conditions for profitable production. By and large this involved substantial state intervention (often in response to forcefully articulated demands) via infrastructural renewal, reorganisation of declining industries, and incentives to business formation or relocation, in addition to the considerable aggregate expense of transfer payments to the unemployed. In a variety of ways, governments became deeply and integrally involved in the recomposition of these older industrial regions.

This chapter examines some of the changes which have in fact taken place, focusing on their implications in the 1990s in terms of class restructuring and new forms of marginality. It first analyses the limits to policy efforts at reindustrialisation, particularly in relation to the scale of the problems which were faced. Despite grand claims, it is evident that much still remains to be done even in the terms by which proponents of "conventional" measures set themselves for evaluation (for instance

Europe at the Margins: New Mosaics of Inequality. Edited by Costis Hadjimichalis and David Sadler
© 1995 European Science Foundation. Published in 1995 by John Wiley & Sons Ltd

reducing regional income inequalities or lowering unemployment rates). The kind of new economy which has emerged is identified, and its potential for longer-term growth and/or stability is assessed. Then the significance of deindustrialisation for class recomposition is explored further, via the interaction between "old" and "new" sources of employment and forms of social practice. The discrepancy between constructed image and reality is also considered in this section. Finally, the chapter concludes by interpreting the ways in which new forms of marginality have emerged in old industrial regions as a political process, and comments on the present and future role of *place* as a socially contested concept.

Much of the account which follows is drawn from the UK, and northeast England in particular, as a condensation of several different strands of research. Many of the arguments, however, apply — with greater or lesser validity but with similar outcomes — far more broadly (see for instance Bade and Kunzmann, 1991; Hudson, 1989; Sadler, 1992; Zukin, 1985). This chapter is therefore not meant to be read as an account of change in just one state or region, nor as a denial of the difference which place makes, but as an attempt to generalise from such experiences, in the light of evidence from elsewhere. It aims to pose some broad questions about the nature of contemporary restructuring in Europe's old industrial areas, the marginalisation of certain groups, and the terms under which reintegration might occur.

THE LIMITS TO REINDUSTRIALISATION

During the 1980s, a great deal of faith was placed in the ability of "conventional" reindustrialisation policies to cope with the aftermath of economic collapse in localities which had previously been dependent upon one industry or employer. Self-proclaimed "success stories" abounded from many such areas by the end of the decade, and these places were not just confined to northern European heartlands; they included textile and other industrial areas in southern Europe too. Unfortunately, however, far less emphasis was placed upon independent and impartial analysis into the impact of those policies. Attempts to initiate closer investigation frequently met with opposition, on the grounds that even to raise suspicion over proclaimed economic recovery (presuming that there was some doubt to be cast) could be damaging to commercial (self-) confidence.

Far less frequently stated but implicitly accepted, there was also an assumption that criticism might lead to political challenge to the government(s) of the day. Locally based reindustrialisation policies which set the blame squarely on the victims and cast the basis for solutions in terms of "market forces" were central to the increasingly dominant neo-liberal ethos of that decade. This section therefore seeks to consider the true effectiveness of reindustrialisation policy, drawing briefly on more detailed analyses reported elsewhere (see for instance Hudson and Sadler, 1985, 1987, 1992; Hudson et al., 1992), and to reflect with the benefit of hindsight on its impacts.

The typical policy emphasis in old industrial areas was upon recovery through the creation of a new generation (effectively the first, in many cases) of small businesses, and the attraction of inward investment. Several of the towns concerned (for instance Consett and Corby in the UK: see Boulding et al., 1988) were frequently portrayed as shining examples of industrial regeneration in practice. Unfortunately, however, a more detailed appraisal of the evidence pointed to a slightly different conclusion. While a very few places did indeed make a remarkable recovery (partly because of contingent factors such as proximity to other, more rapidly expanding areas, or particularly intensive government policy prioritisation), far more were characterised by continuing problems of high unemployment even after relatively strong economic growth during the late 1980s.

Problems deepened still further during the recessionary early 1990s, as decline in the old economic base — often to the point of extinction — continued to outpace growth in new sectors. In north-east England, for instance (a region which in the late nineteenth century produced one-third of the world's shipping and literally fuelled the expansion of the British Empire — for better or for worse), the last major deep coal-mine and the last shipyard both closed in 1994. In the mid-1970s, the three once-linked sectors of coal, steel and shipbuilding accounted for over one-third of the region's industrial employment, some 150 000 jobs. Twenty years later this proportion was down to around 2% of the industrial workforce, with just 7000 jobs remaining in the one-time staple industries. While north-east England was in some ways an extreme case, processes of terminal decline affected many other European coalfield regions, steel towns and ship-building communities. After a decade or more of concerted effort, jobs lost in traditional industries had still not been replaced in most of these localities. It is debatable whether it was ever realistic to expect such an outcome, given the scale of economic changes taking place. Only a relatively limited number of areas could hope — let alone expect — to return to their formerly prosperous heyday, once the decline of "older" industries was accepted as a somehow inevitable or "natural" consequence of world market forces.

At the same time, other changes were also significant. During the late 1980s, there was a surge of foreign direct investment (FDI) into the EU, as American and Asian companies in particular brought forward their plans for international expansion in order to secure a place inside what they saw as (potentially) a new "Fortress Europe". This meant that in theory at least there was more opportunity for declining industrial regions, possessing large pools of surplus labour, to attract such projects as a basis for their economic revival. In practice, however, they faced increasingly intense competition from other parts of Europe, which offered a wide range of fiscal and other incentives to potential investors. One consequence was that the late 1980s wave of FDI actually did very little to reduce interregional disparities in the EU, which continued instead to widen rather than narrow (Dunford, 1994). As boom conditions turned to recession in the early 1990s, and as the flow of FDI lessened, old industrial places faced the even more difficult task of competing with a still broader range of organisations and regions for a share of a smaller cake.

One way for reindustrialisation agencies to rationalise the difficulties attached to the attraction of FDI — particularly the major projects — was to argue that they ran the risk of re-creating a dependence upon one or a limited number of employers that had characterised previous eras, and had led to the problem of many districts in the first place. Partly in consequence of these changes, support for the creation of new small businesses, and for the expansion of existing small and medium-sized enterprises, became an increasingly significant route towards attempted recovery. This carried its own downside, however. A new industrial base, fashioned largely from small companies dependent (at least initially) upon financial incentives, low-cost provision of premises and professional management advice, was almost inevitably in a constant state of flux. The typical emergent economy was therefore highly insecure, as many companies folded while only a few others grew stronger. In Derwentside in north-east England (which included the ex-steel town of Consett), for instance, only one in two new businesses founded in the early 1980s survived to the late 1980s (and that was in a period of national economic growth). This carried a very real price for the founders and owners of many such firms, leading some to question the ethics of what was frequently self-employment forced onto unwilling "entrepreneurs" through the lack of any alternative.

Such insecurity was mirrored in the labour market. The existence of vast pools of unemployment acted to intensify competition for work at (almost) any price, leading to low wages and poor conditions for those in work. Government-sponsored retraining schemes served more to reduce the headline count than to act as a bargaining counter in the search for new employment, because many of the new jobs created needed little in the way of significant or general (as opposed to highly task-specific) skill training. Therefore many men in their fifties became resigned to the harsh fact that they would probably never work for a wage again, while many young people — including some in their early twenties — still sought their first experience as waged labour despite several experiences on training schemes. In that sense they were effectively marginalised from the formal labour market either for life, or for very long periods at a time.

Even those new inward investment projects which did emerge rested upon certain, very distinctive, forms of labour recruitment and organisation, made possible by prevalent levels of unemployment. Reindustrialisation in this context meant a deepening of labour market inequalities and the construction of new forms of employment contract. It not only separated those in existing kinds of work from those elsewhere in the economy, but also exerted a price on those workers in relatively secure jobs in terms of heightened workplace performance norms, partly through socially constructed peer group pressure.

The largest single Japanese inward investment project in Europe — the Nissan car assembly plant at Sunderland — was a case in point (see Garrahan and Stewart, 1992; Hudson, 1992). Drawing on rigorous selection procedures rendered possible and legitimate by the sheer volume of applications (11 000 were received for the first 240 manufacturing jobs), a distinctive employment structure was established which rested on a British version of company unionism (Nissan "appointed" the AEU as its trade union), functional flexibility within team groups, flattened hierarchies and — perhaps most significantly — considerable intensification of the labour process. This was evident not just in the line speed but also in the range of operations which each task on the line demanded. The average age of the manufacturing employees among the 4700 workforce in 1993 was in the early twenties. Fitness and physical dexterity were key attributes. The workforce was overwhelmingly white and male, one further indication of the new employment structure emerging in the shadow (or more accurately, reflection) of the old. Only 30 manufacturing staff were women, and even fewer were black employees. It is not without significance that when the company announced its intention to lay off workers in the face of market downturn at the end of 1993 (with a considerable financial incentive attached), it was faced with more than enough volunteers, even in the midst of recession and with local unemployment rates standing at around 15%. Money aside, working for Nissan was clearly genuine physical toil.

Nor was the question of new employment practices confined to the "peak" companies, the major projects. In Nissan's wake came some investment by automotive component companies (though not on such a scale as to amount to a regional regeneration strategy in its own right; such an interpretation ignored the way in which the company, and other Japanese car manufacturers in Europe, chose instead to link up with an existing, continent-wide, supply base — see Sadler, 1994). In these smaller factories — crucial to the just-in-time supply system of the car assembly lines — there is some evidence to suggest that not only were the core benefits of working for Nissan (a degree of job security, for instance) not reproduced, but also that working conditions were even more intense. In that sense, there was some speculation that the "Japanese" model with all its forms of labour market inequality and segmentation might be emerging. Certainly the AEU and other trade unions reported considerable difficulties in obtaining the right to representation, let alone recruitment, at many of those plants, which remained stubbornly anti-union. This pattern was widespread. Peck and Stone (1992) found that two-thirds of the post-1980 investment projects in north-east England were non-union, compared to 38% of a matched sample of longer-established plants, and that the trend was for only the largest new plants to have any form of union agreement.

Projects such as Nissan's plant at Sunderland were few and far between, however (although of considerable significance for their demonstration effect upon existing and potential employers and on labour). Other, more widespread facets of economic restructuring elsewhere in these old industrial regions involved a marked shift towards increased proportions of part-time, service sector and female employment. In many cases this meant catching up with national trends, for the previous industrial structure had led to an above-average dependence on male, manual, full-time work in manufacturing industry. The service-sector growth which did take place, though, was not usually characterised by high-order activities such as financial and business services. It was instead more frequently associated with the changed composition of retailing (particularly the growth of large outlets with predominantly part-time workforces), the privatisation of public services, and the provision of leisure, recreation and tourist facilities for those in better-paid employment there or elsewhere (the latter being particularly susceptible to seasonal fluctuations). Increased participation by women in the waged labour force occurred in a context where existing gender inequalities (see Rubery and Tarling, 1988) were massively reinforced by the depressed state of local labour markets. In addition, there was very little evidence that the domestic division of labour underwent substantial change, even in those (increasingly prevalent) households where women became the main wage-earner (see Morris, 1990).

Interpreted in this way, there were a number of question marks over the longer-term prospects for substantial economic recovery in many of these older industrial areas. A comprehensive survey in the county of Cleveland (one of the UK's most intractable problem areas and a prime object of policy attention: see Beynon et al., 1994), for instance, identified many of the limits to a policy of growth through new small business creation there in the 1980s (Storey and Strange, 1992). There were only 2300 jobs in firms new to the region in 1990 compared with 7400 in 1979. To put these figures into context, the county's two major industrial companies — British Steel and ICI — shed around 30 000 jobs between them during the course of that decade. More significantly, many of the 1600 jobs in "wholly new" firms (that is, new business start-ups) were highly insecure;

around four-fifths depended on sales just to a precarious local economy. The prime motivation for 44% of new business founders had been the threat or reality of unemployment; that is to say they were forced or tempted into starting their own business through the prospect or experience of redundancy. The type of business activity encompassed remarkably limited variation: 26% of wholly new firms were in hairdressing, car breaking or vehicle repair garages. As the authors noted, with some understatement, this pattern represented a heavy concentration in sectors "unlikely to influence the competitiveness of the UK economy" or even "to provide the self-sustaining growth which Cleveland requires" (Storey and Strange, 1992, p. 75). They were economically marginal activities (though very significant to those engaged in them) in a marginalised corner of the UK.

Effectively what had happened in the UK (and elsewhere) was a redefinition of the political terrain on which reindustrialisation might be encouraged, and also of the structures through which policy might be delivered. Partly in response to the increasingly evident limitations of 1950s and 1960s-style regional policies (which Damette, 1980 argued had led to the "hypermobility" of capital), and partly in pursuit of neo-liberal ideologies, governments had ostensibly withdrawn from significant areas of what had previously been considered to be legitimate political territory (see Albrechts et al., 1989). Nationalisation was no longer on the agenda, and indeed it was increasingly evident that all it had done — in many cases — was to provide a framework for continued contraction rather than broader demand management. In that sense, then, reindustrialisation policy needs to be seen as one part of a broader political shift. "Letting the market rule", however, was not about reducing state intervention, but rather entailed a different kind of relationship between state and market. This had a resonance within the EU, too.

Within parts of the EU there was considerable pressure to "roll back" the frontiers of intervention. This general trend concealed many tensions between different goals. That the Single European Market was likely to lead to deepened problems in many other peripheral and older industrial areas was implicitly recognised by the designation of "objective two" regions affected by industrial decline, as part of the late 1980s reform of European regional policy (see CEC, 1992). The focus of such measures remained largely on encouragement to indigenous small firm creation, however, and this was unlikely to prove a sufficient corrective against the centralisation of power in core regions (Amin et al., 1992). On a broad European scale, it was difficult to envisage the long-term and far-reaching renewal of most older industrial regions, even though by the early 1990s the limitations of neo-liberal policies were becoming increasingly apparent. This, however, raises a different set of questions, to do with *why* policies took the form that they did during the 1980s.

THE POLITICS OF TRANSFORMATION

Central to the brand of reindustrialisation policies adopted in the UK and widely mirrored elsewhere in Europe during the 1980s was a particular vision of social and economic transformation (see also Amin and Tomaney, 1991). This entailed abandonment (forced, if necessary) of older collectivist values and a commitment to privatisation in a variety of spheres. As such, it is important to recognise that what was taking place was a highly political process of recomposition, resulting in a society unequal in various ways.

This is not to suggest that previously established norms had been wholly egalitarian; far from it. Although previous forms of workplace representation and political organisation were the result of long and bitter struggles and epitomised the social values of collective identity and community, they were very much the terrain of a white, male working class. Women's identity had historically been defined in relation to that of men. Migrant groups coexisted in uneasy proximity, simultaneously part of the working class and yet not part of it, in the region and yet not "belonging" to it. The "new" society which was tentatively emerging as part of the process of reindustrialisation contained different forms of inequality from the old; different fault lines and fractures, and alternative ways in which the fragments pieced together.

In the labour market, for instance, the young and the over-fifties were sharply disadvantaged. One group was seen as too old to work again, the other lacked the experience as waged labour necessary to secure a job. Dominant patriarchal images of labour as men's physical toil, and of women's place being in the household, together with the temporal rhythms of shift work, were somewhat shaken as shipyards, steel mills and coal-mines closed, but such ideologies were re-established in different ways. Women increasingly combined long hours of both paid and domestic labour, an even more intense form of gendered discrimination (particularly when added to the conditions of work under which they found employment). Previous racist practices were reinforced as one form of (apparent) employment protection for some. Migrant labour attracted in the boom years of the 1950s and 1960s found itself victimised and shunned by a "resident" population, much of which had only moved to these places as they grew and demanded labour power in the latter part of the nineteenth century. Inequality in the labour market was reinforced by change in the housing market, particularly as public-sector provision was sharply reduced. Many of these changes were not just historical circumstance, but were directly contingent upon the existence of massive local unemployment (see Sadler, 1992, pp. 211–242). In a buyer's market for labour power, the rules could be (and frequently were) not just flouted, but rewritten.

One reason why a wide-ranging social reconstitution took place on terms which led to new and heightened forms of inequality lay in the limits to oppositional politics and policies. Not a few old industrial places were characterised by moments of active resistance to the decimation of long-established norms of economic and social reproduction, particularly those once dominated by the coal and steel industries (see for instance Hudson and Sadler, 1983, 1986). Such resistance was exemplified by the year-long miners' strike against pit closures in the UK (see Beynon, 1985). Ultimately, however, the harsh fact remained that practically all of these anti-closure campaigns were unsuccessful. The oppressive power of the state plus the (questionable) promise of new job creation, combined with divisions between groups of workers and between different places, proved a powerful combination.

With the limits to resistance so openly exposed, it was difficult to develop truly alternative economic strategies, despite the continuation of high levels of unemployment. Passive acceptance characterised the lot of many. Moreover, within the ranks of the unemployed there was considerable fragmentation, not just between those with the necessary skills and acumen to earn a living in the informal economy and those without, but also fostered by government efforts to blame the victims. Not only did the redefinition of welfare as workfare sharpen differences within the "working" class (between those in paid employment at any point in time and those without, even though one state could rapidly and easily lead to the other), it also set the unemployed against each other. The ideology of "benefit fraud" led to frequent accusations *by* the unemployed *of* the unemployed in the form of anonymous telephone calls and other communications to benefit offices, heightening a climate of fear (see Beynon et al., 1994, pp. 121–126).

That the problem of deindustrialisation and resultant unemployment had been effectively sidelined in the broader political agenda was symbolised in a "resort to the local" which characterised much development effort. Frequently guided by (arguably illusory) notions of some kind of more egalitarian post-Fordist society, many of those seeking economic regeneration — from both left and right — saw flexible specialisation as their salvation. In particular, locally based self-sustaining growth came to be portrayed as a way to reduce vulnerability to the whims of multinational capital. In the process, the complex network of power linking even the smallest firm to an increasingly global market-place was disregarded. More significantly in the longer term, the possibility of genuinely alternative development was effectively closed off (see especially Graham, 1992).

Yet much of this picture is heavily at odds with a more positive upbeat promotional image generated by practically all of the organisations responsible for securing economic regeneration in these old industrial areas. In the UK, for instance, the job-creation subsidiaries of the major coal and steel companies, British Steel (Industry) and British Coal (Enterprise) (BCE) claimed to have replaced (in the case of the former) or to be able to replace (in the latter) somewhere in the region of 250 000 jobs lost from these two industries alone during the 1980s and early 1990s. In part, such assertions raised fundamental questions about the basis on which job creation could be measured and apportioned to different institutions, and about the extent to which present or prospective "job opportunities" translated into long-term productive employment. It was clearly important to such agencies that they be seen to be successful, or at least viewed in the best possible light, in a broader political context. British Coal (Enterprise) could therefore proudly proclaim in a review of its activities that one measure of its achievement in the UK was that it had begun to offer its "products and services" on a commercial basis overseas, particularly in the emergent east European democracies of Hungary and (what was then) Czechoslovakia (see BCE, 1992). That the latest export from a deindustrialising UK should be such job-creation agencies was perhaps somewhat ironic.

More generally, however, there was a proliferation of governmental and public/private partnership organisations across Europe during the 1980s in the pursuit of reindustrialisation. While some of their optimism was directed at restoring local economic confidence, much of it was pitched at the elusive but potentially lucrative audience of corporations evaluating investment decisions. Highly sophisticated and professional marketing operations were established in order to "sell" the merits of one particular region as against any other. It was extremely difficult to measure objectively the effectiveness of such activity. One survey of inward investment promotion (in northern England) concluded that much of it was "largely window-dressing and quite marginal in influencing actual investment decisions" (Dicken and Tickell, 1992, p. 106). At best, perhaps, it put a place on the map of investment possibilities. This was not insignificant, in that the risk of ceasing such activity was to disappear from the map; but it was hardly the solution to deep-seated economic problems.

In this process of selling carefully selected attributes of particular areas, place was effectively packaged as a commodity to be bought and sold (see Sadler, 1993). This was encapsulated by one agency, Sheffield Development Corporation (SDC), in the late 1980s, which described a marketing programme organised "with a view to understanding the perception of the 'product' that is Sheffield" (SDC, 1989, p. 17). Crucially, however, the image that was portrayed was invariably a highly tailored one, conditioned by a particular class project. Place-marketing strategies frequently appropriated selected aspects of a locality's culture to create a heritage. To give just one example from north-east England, Tyne and Wear Development Corporation (TWDC) managed to identify within the area the following collective consciousness:

The new north east takes the best of the tradition of the past and applies it to the technology of the future. The productive tradition has been passed from generation to generation, from shipwright to automotive engineer, from draughtsman [sic] to CAD technician. The people of Tyne and Wear have inherited a deep understanding of the processes of production (TWDC, 1992, p. 1).

This created heritage was (like many others; see Thrift, 1989) highly partial. Its eulogy to the past, and particularly to late-nineteenth-century industrial dynamism, erased many issues to do with squalid housing conditions and social conflict.

The environmental legacy of early industrialisation was something which promotional strategies sought to reproduce particularly selectively. For in addition to the apparent advantages (such as a "skilled" labour force, accustomed to the physical and temporal realities of waged labour), the very fact of having an industrial history meant that many old industrial regions had enormous costs to bear. Fifty years ago the author J.B. Priestley's *English journey* took him to the coalfield of east Durham, where he witnessed and subsequently described the impact of coal-mining on the landscape. His words are worth quoting at length, if only as a corrective to other interpretations. He was particularly appalled by what he saw in the colliery village of Shotton:

Imagine then a village consisting of a few shops, a public-house, and a clutter of dirty little houses, all at the base of what at first looked like an active volcano. This volcano was the notorious Shotton "tip", literally a man-made smoking hill. From its peak ran a colossal aerial flight to the pithead far below. . . . The "tip" itself towered to the sky and its vast dark bulk, steaming and smoking at various levels, blotted out all the landscape at the back of the village. Its lowest slope was only a few yards from the miserable cluster of houses. . . . But it was not merely a matter of sight. That monster was not smoking there for nothing. The atmosphere was thickened with ashes and sulphuric fumes; like that of Pompeii, as we are told, on the eve of its destruction. I do not mean that by standing in one place you could find traces of ash in the air and could detect a whiff of sulphur. I mean that the whole village and everybody in it was buried in this thick reek, was smothered in ashes and sulphuric fumes. Wherever I stood they made me gasp and cough. (Priestley, 1934, pp. 336–337)

His words might perhaps strike more than a distant chord in many other places, like Longwy in eastern France, which have carried a similar environmental burden as the price for nineteenth-century prosperity.

Such problems could only partly be tackled by infrastructural renewal. Shotton stands today for instance in the shadow of Peterlee New Town, with its pit heap flattened but still recognisable. Other environmental impacts — particularly groundwater and coastal pollution, and patterns of ill health due to atmospheric pollution (see Townsend et al., 1988) — take much longer to resolve.

Given the stress in much promotional activity upon the merits of earlier entrepreneurs, it is perhaps appropriate also to quote at length in this context from one of a new generation of business leaders in the north-east of England. Sir John Hall was one of a select band of entrepreneurs which emerged in the UK in the 1980s, whose success — typically property-based — was eulogised by the government of the day in an effort to prove the effectiveness of its policy of encouraging business to set the agenda (see also Lowe, 1993). He came from an area with a long tradition of celebrating and paying deference to its paternalist business leaders, men such as Armstrong and Vickers who developed Tyneside's armaments industries in the nineteenth century, or the coal-owner Lord Londonderry.

Hall was developer of the MetroCentre at Gateshead. This vast complex of shopping malls and leisure facilities epitomised much of the new economy that emerged in this region during the 1980s. It employed thousands, with the vast majority on part-time contracts. As an out-of-town development it was dependent upon and reinforced patterns of consumption which reflected sharp divides between those in secure employment with relatively high disposable incomes, and those either unemployed or in greyer areas of the labour market. At the end of the 1980s Sir John Hall spoke in the following terms, which epitomised a particular version of the region's inherited past, and its role for the future:

> The north east is an area which is a family area. We all lived in villages, we were very much family oriented. That's dissipated to a degree with the way society's gone. I'm trying to bring it back here [at the MetroCentre]. I'm trying to take what's good from the past and put it into a modern idiom. I learn from the past. I don't want to live in it. This Centre's built around the family unit. This is what the north east is, a family unit.

He went on as follows to account for his commercial success:

> The main thing is we did it ourselves, here in the north east. We didn't use any of the pundits from London or the experts from the south-east. We did it here. The talent of the people has always been here. We built the biggest ships, the biggest engineering products and the biggest armaments in our industrial time. Now, in a sense, we have to bring ourselves forward and do things in the new way, the modern way, whatever that may be. And that's what this place represents. It embodies everything that I think Thatcherism says. Provincial regeneration is going to happen because people in that area want it to happen (speaking on BBC TV, 1989).

Deeply embedded in local culture, Sir John Hall subsequently acquired control of Tyneside's leading football team, Newcastle United, and developed another leisure complex at Wynyard Hall, former seat of Lord

Londonderry. There was no denying his impact in the "new" north-east. Yet behind his words lay a clear expression of a particular conception of the region's future, and the way in which it could be built from the past; one that was dependent upon "family" values and local expertise. In this way (and this is but one example of a broader trend) the ideology of redevelopment was a carefully constructed one.

While the engagement between local business leaders and élites, and local politics, was far from new, it posed some serious questions to do with accountability, legitimacy and authority (see Business in the Community, 1991; Peck, 1992). Ultimately, however, the different strands of regeneration pointed in one direction: localisation of both problem and solution. Whether through place-marketing strategies targeted at inward investment or a stress upon indigenous skills and abilities, the net result was to pitch places in apparent competition with each other. "Success" became defined in terms of ability to attract branch plants, to create new businesses, or to encourage new (socially divisive) forms of consumption, in one locality as opposed to any other. It is in this context too that the disparity between image and reality of reindustrialisation has to be situated; for redevelopment efforts depended upon the manipulation and reinforcement of partially constructed images as an integral part of their operation. Apparent competition between places was central to the maintenance of particular hegemonic projects which proclaimed the inevitability of decline in older industries in the first place (see Sadler, 1993). Moreover — and importantly — such strategies also contained an implicit conception of the "appropriate" route to reintegration with the mainstream of national economies which was from the outset dependent upon new forms of marginalisation. Far from an unfortunate outcome of restructuring processes, the creation of new forms of inequality — the refracturing of society in a way which created new marginal groups, many of them from the remnants of an older mosaic — was an integral and central feature.

CONCLUSIONS

This chapter has briefly surveyed the impacts of reindustrialisation policies in Europe's old industrial places and regions, drawing on the lessons from one state (the UK) and generalising in the light of similar evidence from elsewhere. Policies were designed to ease the exit from the downward spiral of decline which old industrial places faced as a consequence of international economic changes and constraints upon the capacity of national state economic strategies. It was argued that such measures have been far from successful, however, even in their own terms, except in a very few cases. In a context of continued high levels of unemployment, new and arguably harsher inequalities have emerged in many of these areas.

This picture is in stark contrast to the images portrayed by many of the agencies and organisations concerned with economic renewal. In part, this is due to a need to be seen to be, or at least appear to be, successful. Such pictures have been carefully crafted, however, so as to appropriate selected aspects of local culture and heritage in a fashion which depoliticises the past and localises the search for a future. In the process, "place" becomes a commodity to be bought and sold, pitching one area against another in a struggle for inward investment or business creation. Yet — and crucially — this basis for division, upon which many forms of marginalisation are founded, is an outcome of conscious political projects. National and local state policies, as well as those of the EU (for instance via its Structural Funds) have been integrally and directly involved in the re-creation of new forms of marginality. The present crisis of political regulation — in its various forms — is manifest only too clearly in the limits to state policies in such areas, and in the devastating social and economic consequences of high and lasting unemployment. Reindustrialisation has most definitely not led to wholesale and equitable renewal. Construed in this way as a socially and politically constructed concept, place has been instrumentally associated instead with the reproduction and indeed intensification of inequality. The challenge is to recognise the significance of that geography, and to reconceptualise its potential.

REFERENCES

Albrechts, L., Moulaert, F., Roberts, P. and Swyngedouw, E. (eds) (1989) *Regional policy at the crossroads: European perspectives*, Jessica Kingsley, London.
Amin, A., Charles, D.R. and Howells, J. (1992) Corporate restructuring and cohesion in the new Europe, *Regional Studies*, **26**, 319–331.
Amin, A. and Tomaney, J. (1991) Creating an enterprise culture in the North East? The impact of urban and regional policies of the 1980s, *Regional Studies*, **25**, 479–487.
Bade, F-J. and Kunzmann, K.R. (1991) De-industrialisation and regional development in the Federal Republic of Germany, in Rodwin, L. and Sazanami, H. (eds), *Industrial change and regional economic transformation: the experience of Western Europe*, Harper Collins, London, pp. 70–105.
BBC TV (1989) *The kingdom of fun* (broadcast on BBC2, 19 January).
BCE (British Coal (Enterprise)) (1992) *A review of activities 1991–92*. Mansfield.
Beynon, H. (ed.) (1985) *Digging deeper: issues in the miners' strike*, Verso, London.
Beynon, H., Hudson, R. and Sadler, D. (1994) *A place called Teesside: a locality in a global economy*, Edinburgh University Press.
Boulding, P., Hudson, R. and Sadler, D. (1988) Consett and Corby: what kind of new era? *Public Administration Quarterly*, **12**, 235–255.
Business in the Community (1991) *Directions for the nineties*, London.
CEC (1992) *Reform of the structural funds: a tool to promote economic and social cohesion*, Brussels.
Damette, F. (1980) The regional framework of monopoly exploitation: new problems and trends, in Carney, J., Hudson, R. and Lewis, J. (eds), *Regions in*

crisis: *new perspectives in European regional theory*, Croom Helm, London, pp. 76–92.

Dicken, P. and Tickell, A. (1992) Competitors or collaborators? The structure of inward investment promotion in Northern England, *Regional Studies*, **26**, 99–106.

Dunford, M. (1994) Winners and losers: the new map of economic inequality in the European Union, *European Urban and Regional Studies*, **1**, 95–114.

Garrahan, P. and Stewart, P. (1992) *The Nissan enigma: flexibility at work in a local economy*, Mansell, London.

Graham, J. (1992) Post-Fordism as politics: the political consequences of narratives on the left, *Society and Space*, **10**, 393–410.

Hudson, R. (1989) *Wrecking a region: state policies, party politics and regional change in north east England*, Pion, London.

Hudson, R. (1992) *The Japanese, the UK automobile industry, and the automobile industry in the UK*, Change in the automobile industry DP 9, Department of Geography, University of Durham.

Hudson, R. and Sadler, D. (1983) Region, class and the politics of steel closures in the European Community, *Society and Space*, **1**, 405–428.

Hudson, R. and Sadler, D. (1985) Coal and dole: employment policies in the coalfields, in Beynon, H. (ed.), *Digging deeper: issues in the miners' strike*, Verso, London, pp. 217–230.

Hudson, R. and Sadler, D. (1986) Contesting works closures in Western Europe's industrial regions: defending place or betraying class? in Scott, A.J. and Storper, M. (eds), *Production, work, territory*, Allen and Unwin, Boston, pp. 172–193.

Hudson, R. and Sadler, D. (1987) National policies and local economic initiatives: evaluating the effectiveness of UK coal and steel closure area re-industrialisation measures, *Local Economy*, **2**, 107–115.

Hudson, R. and Sadler, D. (1992) New jobs for old? Re-industrialisation policies in Derwentside in the 1980s, *Local Economy*, **6**, 316–325.

Hudson, R., Sadler, D. and Townsend, A. (1992) Employment change in UK steel closure areas during the 1980s: policy implications and lessons for Scotland, *Regional Studies*, **26**, 633–646.

Lowe, M. (1993) Local hero! An examination of the role of the regional entrepreneur in the regeneration of Britain's regions, in Kearns, G. and Philo, C. (eds), *Selling places: the city as cultural capital, past and present*, Pergamon, Oxford, pp. 211–230.

Morris, L. (1990) *The workings of the household*, Polity, Oxford.

Peck, F. and Stone, I. (1992) *New inward investment and the Northern Region labour market*, Employment Department Research Series 6, Sheffield.

Peck, J.A. (1992) TECs and the local politics of training, *Political Geography*, **11**, 335–354.

Priestley, J.B. (1934) *English journey*, Heinemann, London.

Rubery, J. and Tarling, R. (1988) Women's employment in declining Britain, in Rubery, J. (ed.), *Women and recession*, Routledge, London.

Sadler, D. (1992) *The global region: production, state policies and uneven development*, Pergamon, Oxford.

Sadler, D. (1993) Place-marketing, competitive places and the construction of hegemony in Britain in the 1980s, in Kearns, G. and Philo, C. (eds), *Selling places: the city as cultural capital, past and present*, Pergamon, Oxford, pp. 175–92.

Sadler, D. (1994) The geographies of "Just-in-Time": Japanese investment and the automotive components industry in Western Europe, *Economic Geography*, **70**, 41–59.

SDC (Sheffield Development Corporation) (1989) *Annual report and accounts 1988/89*, Sheffield.

Storey, D.J. and Strange, A. (1992) *Entrepreneurship in Cleveland 1979–1989: a study of the effects of the enterprise culture*, Employment Department Research Series 3, Sheffield.

Thrift, N. (1989) Images of social change, in Hamnett, C., McDowell, L. and Sarre, P. (eds), *The changing social structure*, Sage, London, pp. 12–42.

Townsend, P., Phillimore, P. and Beattie, A. (1988) *Health and deprivation: inequality and the north*, Croom Helm, London.

TWDC (Tyne and Wear Development Corporation) (1992) *The European flagship*, Newcastle upon Tyne.

Zukin, S. (1985) The regional challenge to French industrial policy, *International Journal of Urban and Regional Research*, **9**, 352–367.

10 Growth at the Margins: Contract Labour in a Core Region

JOHN ALLEN
The Open University, Milton Keynes, UK

NICK HENRY
University of Birmingham, UK

INTRODUCTION

One of the themes stressed in earlier chapters, especially those by Hadjimichalis and Sadler (Chapter 1), and by Mingione (Chapter 2), is the importance of locating present trends within a historical context. The shift towards more diversified, fragmented employment structures within the major industrial economies and the greater inequality associated with this trend is obviously one that has its roots in the demise of an industrial landscape based upon large-scale manufacturing and a mass workforce. Whether one refers to this shift in terms of the decline of Fordist mass production is less significant here than the recognition that the long post-war period of full employment and growing real wages is over. In its place, within the European core, is the prospect of a decline in employment opportunities, a reversal of the trend towards income equality, and a halt on state welfare spending (Glyn, 1992). Obviously, these shifts will take an uneven form across and between countries, but it is interesting to register the general appearance of a more diversified, fragmented employment structure as part and parcel of this broad direction of change.

One reason for this, noted by Mingione and others, is the growth of service sector jobs in all the major industrial economies. According to Mingione (1991), the shift to services, in itself, is partly responsible for the greater diversity of employment practices, both formal and informal, and the increase in the numbers of precarious and irregular forms of employment. Indeed, Mingione's notion of Western, *fragmented* societies is partly an attempt to convey the thrust of these changes, as is his notion of "fragmented polarisation", which draws attention to the cross-cutting nature of social groupings at both ends of the social structure.

In this chapter, we wish to explore certain aspects of the emergence of a more diversified, possibly fragmented, employment structure within the

Europe at the Margins: New Mosaics of Inequality. Edited by Costis Hadjimichalis and David Sadler
© 1995 European Science Foundation. Published in 1995 by John Wiley & Sons Ltd

dominant region of the UK — London and the south-east of England. Broadly, we take our brief from an earlier thesis (Allen, 1988, 1992a) that in the 1980s a particular form of service growth moved across London and the south-east which laid down new lines of social division. The constellation of events from the late 1970s onwards which produced this shift in the social base of the region was considered to be profoundly inegalitarian in its forms. The precise contours of this form of inequality are uncertain, although Sassen (1991) and others have argued that the direction of change in global spaces such as the London city region is one of increasing social polarisation based upon two very different kinds of growth: on the one hand, the emergence of highly dynamic, technologically advanced sectors centred on international finance and commerce and, on the other, the expansion of low-wage, unstable sectors of manufacturing and service employment. More importantly, the two sides to growth are said to be interconnected, with the spread of poorly paid, "marginal" work regarded as a consequence of dynamic industrial growth rather than a sideline development. While it is only possible to indicate rather than establish such an interconnection, the following section builds up a picture of the "two sides to growth", drawing in particular upon evidence of the significant expansion of the labour-intensive, servicing industries throughout the 1980s across London and the south-east.

Discussions of the "downside" of growth or indeed of casual or informal labour markets almost always revolve around such activities as cleaning, catering, delivery, retail, security, and various manufacturers such as furniture and clothing. In London and the south-east, the activities which *are* integrally related to the growth of international finance and commerce are those of contract servicing: cleaning, catering and security. As office space has increased, so too has the demand for these services. These are among the activities most regularly contracted out by banks, insurance companies and other financial and commercial institutions in the City.[1] More importantly, they lie behind what Castells in his account of the *Dual City* has referred to as "a highly dynamic, growth-orientated, and often very profitable sector" (1989, p. 225). What is frequently overlooked, however, in accounts of the expansion of low-paid, low-status service work is that it is *formally* organised by national and, often, multinational contract service firms. The implications of this situation are discussed in the second section.

In the final section, we look briefly at the intensification of exploitation among poorly paid contract service workers and the way in which this process is promoted by a state which, in the name of market efficiency, is shifting the UK in the direction of a low-wage, low-skilled economy. Central to this possibility is the manner in which certain forms of contract service work are *represented* as "marginal" and thus less able to resist the direction of change. First, however, we take a closer look at the dynamics of growth that lie behind the expansion of contract services.

TWO SIDES TO GROWTH

During the 1980s, London and the south-east experienced a significant period of growth as a series of growth dynamics including, among others, finance, high technology, property, consumption and state action combined in a reinforcing cycle of "boom". The exact form that this "combination" took varied across the region to provide a pattern of uneven growth *within* the south-east as well as between the south-east and other regions of the UK (Allen, 1992b).[2] Thus, London experienced a dynamic of growth centred on finance and property, whereas Cambridge, for example, rose to prominence through the growth of high-technology industry and the Medway towns of Kent largely saw growth pass them by.

Following on from the arguments of Sassen (1991), this section will concentrate on that particular bundle of dynamics concerned with finance and property to highlight the "two sides to growth" during the 1980s boom. Both sides are elements of a particular form of service growth in the south-east region, with growth in finance and commerce running alongside that which occurred in the labour-intensive *servicing* industries.

The rise to prominence of finance and commerce during the 1980s represented a significant shift in the structure of the UK economy. By 1990, when the nation's current account balance was in deficit to the tune of £14.4 bn, financial and other services contributed almost £9.8 bn to net national earnings, an increase of more than 150% over the 1980 figure (taken from Table 1, Court and McDowell, 1993). Over the same period, the share of gross domestic product (GDP) accounted for by finance and commerce increased from 12% to 18% representing a growth in output greater than any other major industry in the UK.

This growth in national earnings and output was mirrored by growth in employment (see Table 10.1). Between 1981 and 1989, employment in finance and commerce grew by over 50% or 876 000 jobs, representing an absolute growth in jobs more than double that for any other industrial division. By 1989, over 2.5 million jobs were located in finance and commerce, almost 12% of total employment in the UK.

Moreover, it is the south-east of England which represents the backbone of finance and commerce. In output terms, while the industry accounted for 18% of UK GDP it represented over 27% of the output of the south-east in 1990 (Table 5, Court and McDowell, 1993). The industry's importance in the south-east is matched by the south-east's importance to the industry (see Table 10.1). In 1981, 49% of employment in finance and commerce was located in the south-east.[3] Already dominant as the location of finance and commerce, during the rapid expansion of the 1980s the south-east was the major recipient of this growth. Over 500 000 new jobs, representing 58% of all new jobs created nationally in the industry, increased the south-east's dominance of employment in the industry. Thus, by 1989, over half of all

Table 10.1. Employment in banking, insurance and finance, 1981–89 (June), by region

Region	Location quotient 1981	Employment (000s) 1981	Employment (000s) 1989	Employment change 1981–89 000s	Employment change 1981–89 %	Share of GDP 1987 %
South-east	1.45	844	1352	+508	+60.1	26.5
Greater London	1.96	568	847	+279	+49.1	33.4
Remainder	0.96	276	505	+229	+83.0	21.4
East Anglia	0.82	45	75	+30	+66.7	14.8
South-west	0.92	113	199	+86	+76.1	17.4
East Midlands	0.65	77	106	+29	+37.7	10.6
West Midlands	0.75	123	176	+53	+43.1	14.4
Yorkshire and Humberside	0.71	105	137	+32	+30.5	13.6
North-west	0.85	168	226	+58	+34.5	14.7
North	0.66	59	79	+20	+33.9	11.9
Wales	0.65	50	67	+17	+34.0	12.9
Scotland	0.81	129	172	+43	+33.3	15.0
Great Britain	1.00	1712	2588	+876	+51.2	18.7

Note: Data relate to Industrial Division 8 and to employees only, excluding self-employed.
GDP = Gross Domestic Product.
Source: Champion and Townsend (1990).

employment in finance and commerce (1 352 000 jobs) was to be found in the south-east.

However, such growth has been uneven within the region. In this sense, the dominance of London in both the regional and national economy cannot be ignored. In 1981, Greater London held the highest concentration of employment in finance and commerce in the country, representing a third of national finance employment and over two-thirds of the industry's employment in the south-east region. Over the decade, a further quarter of a million finance jobs, representing one-third of the national growth figure, located in Greater London.[4] Moreover, the symbolic representation of this dominance in finance and commerce is the City of London itself ("the square mile"). Between 1981 and 1987, the City of London grew by 39 600 jobs (22%) and the City of Westminster by 34 800 jobs (32%) (Champion and Townsend, 1990). Since 1987, Rajan (1990) has mapped further employment growth in the City averaging 3.5% growth per year or an additional 35 000 jobs by 1990.[5]

The growth of finance and commerce in the national and regional economy has provided a variety of types of job. For instance, we should be careful not to fall into the trap of equating only high-wage and high-status jobs with this "upside of growth" industry. None the less, it is true to say that the sector is one of the highest-paid sectors in the UK economy and it includes some of the highest-paid individuals in the land. In 1992, for example, the average weekly wage of a non-manual, full-time employee in finance and commerce stood at £357.1 (Dept. of Employment, 1992). This figure compares favourably to the average weekly wage for all manufacturing industries of £299.7 and a figure of £303.6 per week for all service industries. In terms of individuals, a Labour Research report in the mid-1980s identified over 400 individuals in just over 50 City companies earning £100 000 or more a year (Labour Research, 1986). Yet a breakdown by gender of earnings figures provides a different story. First of all, it reveals considerably higher wages in the industry in London and the south-east than elsewhere. Thus, in 1992, men working in non-manual occupations in finance and commerce earned an average of £467.9 a week. Furthermore, the average wage figure for males employed in the industry in the south-east rises to £547.6 and for males in Greater London average earnings reach £601 a week. Second, however, this breakdown also reveals the male domination of the high-paid jobs in the industry. Nationally, non-manual women in the industry earned an average weekly wage worth 56% of the male equivalent (£261.5) and, in Greater London, the higher weekly wage of £345.9 only translated as 57% of the male equivalent. Thus, in the portrayal of City workers provided by Labour Research in 1986, the £100 000 annual salaries of the highest paid (men) stood in stark contrast to the average yearly earnings of under £7500 of the receptionists, secretaries, typists and clerks with many earning less than £100 a week.[6]

In summary, during the 1980s the south-east region dominated the UK's finance and commerce industry, with the City and Greater London representing the region's hub. This dominance has provided the region with a significant amount of jobs, a high proportion of which are high waged and high status. Yet this was not the only type of employment growth taking place in the region during the 1980s. For the growth of finance and commerce was paralleled by another side to growth; namely, the growth of private, labour-intensive services.

In particular, we wish to concentrate on three of these services — contract catering, contract cleaning and contract security. In 1992, turnover in the UK contract catering industry stood at over £1.5bn (BHA, 1993). Indeed, between 1980 and 1988, the industry saw over 50% growth in real turnover (HCTC, 1992). By 1990, contract catering employed 131 000 workers nationally, an employment growth of over 25% during the decade. Once again, London and the south-east were the focus of this growth. In 1984, after several years of particularly dynamic growth, London accounted for 22% of national employment in contract catering and the rest of the south-east a further 15% of national employment. In total, over a third of national employment in the catering industry is located in the south-east region (HCTB, 1989).

Similarly, the contract cleaning industry has experienced continued expansion of both turnover and employment throughout the 1980s. In

1985, turnover in the industry stood at £400m and, by 1990, had increased to about £1.2bn (Key Note, 1991a). Regionally, a membership survey of the Contract Cleaning and Maintenance Association in 1987 revealed that 38% of contracts held were based in London and the Home Counties. Moreover, in 41 of the 83 companies surveyed, London and the Home Counties was the total source of turnover, with a further 14 companies recording that over 50% of their turnover was generated in the region. Overall, the south-east was the major source of turnover for 64% of companies in the contract cleaning sector (CCMA, 1987).

The growth of the cleaning industry and its concentration in the south-east is also reflected in its employment statistics. In 1981, the census of employment registered a national workforce of 190 000 in "cleaning services". By 1989, the figure had increased to over 293 000 employees representing an employment growth of more than 50% in the industry. At the beginning of the 1980s, the south-east region accounted for 50% of all employment in cleaning services, representing over 95 000 jobs. The dominance of the region in the industry's employment profile has also ensured that the south-east has been the major recipient of the industry's growth during the 1980s, accounting for over one-third (38 000 jobs) of national employment growth. Once again, within the south-east region it is London and the City which dominate employment in cleaning services. In 1989, 76 000 cleaning workers were located in London, of which 46 500 were within the City area as defined by Rajan (1990).

Two recent reports estimated the total market of the UK security industry as at least £2bn in 1990, at the end of a decade which saw year-on-year growth of around 10% per annum (McAlpine, Thorpe and Warrier, 1991; Key Note, 1991b). Within the industry, guarding represents one of the largest sectors, accounting for about £250m of business in 1991, as against £151m in 1986. The growth of the industry is reflected in the history of its major trade association, the British Security Industry Association (BSIA), which celebrated its twenty-fifth anniversary in 1992. Created with a membership of 10, the association now has a membership of over 160 companies with a combined turnover of over £1.2bn. This represents an increase in turnover of 325% on 1981. This growth in turnover is also related to employment growth, with member companies employing over 73 000 employees in 1991 (Security Spokesman, 1992). The estimates of employment in contract guarding alone give a figure of 60 000 employees and although no figures on regional breakdown of employment are available, a regular survey of guards' pay is carried out by the BSIA.[7] The 1991 survey covered over 27 000 guards across the country and a breakdown of guards by region revealed 27% to be employed in central London and a further 23% employed in the rest of the south-east. In total, 50% of the guards surveyed, numbering nearly 14 000 individuals, were employed in the London and south-east region.

In summary, throughout the 1980s, the contract service industries of catering, cleaning and guarding experienced consistent, impressive growth. Moreover, this growth took place, first and foremost, in London and the south-east. Thus, we estimate that over the decade the region gained about 60 000 jobs in these industries, giving a recent total regional employment figure of about 200 000 employees in the contract services. At this point, however, we should be clear about what this growth represents. Much of this employment growth in contract services is strictly speaking not new employment, but rather "in house" jobs transferred to subcontractors. Yet it is the type of job provided by these industries which distinguishes them as the second (and "down") side to growth.

The contract service industries, for example, are characterised by a high proportion of low-paid and low-status labour; 70% of contract catering employment is in the lowest occupational category of "general worker" (BHA, 1993). In 1991, the average hourly wage for a general worker was £3.00 per hour. In the south-east, this figure rose to £3.24 and in London to £3.47 (BHRCA, 1991). In security, the dominant occupational category is that of guard. In 1991, the average hourly rate was £3.39 per hour rising to £3.85 in London (BSIA, 1992). For cleaners, the *New earnings survey* (Dept of Employment, 1992) provided a wage figure of £3.63 for part-time, female cleaners, who comprise the bulk of the workforce. Moreover, the fact that hourly rates have been quoted highlights another characteristic of these industries, namely the extreme variation in the hours worked. While part-time work is the norm in cleaning, in contract catering, 14% of employees work part time (under 16 hours) (BHA, 1993) and, in contrast, the security industry is characterised by long working hours (a national average of 60 hours per week).

To conclude, the two sides to growth in London and the south-east in the 1980s have been described. On the one hand, there is the familiar growth dynamic of finance and commerce, which has provided some of the most highly paid, full-time employment in the UK. On the other hand, one finds the labour-intensive contract service industries of catering, cleaning and security which are among the lowest-paid and lowest-status jobs in the economy.

FRAGMENTS OF INDUSTRY

At best, therefore, we can infer a connection between two equally dynamic sectors; one characterised by a predominance of high-wage, high-status labour, and the other by a high proportion of low-wage, low-status labour. Although, as indicated, we should be careful not to draw superficial parallels between the divergence of skills and incomes on the one hand and the emergence of advanced and less advanced sectors on the other, it is perhaps reasonable to assert that the growth of low-wage, unstable service work in the south-east, and London in particular, is in part a function of contemporary restructuring in the financial and commercial services sector. It is in this sense that it is possible to talk about the margins *in* the centre of economic activity in the region. We need to be careful however, how we unpack this statement.

In terms of employment structures, it is commonplace to point to the casualisation of the employment relation, the growth of temporary and irregular work, as well as the proliferation of part-time work. In our intensive survey of some of the leading operators in the contract cleaning, catering and security sectors, however, this set of trends which usually implies a general downgrading of labour fails to capture the complexity of the current situation.[8] There is indeed a more diversified employment structure in these economic activities, but it is equally important to note the continuity of old patterns — which embrace each of those mentioned above — and the changing organisational forms under which they operate. Part-time work, irregular work or casual forms of employment are hardly new to the cleaning sector, for example. What has principally altered, however, are the firms which *organise* these kinds of work. There are two trends worth noting here.

First, that the major operators in each of the three sectors expanded in size at a rapid rate throughout the 1980s (Ascher, 1987; Brosnan and Wilkinson, 1988; Michie and Wilkinson, 1992). Largely on the basis of the acquisition of small companies, a handful of lead firms dominate each sector and exercise a barrier to entry through their ability to service the multiple sites of equally large clients. At the risk of exaggeration, many of these contract "giants" are hollow corporations who formally organise labour at a distance on an infinite variety of sites. In every sense of the word, they represent *fragments of industry*. Second, that in contrast to large firms in the manufacturing sector which have tended to pay relatively high wages and provide reasonable terms and conditions of employment, the large contract service firms have generally responded to growth by further eroding the pay and conditions of labour. Their ability to do so rests upon both the explicit strategy of recent conservative governments to "free up" pay and employment protection legislation and the relative powerlessness of a contract workforce that is, literally, fragmented. We shall consider the implications of the first trend in this section and consider those of the second in greater depth shortly.

As noted above, each of the three sectors — cleaning, catering and security — is highly concentrated, with a few large firms dominating the expanding UK markets. It is impossible to say with any certainty whether oligopolistic practices operate or whether a tacit collusion exists between the lead firms, but whatever the situation it is evident that these firms shape their respective markets and exercise wide influence over the employment standards and work practices of thousands of private service workers.[9] In the contract cleaning industry, for example, five firms hold around one-third of the UK contract cleaning market, with a combined cleaning workforce of over 58 000, the vast majority employed on a part-time basis.[10] Of the five firms, one is a Danish-based multinational, which, despite drawing most of its business from the USA and Scandinavia, has a cleaning workforce of over 12 000 in the UK alone. Another firm, a subsidiary of a UK-based industrial services conglomerate, employs just under 10 000 on the cleaning side. Both companies expanded rapidly in the 1980s on the basis of acquisition and virtually doubled their UK workforce in the second half of the decade. A third, a private cleaning company established at the turn of the century, employs around 16 000 cleaners across the UK, although like the others, its activities tend to be concentrated in London and the south-east.

Within contract catering, the measure of market concentration is even higher than that of contract cleaning, with just three firms holding 80% of the UK market. The leading operator, part of a broader service group whose core activities are catering and health care, has a workforce of just under 20 000 on the catering side. Its close competitor is a UK-based catering multinational with operations in the USA, Belgium, France, the Netherlands, Spain, Australia and South East Asia. World-wide, it has a workforce of just under 44 000, of which 75% are based in the UK. Interestingly, both companies were formed in the last five years through management buyouts from larger hotel and catering chains and both have pursued an active acquisition strategy since the mid-1980s. The third firm is the catering arm of a major, diversified international company with operations in more than 40 countries. Its UK catering operation employs 22 000 staff on 2000 sites. Overall, the three firms employ around 75 000 on 10 000 sites across the UK, with the majority working more than part-time hours. Again, London and the south-east is the main focus of their UK operations.

The measure of concentration in contract security lies between that of the other two contract sectors, with three firms holding just under 60% of the market in the UK. Of the three, the largest is a Netherlands-based multinational of Swedish parentage which draws one-third of its business from the UK. The firm employs over 35 000 world-wide, operating in 36 countries, with major interests in both west and east Europe, as well as Argentina and India. Its UK workforce numbers just under 7000, of which 4000 are in contract guarding. Close behind the market leader in terms of share, is another multinational security firm operating in 22 countries with a total workforce of 30 000 across all its divisions. In the UK, it employs 3300 guards, of which just under a third are in London and the south-east. The third security company also has its base in the region, with 25% of its turnover accounted for by London alone. Smaller than the other two security firms in terms of general market share, nevertheless it employs over 4000 guards. Together, the three firms employ around just under 12 000 security guards, most of whom work on a full-time, shift-work basis with an average working week of 60 hours. Moreover, all three firms increased their numbers throughout the 1980s, in part through the acquisition of smaller firms.

Overall, then, across the three sectors some 145 000 people in the UK rely upon this handful of firms for their economic livelihood, especially in London and the south-east (which is of some significance if you compare the figure with British Steel's 40 000 workers). In cleaning, it is predominantly women working on a part-time basis; in catering, it is mainly women working a range of hours, often above the part-time threshold, and in security it is overwhelmingly men employed on a full-time, shift-work basis. Cutting across this is an ethnic division of labour which has tended to produce distinct job concentrations, with non-Commonwealth groups, especially south European migrants, meeting much of the demand for labour in contract cleaning and catering, and Afro-Caribbean and white groups dominating security work (see Cross and Waldinger, 1992). Indeed, while the complex manner in which gender and ethnicity cut across one another in these industries belies any simple polarisation thesis, it does none the less point to the fact that a significant number of people — young and old, male and female, migrant and non-migrant — are currently experiencing a transformation in their working lives as their employment is reorganised by multinational contract service firms.

Contract cleaners, caterers and guards in the City of London, for example, work on the borderlines of formal employment. They are employed by large national and international service firms which, somewhat paradoxically, have large workforces yet few tangible assets, in the forms of buildings and machinery. Their major asset is goodwill; the goodwill of a client to renew a contract and release a stream of profits for the contractor. Such profits arise from contracts over a multitude of sites, even in the City. More importantly, the contractors merely "place" their workforce on the client's site, be it a merchant bank, insurance company, accountancy firm, law firm or whatever. A typical commercial site in cleaning, for instance, would have around four to five cleaners, in security around two to three guards, and in catering significantly more depending upon the size of the operation. In sum, the contract service firms, despite their apparent size, are "hollow" entities composed of *fragments*, with each site isolated from every other and with no interdependent division of labour to bind the units across space (as in many parts of manufacturing production).[11]

One consequence of working in a fragmented industry is that the organisation and control of work is devolved to the site supervisor or unit manager. In cleaning, for example, their authority and power are almost akin to that of a contract gangleader in the nineteenth century. Scattered across sites, cleaners are vulnerable to the arbitrary power of supervisors, as well as being open to the possibility of working informally and thus avoiding regulatory practices covering taxes, health and safety, and such like. The intrusion of personal authority, particularistic relationships, is also a marked feature of catering and security work and the spread of such conditions adds a high degree of insecurity and vulnerability to this type of employment.

It is important to stress, however, that we are referring here, in the main, to regular, formal employment. All of the large firms mentioned employ labour on a casual or a temporary basis, but not in sufficient numbers as to warrant generalisation about the emergence of a casualised contract work-force — in London at least. Within security, "floater" guards are employed to cover unanticipated shortages across sites and part-timers are used to cover weekend shifts, but on a regular, quasi-permanent basis. Temporary workers are frequently used for one-off events within catering and to cover gaps created by sickness and holiday leave, but the overwhelming number of workers are employed on a permanent basis. The same is true of contract cleaning, although in this case there is greater scope for the use of informal labour practices. Even here, however, much of the work is likely to be performed on a regular basis, implying a form of tacit permanency. We should be wary, therefore, about identifying work characterised as vulnerable or insecure, such as part-time employment or work involving lengthy shifts, with a movement towards casualisation.[12] On the contrary, we appear to be witnessing the growth of a new working poor whose regular employment is formally precarious. Formal in the sense that the work is organised by expanding multinational service firms based within and beyond the UK.

If, as some would argue, it is precisely this kind of work that has been accorded a marginal status, it is not simply because of the *kinds* of work undertaken. The notion of marginal employment here refers to an econ-omic position, not to any intrinsic characteristic of the work itself. It is not simply because of what they do that the workforce in these contract service industries *lives* a marginal status. It is precisely because of their *relationship* to a client's workforce; that is, a relation which gives the latter workforce the power to define itself as central and others as marginal or secondary to their activities. Not all contract work is represented as economically marginal, as for example, in the case of professional contract work, but the notion of marginality constructed around cleaning, catering and security is reified when it becomes *contract* cleaning, *contract* catering and *contract* security.

Moreover, this is *not* a "peripheral" workforce in so far as those working on the borders of formal employment are part of the "core" of a company's activities. Such workers are engaged in the *central* operation of the lead firms in cleaning, catering and security.[13] To suggest otherwise is to conflate those activities peripheral to a client firm, that is, those which have been contracted out, with those employed by the contractor to carry out those activities. The activities may be peripheral to the client, but the workforce performing these activities is certainly not peripheral to the contract company. The workforce is a key source of profits for such companies, especially in the labour-intensive operations of cleaning and security.

WIDENING THE MARGINS

While there are obvious benefits to be realised by the large contract service firms from the use of vulnerable forms of labour, the spread of these conditions may also be interpreted as part of a broad direction of change within the UK economy. While it would be reckless to claim that recent, successive conservative administrations in the UK look, for example, to the cleaning and security industries to deliver a competitive advantage strategy for the economy, it is accurate none the less to suggest that the contract services industries have been held up as a positive example of low pay operating as a competitive strategy; that is, industries which have loosened the "rigidities" of the labour market by taking advantage of the removal of government restrictions and, perhaps more importantly, adopting the practical norms laid down by government.[14]

Since 1979, conservative governments in the UK have adopted a range of policies to reduce the low-pay threshold and to dismantle various forms of employment protection (Brosnan and Wilkinson, 1988; Deakin and Wilkinson, 1992). The powers of the wages councils have been reduced, removing their ability to set a minimum wage for the under-21s or to regulate holiday pay, unsocial hours and overtime rates; unfair dismissal protection rights have been weakened; wage levels of young workers on government employment schemes pegged down; unemployment and social welfare benefits made more difficult to claim; trade union legislation passed to frustrate effective organisation at the workplace; and so on. Currently, the UK government is enacting legislation which will abolish what remains of the wages council system, leaving the UK as the only country in the EU without some kind of legally enforceable minimum rate of pay.

The message of this legislative thrust has not been lost on the contract service industries, although the most significant impact has come from the government's privatisation programme.[15] The contracting-out of public services, with the explicit intention of lowering pay and restricting conditions of employment, has given a considerable boost to the market share of the large contract firms. The Ministry of Defence and the National Health Service, for example, have proved to be attractive markets for cleaning and catering firms, especially in the south-east (Ascher, 1987, Mohan, 1988). In security, the privatisation of the prisons is at an early stage and, indeed, overall the shift from public to private service provision in this area is, as yet, not particularly extensive. For the contract service firms, these markets are growing from a small base, but their major market is still that of commerce and industry. The significance of this array of legislative activity, however, cannot be measured by its direct impact, but rather by its *pervasive influence*.

In one sense, the contract cleaning, catering and security industries are held up as a catalyst for change by the post-1979 governments. They are regarded as a positive role model which, if carried across other sectors of the UK economy, will have the effect of realising low pay and unregulated labour as a competitive strategy in the international economy (see Brosnan and Wilkinson, 1988; Machin and Manning, 1992). It is not that all industries would have to adopt the labour-intensive strategies of the contract services; rather it is assumed that the adoption of a low-wage strategy would enable other, more capital-intensive sectors to achieve a competitive advantage.

Leaving to one side the somewhat bizarre logic of the UK developing vulnerable, "cheap labour" sectors as a form of competitive advantage, there are reasons other than legislation and a high rate of unemployment which account for the marginal status of jobs in cleaning, catering and security — reasons which limit the transfer of such a status to other sectors. We will restrict our attention to two factors: the first is the representation of skill in the three service industries and the second is the structure of the work itself, in particular the conditions under which the work is performed.

On the question of skills, the cleaning and security industries are rarely, if ever, associated with skilled work. At best, they are seen to involve a range of practical tasks, most of which anyone can do by learning on the job. The notion of formal training or formal instruction to perform cleaning tasks, for example, would sit oddly with the unskilled label attached to such work. From our survey it was apparent that cleaners undervalued the skills required to clean the variety of surfaces found in the City of London's finance houses. The varied combination of skills, machinery and chemicals required to clean desk tops, terminals, chrome panels, and numerous types of floor covering — ranging from marble, wood, tile, non-slip, to carpet, were invariably translated as tasks involving little or no skill. The practical, *use value* of the skills, however, was recognised, whereas the *exchange value* of the work was denied. Indeed, this is an accurate reflection of the situation as employers in the industry do not reward such skill by promotion or financial gain. It is invariably to the employer's advantage where possible to downgrade the exchange value of such "practical" skills. Aside from chefs, who have achieved a degree of success in representing their work as skilled, much the same is true in catering, with the work of catering assistants, waiters and kitchen porters receiving little or no skill acknowledgement.

It is not just the unskilled status of cleaning work that is being constructed and reinforced, however, it is also the marginal status of the work. Skilled or semi-skilled work, because it is endowed with a social significance and value that flows from the skilled label, is less likely to be represented as marginal employment. Recently, within the contract services, especially catering, there has been a shift to more "flexible" forms of work, with demarcations between tasks progressively broken down and workers required to learn new tasks. Yet, instead of attracting the label of a multi-skilled worker, as in some of the advanced manufacturing plants for example, it has merely served to confirm the unskilled nature of the work. In this context, the *fragments of skill*, albeit of a low level, merely add up to an unskilled rather than a multi-skilled status.

Another characteristic of contract service work which has helped to construct its marginal status is the structure and timing of the work (see also Walsh, 1990). All contract service work, by definition, is separate from the client's work, but this social distance is exacerbated by the fact that the majority of tasks are undertaken out of sight of the client's workforce. The vast majority of cleaning, for example, takes place either before or after the "working day". Most cleaning is done in the twilight hours between 6 and 8 in the morning and between 5.30 and 7.30 in the evening. The relative isolation of the activity, coupled with its unseen nature, tends to erase all traces of the presence of a cleaning workforce — unless, of course, the work is not done or poorly done. Somewhat ironically, the visibility of contract cleaners is registered only by their lack of work.

In the case of security work it is even harder to discern the product. Most security work takes place at night on a shift-work basis, usually of a 12-hour duration, and involves blocks of empty time punctuated by regular "walks" around a building in virtual silence. The slow tempo of the work, the relative isolation and the limited overlap with the client's workforce all contribute to the separation of security "work" from most other work, apart from that undertaken by contract cleaners. The relative lack of visibility of security work is perhaps best exemplified by the fact that the tangible product of security is, in fact, that "nothing happens". In the day, the visibility of guards at entrances and exits is naturally high, although even here their presence is often remote from that of the client's workforce — as an intended characteristic of the job.

Contract catering staff are perhaps less remote than those involved in either cleaning or security work. Catering work takes place throughout the day, although the intensity of the work revolves around the lunch period of the client's workforce. When others are at rest, the catering workforce are under pressure to deliver a very visible product. Apart from those who deliver the service, however, the catering assistants, waiters and butlers, the rest of the workforce are less visible than the product. Indeed, in the City finance houses, even those who do deliver the service are not always "seen", in so far as waiters, for example, occupy an unacknowledged presence in the directors' dining rooms.

Working under a different employer from that of the majority of a workforce in a building represents, in itself, a form of social distance, but it is perhaps the fact that the work is also *fragmented by time* which reinforces the marginal status of contract cleaning, security and catering work. By this, we do not mean that something like part-time work should necessarily be equated with marginal employment, but rather that the timing of work itself is part of the construction of a marginal work status. In sum, the relative powerlessness of this expanding group of service workers can, arguably, be attributed largely to its fragmentation — by workplace, by skill and by time.

CONCLUSION

If indeed the "two sides to growth" across London and the south-east in the 1980s are interconnected, with the increase in poorly paid, insecure contract service work tied to the growth of the financial and commercial sectors, then the main argument of this chapter is that the "downside" is every bit as formalised as the "upside". In contrast to those who have argued that the informalisation of work is growing apace in first world cities such as London, the contention here is that much of the shift in the fragmentation of employment and work at the lower end of the labour market is formally organised by expanding national and international service organisations.

As to why this should be so in London, an answer may be sought in the activities of recent conservative governments intent on legalising low-paid, vulnerable employment in the UK. Quite simply, it is not in the interests of the dominant companies to pursue strategies of informalisation when the UK government has effectively removed many of the controls and regulations that informal labour market strategies would seek to undermine. One outcome has been a growth in precarious, marginal forms of work — of limited security and of negligible pay — all of which are quite legal.[16] And if Mingione's contention holds that the two ends of the labour market are fragmented socially, then some groups, such as older unskilled, manual workers, lone mothers and non-Commonwealth migrants are trapped legally, with little prospect of alternative employment, whereas others, such as students, actors and middle-class youth will move through the margins.

ACKNOWLEDGEMENTS

We wish to acknowledge the funding received from the Economic and Social Research Council to conduct this research (Grant no. R 000233008).

NOTES

1. From a related survey by McDowell and Court in the South East Programme, which found that 95% of the financial institutions in the City who responded had contracted out cleaning services, 80% had contracted out security, and 72% had contracted out catering services. In 482 cases where contracting out of these services was possible, 403 were contracted out, representing an overall rate of 84% (McDowell and Court, 1991).

2. Allen (1992b) outlines the arguments of the South East Programme concerning the *particular* form of growth during the 1980s and how this particularity constructs our conceptualisation of the region. The South East Programme involves John Allen, Julie Charlesworth, Allan Cochrane, Gill Court, Chris Hamnett, Nick Henry, Doreen Massey, Linda McDowell, Beverley Mullings, Phil Sarre and Jenny Seavers.

3. The proportion of total employment accounted for by the south-east has remained at about 34% throughout the 1980s.

4. It should be noted, however, that this growth rate was below the UK average and it was the rest of the south-east which experienced the greatest growth rate of the period. Thus, continued concentration of finance and commerce employment in the south-east occurred but this growth was more widely dispersed within the region than at the beginning of the decade.

5. It should be noted that Rajan (1990) defines the City as encompassing not only the borough of the City of London, but also the Inner London boroughs of Camden, Islington, Hackney, Tower Hamlets, Southwark, Lewisham, Lambeth, Wandsworth, Hammersmith and Fulham, Kensington and Chelsea, and Westminster.

6. See Court and McDowell (1993) for more detail on the gendered nature of jobs in the financial services sector in the south-east.

7. Employment figures for contract security cannot be identified from the Census of Employment. Contract security comes under the heading "Business Services not elsewhere specified" (AH 8395).

8. Sassen (1991, Chapter 9) tends to equate casual and part-time work in London with the downgrading of work, although the evidence for such an assertion is scant.

9. The following company profiles were compiled from a variety of sources, in particular company interviews at the corporate level, interviews with the trade association for each industry, and secondary sources, both private and government based.

10. For the purposes of definition, a part-time worker in the UK is legally defined as someone who works less than 16 hours a week.

11. An exception here would be the transfer of workers and unit managers/ supervisors from site to site, although this type of interconnection does not amount to an interdependent division of labour.

12. See also recent evidence presented in the *Employment Gazette* by McGregor and Sproull (May 1992) and by Hunter and MacInnes (June 1992).

13. See Baggaley (1990) for a similar argument in relation to the hotel and catering industry.

14. See *Financial Times*, 6 November 1992, and *The Guardian*, 10 February 1993. Recently, the Employment Minister, Michael Forsyth referred to the cleaning and security industries as positive examples of sectors unaffected by interference from wages councils.

15. Privatisation refers to a number of governmental strategies, including the denationalisation of the public utilities and the deregulation of economic

activities. Here, we focus specifically upon the contracting-out of public services. For the impact of contracting-out on public workforces see, for example, Cousins (1988) and Pulkingham (1992).

16. For a similar argument in relation to New York, see Waldinger and Lapp (1993). Hakim (1992) also charts the growth of legal forms of marginal work in the UK.

REFERENCES

Allen, J. (1988) The geographies of service, in Massey, D. and Allen, J. (eds), *Uneven development: cities and regions in transition*, Hodder and Stoughton, London, pp. 124–141.
Allen, J. (1992a) Services and the UK space economy: regionalization and economic dislocation', *Transactions, Institute of British Geographers*, New Series, 17, 292–305.
Allen, J. (1992b) The nature of a growth region: the peculiarity of the south east, in *The South East Programme Occasional Paper Series No. 1*, Faculty of Social Sciences, The Open University, Milton Keynes.
Ascher, K. (1987) *The politics of privatization: contracting out public services*, Macmillan, London and Basingstoke.
Baggaley, P. (1990) Gender and labour flexibility in hotel and catering, in *The Service Industries Journal*, 10, 737–747.
BHA (British Hospitality Association) (1993) *Contract catering survey 1993*, London.
BHRCA (British Hotels, Restaurants and Caterers Association) (1991) *Wages and salaries in the hotel and catering industry 1991 survey*, London.
BSIA (British Security Industry Association) (1992) *Wages survey comparisons*, January, Worcester.
Brosnan, P. and Wilkinson, F. (1988) A national statutory minimum wage and economic efficiency, *Contributions to Political Economy*, 7, 1–48.
Castells, M. (1989) *The informational city*, Basil Blackwell, Oxford.
Champion, A. and Townsend, A. (1990) *Contemporary Britain: a geographical perspective*, Edward Arnold, London.
CCMA (Contract Cleaning and Maintenance Association) (1987) *Second CCMA membership survey 1987*, London.
Court, G. and McDowell, L. (1993) Serious trouble? Financial services and structural change, in *The South East Programme Occasional Paper Series No. 4*, Faculty of Social Sciences, The Open University, Milton Keynes.
Cousins, C. (1988) The restructuring of welfare work: the introduction of general management and the contracting out of ancillary services in the NHS, *Work, Employment and Society*, 2, 210–228.
Cross, M. and Waldinger, R. (1992) Migrants, minorities and the ethnic division of labour, in Fainstein, S. et al. (eds), *Divided cities*, Blackwell, Oxford, pp. 151–174.
Deakin, S. and Wilkinson, F. (1992) European integration: the implications for UK policies on labour supply and demand, in MacLaughlin, E. (ed.), *Understanding unemployment: new perspectives on active labour market policies*, Routledge, London, pp. 196–214.
Department of Employment (1992) *New earnings survey*, HMSO, London.
Glyn, A. (1992) The costs of stability: the advanced capitalist countries in the 1980s, *New Left Review*, 195, 71–95.
Hakim, C. (1992) Unemployment, marginal work and the black economy, in MacLaughlin, E. (ed.), *Understanding unemployment: new perspectives on active labour market policies*, Routledge, London, pp. 144–159.

HCTB (Hotel and Catering Training Board) (1989) *New employment forecasts: hotel and catering industry 1988–1993*, London.

HCTC (Hotel and Catering Training Company) (1992) *Meeting competence needs in the hotel and catering industry — now and in the future*, London.

Hunter, L. and MacInnes, J. (1992) Employers and labour flexibility: the evidence from case studies, *Employment Gazette*, June, 307–315.

Key Note Report (1991a) *Contract cleaning*, Key Note Publications Limited, London.

Key Note Report (1991b) *Security*, Key Note Publications Limited, London.

Labour Research (1986) Divided city , November, pp. 11–14.

McAlpine, Thorpe and Warrier (1991) *Report on the European market for security products and services 1991–95*, London.

McDowell, L. and Court, G. (1991) OU survey of city institutions (unpublished).

McGregor, A. and Sproull, A. (1992) Employers and the flexible workforce, *Employment Gazette*, May, 225–234.

Machin, S. and Manning, A. (1992), *Minimum wages, wage dispersion and employment: evidence from the UK wage councils*, Discussion Paper 80, Centre for Economic Performance, London School of Economics and Political Science.

Michie, J. and Wilkinson, F. (1992) Inflation policy and the restructuring of labour markets, in Michie, J. (ed.), *The economic legacy 1979–1992*, Academic Press, London and San Diego, pp. 195–217.

Mingione, E. (1991) *Fragmented societies: a sociology of economic life beyond the market paradigm*, Basil Blackwell, Oxford.

Mohan, J. (1988) Spatial aspects of health-care employment in Britain 1: aggregate trends, *Environment and Planning A*, **20**, 7–23.

Pulkingham, J. (1992) Employment restructuring in the health service: efficiency initiatives, working patterns and workforce composition, *Work, Employment and Society*, **6**, 3, 397–421.

Rajan, A. (1990) *Capital people: skills strategies for survival in the nineties*, The Industrial Society, London.

Sassen, S. (1991) *The global city: New York, London, Tokyo*, Princeton University Press, Princeton, New Jersey.

Security Spokesman (1992) BSIA 25th Anniversary Special, September, BSIA, Worcester.

Waldinger, R. and Lapp, M. (1993) Back to the sweatshop or ahead to the informal sector? *International Journal of Urban and Regional Research*, **17**, 1, 6–29.

Walsh, T.J. (1990) Flexible labour utilization in the private service sector, *Work, Employment and Society*, **4**, 4, 517–530.

11 Housing the "Guestworkers"

JAN VAN WEESEP
Utrecht University, the Netherlands

INTRODUCTION

In spite of their image as homogeneous societies, most west European countries today maintain an uneasy balance of different ethnic communities. Xenophobia runs rampant under the pressure of mass immigration from less affluent societies; people fear that millions more might follow as eastern Europe makes its transition. The pressure reached a breaking point in the spring of 1993, as the entire world witnessed the violent attacks on Turkish residents and asylum-seekers in Germany. Although the tensions have not led to overt violence of that magnitude elsewhere, other European countries have not successfully integrated their minority populations either. Some categories of foreign-born residents have been able to blend in. But by and large, each country in western Europe now consists of two nations: the indigenous inhabitants and the migrants. Socially and economically, many migrant groups form a marginal population.

The two-track societies of Europe are not created by a deliberate public policy. On the contrary, many migrants remain in a marginal position despite a variety of programmes to promote their cultural and economic integration. Such policies have been unable to compensate for deprivation emanating from the migrants' socio-economic positions, their cultural distinctiveness and their personal coping strategies in a rapidly evolving housing environment.

Among the foreign population, guestworkers comprise a special category. Initially, they were recruited for job vacancies that were hard to fill. They were supposed to rotate back to their homelands. But many have stayed on to become permanent residents. Though no longer guests, even after many years, they are not fully recognised as immigrants. This ambiguous situation often muddles their legal status and weakens their housing market position. Their social status is determined above all by the niche they occupy in the labour market. As manual workers, they bear the brunt of the ongoing economic restructuring, which has curtailed any attempts to improve their lot. The jobs they came to fill in the past have largely disappeared in the meantime, while their qualifications do not generally fit

Europe at the Margins: New Mosaics of Inequality. Edited by Costis Hadjimichalis and David Sadler
© 1995 European Science Foundation. Published in 1995 by John Wiley & Sons Ltd

the new employment opportunities. Culturally, they maintain their distinctiveness. Their separation from the mainstream of their host societies may provide them with a buffer against the growing frictions. But as the populace becomes increasingly hostile towards disadvantaged foreigners, the immigrants are caught up in the surge of popular resentment, no matter how long they have lived in the host country. Yet, they cannot return "home" after so many years abroad. Back in their place of origin, they often no longer fit in socially and economically, having become accustomed to the social relations of their host societies. Therefore, most have no realistic alternative but to stay in marginal jobs abroad or, if unemployed, to remain there as wards of an increasingly reluctant welfare state.

This chapter focuses on one specific aspect of the marginality of the guestworkers in a few west European countries: the quality of their housing. By and large, housing conditions are related to income, social position and previous housing. We would therefore expect this deprived group to live under poor housing conditions, as compared to indigenous low-income households. In this chapter, these poor conditions are perceived to emanate from a weak housing market position, which in turn results from the competition in the housing market. Specifically, we evaluate the quality of their housing in relation to that of the indigenous (low-income) population. We look for signs that the housing conditions of the guestworkers and the indigenous poor are becoming more similar as the migrants' length of residence increases.

Their quality of housing is examined in the context of three countries: the Netherlands, Germany and Switzerland. These are all advanced economies with a wide array of welfare state policies. Each harbours a substantial number of disadvantaged foreign workers. Yet, the three countries differ substantially with respect to policy on immigration and housing. In Germany and the Netherlands, the erstwhile guestworkers became permanent residents. In theory, their altered legal status and the increasing length of stay should have helped them catch up with the indigenous population groups with respect to the quality of their housing. In contrast, until recently, most guestworkers in Switzerland kept rotating back to their country of origin. Accordingly, they would have been unable to improve their housing situation by moving up the housing ladder.

Furthermore, the three countries differ markedly with respect to their housing systems. The Netherlands' housing system is epitomised by its vast social rental sector. This emphasis is an expression of the extensive government intervention in the housing market, a tradition that has been diminishing lately. At the other end of the spectrum, Swiss housing is essentially a market-driven system. German housing lies somewhere between these two extremes. Comparison of the three countries allows us to evaluate the extent to which diverse housing policies promote equity among different population categories.

"GUESTWORKERS" IN WESTERN EUROPE

During the 1960s, the rapidly expanding economies of western Europe were confronted with serious labour shortages. In several countries, guestworkers were recruited to fill the least attractive vacancies. They were employed for a specified period and were required to rotate back to their country of origin when their contract ended. Not surprisingly, most guestworkers were young males with little education or marketable skills, although there have been cases where a trained and experienced workforce was recruited. The contract labourers were not permitted to bring their families. This set them apart from other immigrants in their host countries, predominantly those from the former colonies (Parkinson et al., 1992, p. 98).

In most countries, however, the repatriation clauses were not strictly enforced. Employers were reluctant to invest in training newcomers and thus sought ways to keep the workers beyond their contract period. Eventually, the guestworkers became permanent residents. But while their new legal status entitled them to the provisions of the welfare state, it rarely improved their social position.

The initial sources of guestworkers were the countries on the northern flank of the Mediterranean: Spain, (southern) Italy, Greece and what was then Yugoslavia. Gradually, economic opportunities improved within these countries themselves. Many migrants then returned home, and the recruiters from northern and western Europe set their sights on North Africa and Turkey. It is significant that employees of a particular firm were mostly recruited from a single region. The contingent often included members of individual families or villages. Therefore, people arrived with established social networks and did not feel compelled to integrate into the host community, not even when they stayed beyond their short-term contract period. Chain migration helped individual communities to channel virtually all their migrants to a single town or region, reinforcing their identity as separate from mainstream society.

It is not easy to obtain the exact numbers of guestworkers in each of the west European countries. But the sparse data on the foreign residents from typical recruiting areas give at least some indication of the volume of the migration flows (Table 11.1). These aggregate numbers do not, however, reveal the major fluctuations from year to year and by country of origin. For instance, the 1955 recruitment agreement between Germany and Italy initially generated only a trickle of migrants to the north. But the foreign worker population in Germany increased rapidly after 1961; the Berlin Wall effectively cut off the constant supply of labour from what was then the GDR. In 1960, the number of *Gastarbeiter* (i.e. foreign workers without German ancestry) amounted to a mere 279 000. With active recruiting, this number rose sharply. By 1961, recruiting agreements had also been

Table 11.1. Foreign population in Germany, the Netherlands and Switzerland by nationality, 1978 and 1989 (thousands of persons)

| | Receiving country | | | | | |
| | Germany | | Netherlands | | Switzerland | |
Sending country	1978	1989	1978	1989	1978	1989
Greece	306	294	4	5	9	8
Italy	572	520	21	17	443	379
Portugal	110	75	9	8	8	69
Spain	189	127	25	17	96	115
Turkey	1165	1613	107	192	30	59
Yugoslavia	610	611	14	13	38	117
Morocco	29	62	64	148		
Tunisia	19	24	2	2		
Other	981	1513	185	241	276	294
Total	3981	4839	431	643	900	1041

Notes: For Germany and the Netherlands, the figures are based on "foreigners files" kept at local registry offices. For Switzerland the figures are for annual and "established" permit-holders, not seasonal or frontier migrants.
Source: Adapted from King (1993, Table 2.2).

negotiated with Spain and Greece (1960) and Turkey (1961); these were soon followed by agreements with Morocco (1963), Tunisia (1965) and Yugoslavia (1968). The number of guestworkers subsequently rose to 1.8 million in 1970, topping 2 million in 1980. Many workers from Italy, Spain, Greece and Yugoslavia eventually returned to their country of origin. In contrast, Germany's Turkish population increased rapidly: 511 000 in 1987, just below the peak of 606 000 reached in 1974 (Blotevogel et al., 1993, pp. 86–87). Ever since the arrival of Turkish guestworkers, their position has been undermined by the strong competition — in both the labour and housing markets — from ethnic Germans repatriated from eastern Europe, who received preferential treatment.

Similarly, the homelands of the guestworkers in the Netherlands shifted as time passed. Recruitment began in Italy and Spain in the mid-1960s. Only later did firms concentrate on Morocco and Turkey, the countries of origin of the currently dominant Mediterranean immigrants in the Netherlands. Eventually, the Italian and Spanish populations declined through return migration. The number of Italians slipped gradually from about 20 000 during the mid-1970s to 17 000 in 1988. The population of Spanish origin decreased even more, dropping from 30 000 to 18 000 (Blauw, 1991, p. 48). In 1989, Turkey (192 000 migrants) and Morocco (148 000 migrants) were the most prevalent countries of origin. By then, Turkish and Moroccan "guestworkers" had been allowed to settle permanently. This change in status is reflected in the characteristics of the most recent immigrants from these countries. At first, the workers were joined by their dependants in the context of family reunification; lately, marriage partners have been brought over from the countries of origin for the young adults of the second generation (Dieleman, 1993, pp. 121–122).

Foreigners accounted for no less than 15% of the Swiss population in 1988. But the number of foreign-born residents is substantially higher, as many immigrants eventually become naturalised. This option, available to long-term residents, accounts for the sharp decrease in the number of Germans and Austrians during the 1970s. In addition, numerous Hungarian and Czechoslovak refugees, who arrived after the respective uprisings in their countries in 1956 and 1968, eventually adopted the Swiss nationality (Arend, 1991, p. 156). Meanwhile, the guestworker population grew rapidly during the 1970s, whereby the number of Yugoslavs and Turks more than doubled. The guestworkers also included over 400 000 Italians (44% of the foreign population) and 100 000 Spanish (p. 156). Rather than being allowed to stay — and thereby becoming entitled to naturalisation — they had to rotate back to their country of origin. Only recently has the Swiss government sought to limit the number of new entrants.

FROM "GUESTWORKERS" TO IMMIGRANTS

The mass migration of guestworkers to northern and western Europe lasted until 1974. It came to an abrupt end when the first oil crisis threw western Europe into recession, due to spiralling energy prices. Suddenly, full employment and the concomitant labour shortages in unattractive sectors ceased to exist. As unemployment grew, immigration plummeted (King, 1993, pp. 28–29). A similar drop in immigration occurred again in the early 1980s, when a new wave of recession hit western Europe.

King (1993, pp. 28–29) reports that by the mid-1970s, there were approximately 2 million foreign workers in West Germany, about 1.5 million in France, about 750 000 in the UK and 500 000 in Switzerland. These figures almost matched the number of registered unemployed in these countries. This correspondence, which was frequently flaunted by elements intent on fuelling antagonism towards the guestworkers, had serious social and political repercussions. Consequently, immigration regulations were tightened (Blotevogel et al., 1993, p. 88); several countries tried to entice the resident foreign workers to return to their countries of origin. This might have been achieved by enforcing the repatriation clauses, but political expediency called for a gentler approach. Thus, premiums were offered to help guestworkers resettle in their home countries. In some cases, local development programmes were set up to provide them with jobs upon their return.

Nevertheless, the incentives did not have the anticipated effects, although substantial numbers of guestworkers did indeed leave the host countries. In Germany, the total outmigration was larger than the number of immigrants between 1974 and 1977; this was again the case in the period 1982–84. Likewise, in Switzerland, the balance shifted at roughly the same time. But in the Netherlands, immigration remained significantly higher than the number of outmigrants throughout the period (King, 1993, p. 30).

By and large, the policy to repatriate guestworkers failed because the economy in the countries of origin remained weak. In fact, the average duration of the foreigners' stay increased while the official policy was to entice them to leave. In 1988, some 60% of the 1.5 million Turks in Germany had lived there for over 10 years; this applied to only 46% of its total foreign population. A similar tendency was observed in the Netherlands, where Turkish and Moroccan populations stayed for a longer time (Dieleman, 1993, p. 121).

Although labour recruitment stopped, most countries did allow family reunification, once it was acknowledged that many of the workers had come to stay. The countries of northern and western Europe became *de facto* immigration countries. Consequently, the number of foreign residents kept rising, although the foreign working population remained more or less constant (Table 11.2). The change in immigration policy also led to a shift in the composition of the foreign population. Instead of young, single men, the new immigrants were predominantly dependants.

This shift had some far-reaching social implications. The need to integrate into the host community became a major issue. The debate focused on the desired level of integration and the spheres in which it was considered imperative. But the first generation of migrants have hardly responded to this pressure. To make matters worse, they were seen to compete more directly with the indigenous population for jobs, social services and housing rather than remain separate. This aggravated the sentiments of xenophobia, particularly during periods of economic recession.

Having originally been recruited to work in particular firms, the foreign worker population had been scattered throughout the country, even residing in small towns. But eventually, many migrants drifted towards the large cities, where a more diversified economy provided better job opportunities. The foreign workers and their families are now overrepresented in most of the big cities of northern and western Europe (White, 1993, pp. 66–67). This imbalance was enhanced by family reunification, the high birth rate among the guestworker population, and by the suburbanisation of the indigenous population.

As the guestworker communities grew, it became easier for them to retain their own cultures, but they also encountered new problems. The debate on the consequences for education is a case in point. School segregation emerged as a political issue, as many schools in inner cities became dominated by the children of guestworkers and other

Table 11.2. Annual migration trends 1973–89 for three European countries (thousands of persons)

	1973	1975	1980	1985	1989
Netherlands					
Total inflow	93.7	55.2	79.8	46.2	65.4
Total outflow	—	22.1	23.6	24.2	21.5
Stock total	315	351	521	553	642
Stock workers	160	176	188	166	192
Germany					
Total inflow	869.1	366.1	631.4	398.2	770.8
Total outflow	526.8	600.1	385.8	366.7	481.3
Stock total	3966	4090	4453	4379	4846
Stock workers	2595	2227	2116	1823	1941
Switzerland					
Total inflow	—	46.3	70.5	59.4	80.9
Total outflow	73.0	121.1	63.7	54.3	57.5
Stock total	1030	1013	893	940	1040
Stock workers	596	553	501	549	632

Notes: Data collected on different criteria and with different methods in the three countries. Netherlands: Flows and stocks of total migrants based on aliens' files kept at municipal registry offices; includes asylum-seekers. Outflows are underestimates owing to failure to deregister. Stocks of total foreign population refer to 31 December each year. Stocks of workers are Central Bureau of Statistics estimates of employed foreigners at 31 December each year. Stock includes frontier workers but excludes self-employed and unemployed. Germany: Flows and stocks of total migrants based on central register of foreigners; includes asylum-seekers. Stocks are for 30 September each year. Stock of workers includes unemployed and frontier workers but excludes self-employed. Data refer to former FRG only. Switzerland: All figures are for annual and permanent ("established") permit-holders; seasonal and frontier migrants are excluded, as are asylum-seekers. Stocks of workers are for 31 December each year.
Source: Adapted from King (1993, Table 2.1).

disadvantaged foreign residents. Poor housing conditions form another focus of debate. Not only do housing situations express the spatial segregation tendencies in the host societies, but they also reveal that inequities persist between immigrants and the indigenous population. In the rest of this chapter, we will expand upon the issues raised in that debate. We focus on segregation and inequity in regard to housing in the Netherlands, Germany and Switzerland.

NATIONAL HOUSING POLICIES AND THE POOR

The Netherlands

Over the past 40 years, the Dutch government has built up an elaborate system of housing market regulations. Initially, this endeavour was a

Table 11.3. Completed dwellings by financing category in the Netherlands, 1941–90

	Total	Social	Subsidised	Non-subsidised
1941–50	186 445	107 247	79 198	
1951–60	715 959	408 140	273 192	34 627
1961–70	1 068 839	465 231	332 161	271 447
1971–80	1 236 790	417 413	540 414	278 963
1981–90	1 101 000	447 900	422 500	230 600

Note: Prior to 1950, the categories of subsidised and non-subsidised were not pertinent. Data for 1990 preliminary.
Source: van Weesep and van Kempen (1993a).

response to the severe housing shortage after 1945. But the national government soon took control of what has become a highly centralised housing system, a far cry from the pre-war market-driven system (van Weesep, 1984). Housing policy became a key element in the scaffolding for the emerging welfare state.

The social housing sector expanded from approximately 140 000 dwellings (10% of the stock) in 1945, to more than 540 000 (25%) by 1960. Since then, it has grown by leaps and bounds (Table 11.3), now accounting for over 40% of the stock. This housing is owned and managed by powerful non-profit-making housing associations. They are regulated by the Ministry of Housing and work closely with local government housing agencies, while they remain politically independent. The government also introduced an extensive system of price controls, statutory tenure security and housing allocation rules to guarantee the equitable distribution of housing (van Weesep and van Kempen, 1993a).

Since the 1950s, government funding has played an important role in the Dutch housing system. Initially, it consisted predominantly of construction and operating subsidies. From the late 1960s onward, these producer subsidies were gradually replaced by rent relief for low-income tenants. Housing allowances made new, more expensive dwellings widely accessible. In addition, generous tax deductions became available to home-owners. However, due to progressive taxation, high-income households benefit much more from this measure than low-income home-owners.

By 1975, it seemed that the housing shortage had finally been overcome. Soon, however, talk of a "new housing shortage" resounded. Several social developments lay at its root: young singles demanded housing rights; the number of foreign immigrants continued to increase beyond the projections; and the elderly were encouraged to remain independent much longer than before. Many of these households have to operate in the social rental market because their incomes are low (van Kempen, 1992a).

Nevertheless, the government set out to deregulate the housing market. The ensuing housing policy (Nota, 1989) had its greatest impact on two fronts: cutbacks in social housing completions, and wide-ranging deregulation. At the same time, the construction of more expensive owner-occupier dwellings was emphasised. This was done to encourage high-income households to trade up and vacate low-cost rental dwellings. In theory, as high-income groups move on, low-income households will be able to secure a place of their own.

The process of deregulation brought about a deeper involvement of local and regional authorities in housing policy. They will work along with the non-profit-making housing associations, which in turn gained more autonomy in their management decisions. To ensure that this is not detrimental to the groups with the weakest housing market position, some protective measures have been kept in place. Yet it should be recognised that additional changes are afoot. As the associations run larger financial risks, they will have to adapt their management practices to conform more closely to market forces. This may further erode the already weak housing market position of the disadvantaged.

The effects of the new housing policy are already visible in the current housing completions in the big cities. Their programmes were most blatantly out of step with the newly prescribed tenure structure. In recent years, more market-rate housing has been built than in the 1970s and early 1980s (Dieleman et al., 1993). Sometimes these new dwellings were built in low-rent neighbourhoods, thereby increasing social differentiation. Elsewhere, new and expensive dwellings are filling up vacant sites or areas previously devoted to other functions. Apparently, many occupants of the new housing were lured out of the low-rent social sector. Their departure expanded the housing opportunities for the urban poor in areas that had previously been socially and economically mixed (cf. van Weesep and van Kempen, 1993b). In this way, filtering may contribute to the spatial segregation of diverse income groups. However, the net effect of the policy changes upon segregation is by no means clear, as the measures are still working their way through the housing system.

The segregation trend will be boosted by the adjustments in the rent-subsidy programme. The changes imply that the new "rich" areas are no longer affordable to low-income households. The allocation of older, inexpensive social housing to low-income groups concentrates the poor in older neighbourhoods (van Kempen, 1992a, b). In many places, the indigenous poor feel that immigrants are being given priority for housing there. In these neighbourhoods, the sense of inequity led to rising social tensions.

There is another development that boosts segregation. Since the 1960s, the urban housing markets have increasingly become regional in scope. Suburban development and the completion of planned growth centres tempted many indigenous middle-class families to move to new single-family housing. Consequently, the cities became concentration areas of low-income groups. This process was reinforced by the continuing emphasis on social rental housing provision in the cities, which was meant to redress the urgent needs of the local population.

The Federal Republic of Germany

The post-1945 housing shortage in Germany was catastrophic. The number of dwellings per 1000 inhabitants had dropped to 214 by 1950, down from 263 in 1940 (Jaedicke and Wollmann, 1990, p. 128). Drastic measures were required. All tiers of government — federal, state (*Länder*), and local — became deeply involved in housing policy. Every possible resource was mobilised for the reconstruction of the housing system, and the effects were soon apparent. By the mid-1950s, annual housing production had risen to over 550 000 units, approximately 10 per 1000 inhabitants. The output peaked at more than 700 000 in 1973 but declined rapidly afterwards (pp. 128–129). The construction effort was so successful that within two decades after 1945, people referred to it as a "housing miracle".

The intervention did not follow the state-controlled social-housing trajectory taken by the Dutch. Instead, the German authorities aimed to develop a mixed system fitted to the dominant economic philosophy, known as the socially responsible market economy (Ulbrich and Wullkopf, 1993, p. 99). In addition, the question of accountability for housing policy has long been a bone of contention between the federal and state officials. The federal government has the power to devise housing policy, including the subsidy formula, and provides the lion's share of the funding. But the states decide on actual spending, because they have to match the federal grants. Similarly, local governments determine the kind of projects for which public money is to be used. They can even add subsidies of their own. Moreover, municipalities may resort to land-use planning, a powerful instrument, to promote social housing construction (Jaedicke and Wollmann, 1990, p. 133). Thus, there are strong local variations in the housing system.

The system encourages market participation in the owner-occupier as well as the private rental sector. This shows up clearly in the way the composition of the housing stock in (former) West Germany has evolved. The private rental sector has remained much stronger than in other countries of northern and western Europe, even though the owner-occupier sector has expanded from 25% in 1950 to 42% in 1987 (Ghékiere, 1991, p. 284). The social rental sector has in fact declined, in both absolute and relative terms (Table 11.4). Social housing is provided on contract by non-profit-making organisations and private landlords. In return for subsidies, they must operate their properties as social housing for a specified period. The sector has shrunk due to the expiration of more contracts than are

Table 11.4. Evolving composition of the housing stock in (former) West Germany, 1978–87 (millions of dwellings and percentages)

	1978		1982		1987	
	Number (millions)	%	Number (millions)	%	Number (millions)	%
Owner-occupier	8.5	37.5	9.3	40.1	11.0	42.0
Private rental	10.1	44.8	10.4	45.0	11.9	45.4
Social rental	4.0	17.7	3.5	14.9	3.3	12.6
Total	22.6	100.0	23.2	100.0	26.2	100.0

Source: Adapted from Ghékiere (1991, p. 284).

being replaced by new social housing. Consequently, low-income households are increasingly dependent on private rental housing. To soften the blow, they can take advantage of housing allowances, which have been available since the 1960s.

Much earlier than in the Netherlands, the German authorities took the road to deregulation. National rent control was abolished in the 1960s and replaced by a system of setting rents for new housing at a level comparable to current rents in the district. In turn, local rent control was largely abolished during the 1980s. The deregulation of social housing has also contributed to the preservation of a viable private rental sector, catering to all income groups (Ghékiere, 1991, p. 284).

"Non-profit-making" organisations have also been active. Between 1950 and 1985, they constructed 3.7 million dwellings, of which 2.8 million were rentals (Jaedicke and Wollmann, 1990, p. 132). While these organisations could make a profit — and had to, in order to continue their activities — they were limited to the construction of modest, affordable housing for low-income groups. By the late 1960s, government loans were increasingly replaced by capital market loans. Under these circumstances, the public subsidy was meant to help the private investor pay the interest. The subsidy was designed on a digressive formula. Accordingly, this type of housing was subject to built-in rent rises. As political support for social housing diminished, production declined from over 300 000 annually in the 1960s to less than 50 000 by the late 1980s (Ulbrich and Wullkopf, 1993, p. 106).

Upon the first manifestation of the post-1945 "housing miracle", the time bomb of privatisation was embedded in the German housing system. It went off prematurely when the amount of time for keeping the dwellings in the social rental sector was reduced. The effect was to cut the average remaining contract period from 30 to 15 years (Ulbrich and Wullkopf, 1993, p. 106). This decision in the early 1970s was intended to boost lagging private investment. The result is the present tendency for low-cost rental housing to be converted into luxury accommodation, just when the greatly expanded demand for low-cost rentals by immigrants has led to a new shortage of affordable units. The stock of social housing is decreasing sharply and will have shrunk to about half its former size by the year 2000. Since the late 1970s, it has been getting harder for low-income groups to obtain affordable dwellings. For some time, affordability was the main issue, as the rents at the lower end of the market rose steeply (p. 116). But with the rapid increase in the number of deprived immigrants and refugees, affordability became secondary to access. An actual shortage emerged in the late 1980s, increasing the competition for the short supply of inexpensive housing.

Thus, the recent immigration waves have added new fuel to the burning issue of housing shortage. The real homeless are few, but the number of people living in makeshift accommodation rose in the 1980s and soared after 1989 (Ulbrich and Wullkopf, 1993, p. 119). As the flow of immigrants accelerates, it will take years to accommodate them all at current standards. In the meantime, the effects of the shortage send ripples through the entire housing system. Even government-funded production incentives are not expected to generate an additional supply of rental housing. Investors will most likely stick to their pessimistic expectations, as voiced in the past. Their anxiety is heightened by a high real interest rate and an anticipated decline in population. Consequently, a steady rise in rents over a prolonged period would be needed to stimulate investments (Tomann, 1990, p. 929).

Switzerland

The Swiss maintain a relatively small federal government apparatus with few responsibilities. Basically, it provides a legal framework to be fleshed out by the states (*cantons*) (Lischner, 1988, pp. 3–5). Since the 1960s, a Housing Commission at the federal level has monitored the housing market and advised the government on appropriate action. But much of the policy-making bypasses the Commission; the actors find it more convenient and efficient to deal directly with each other.

During the 1970s, the federal government tried to resolve a number of bottlenecks by financing affordable housing, stimulating home-ownership, and providing statutory tenant protection (Gurtner, 1992, pp. 2–3). Most of the *cantons* and the big cities have since introduced their own ordinances to promote housing, supplementing federal programmes and regulations commensurate with their specific local housing conditions. But by and large, the producers tend to come out ahead in this housing system — one that comes as close to a free-market system as can be found anywhere in Europe. This system can partly be sustained by the population's relatively

Table 11.5. Occupied dwellings by tenure in Switzerland, 1960–90 (thousands of dwellings and percentages)

	1960	1970	1980	1990
Total stock	1581	2050	2413	2801
Owner-occupier	33.7	28.1	29.9	27.0
Rental dwellings	56.9	64.1	63.2	62.7
Co-operatives	3.8	3.8	3.9	3.7
Other	5.6	4.0	3.0	6.6
incl. public housing	3.5	3.6	3.2	3.0

Note: Data from the 1990 Census refer to occupied houses in use as principal dwelling.
Sources: Adapted from Lischner (1988, p. 101); Census of 1990.

high incomes; the consumers have been both willing and able to pay market rents. The system reflects the interests and the financial potential of institutional investors, who are drawn to housing as a safe investment with an attractive yield.

In general, the housing conditions in Switzerland are very good. There are more dwellings than households. The average amount of space consumed is high and growing. And most houses are not only well maintained but also have a full range of modern amenities. During the past two decades, the number of dwellings has increased faster than the population. Consequently, the occupancy rate has decreased progressively; from 3.3 persons per dwelling in 1960, it dropped to 2.4 in 1990 (*Wohnen*, 1993). The national average is 44 m^2 of floor space per capita. This figure is surpassed in the big cities, as many small households reside in urban areas. It should be noted that nationwide some 10% of the dwellings are used as second homes. The housing conditions in the big cities are less favourable than those for the country as a whole.

Overall, the owner-occupier sector is small (30%). In fact, it is even substantially smaller (12%) in the cities. The private rental sector predominates throughout the system (Table 11.5). In relation to income, housing costs are relatively high; on average, well over 20% of income is spent on rent. During the past few years, the rapidly rising interest rates forced the rents up faster than the price of consumption goods. The housing costs have become an increasingly heavy burden for the elderly and other low-income households. Since mortgage rates are directly linked to rents, the rise in interest rates became a major housing issue.

In view of the reliance on free market principles, there has been little direct action to alleviate the housing problems of low-income households. The non-profit-making housing sector has traditionally been weak in Switzerland, due to financial constraints and an inadequate organisation. Other financial support has also been minimal. The instruments provided by the Housing Act of 1974 only resulted in the addition of 50 000 publicly sponsored dwellings between 1975 and 1991 (Gurtner, 1992, p. 18). Government agencies at any level provided less than 3% of the new housing during the 1980s; the share of housing built with public financial aid was never higher than 8% of the total production (Lischner, 1988, p. 111). Excluding guarantees, only 0.18% of the federal government's budget was spent on housing. And even when the contributions from *cantons* and local authorities are taken into account, the amount hardly makes a dent (Gurtner, 1992, p. 2). Financial incentives common in other European countries — such as home savings premiums, housing grants, reduced tax rates on home savings and other fiscal advantages — are practically unknown in Switzerland.

The increased cost of financing, rising construction costs and high land prices caused the production of housing to fall to just over 35 000 in 1991. This number is some 5000 less than the average during the preceding decade. It is the lowest figure since the recession of the mid-1970s and not high enough to meet the growing demand. The new dwellings are barely affordable to households with average incomes, and they are completely out of reach of the low-income population. The government therefore introduced a loan programme to reduce rents of new dwellings to below the amount needed to cover the real costs. The initial rent is fixed at 5.6% of the total investment, independent of the mortgage interest rate. But the system requires the rents to be adjusted upward by 7% every two years (Gurtner, 1992, p. 6). The system of regular rent rises implies a need for a steadily increasing income, which not everyone has. Therefore, this rent reduction programme is woefully inadequate as a way to make new housing affordable to low-income households. And even supplementary subsidies for low-income groups to reduce their rent burden do not give them guaranteed access to housing of average standards.

The financial developments are making the housing situation worse in Switzerland. Moreover, there is a growing problem of misallocation in existing housing. Elderly people remain living in large, inexpensive dwellings, though these often have quality deficiencies. More and more families with children live in overcrowded conditions (Lischner, 1988, p. 103). Underprivileged foreigners live in the oldest stock, generally housing of relatively poor quality. They bear the brunt of the deteriorating housing situation, yet they are frequently blamed for the problems all Swiss renters now have to face.

HOUSING SITUATIONS AND HOUSING MARKET POSITIONS OF "GUESTWORKERS"

Initially, employers of guestworkers were legally required — or felt otherwise compelled — to provide housing for the duration of the contract.

Thus, the workers were mostly accommodated in workers' hostels, makeshift camps of barracks or caravans, or any other accommodation that could be provided quickly and cheaply. When the guestworkers migrated to the cities, they generally moved into private-sector rooming houses in inner-city slums (Huttman, 1991, p. 23), since they remained barred from entry to the formal housing market. Their housing was of poor quality and usually overcrowded; at least it was inexpensive. As long as the workers were single men who subscribed to the idea of a temporary stay, these conditions fitted their individual strategies. The low housing costs allowed them to transfer their savings to relatives back home. Sharing their accommodation with people from their home towns provided a degree of social support. But their needs and preferences sometimes put their individual strategies at loggerheads with official attempts to improve their housing conditions by enforcing more rigorous (safety) standards.

In the event their status changed from contract labourers to immigrants, the guestworkers needed to find room in the formal housing market. Frequently, they had to obtain housing before they were allowed to bring their dependants over. Their special legal status and weak housing market position directed them to the worst housing in run-down parts of the cities. Since these areas were shunned by households with a greater range of opportunity, this also promoted segregation. The inner-city slums where the single workers had previously found shelter also became the main habitat of the workers' families; but in some countries, many moved to peripheral areas (Huttman, 1991, p. 23), sometimes into squatter settlements, sometimes into older housing estates. Housing regulations and waiting lists for social housing put them at a disadvantage with respect to the indigenous low-income households in the host societies.

The initial segregated pattern became entrenched where their own social networks played an important role in gaining access to housing. Segregation created a useful social environment for the newcomers, providing the critical mass to support familiar facilities and services. The guestworker neighbourhoods soon stood out because of their ethnic markets and shops (e.g. Islamic butchers), coffee houses, and eventually mosques and specific services, both social and commercial. But the squalor of their housing conditions became unacceptable. The immigrants, especially those with families, desired housing of higher standards. Thus, the initial assumption that only minimum provision of encampment or barrack housing would be necessary was falsified by subsequent events (Huttman, 1991, pp. 23–24). Eventually, it resulted in a policy debate, especially when urban renewal touched the concentration areas. This debate took on more urgent overtones when social tensions and conflicts with the indigenous population started to accompany the emergence of immigrant enclaves.

The Netherlands

Each of the big cities in the Netherlands has a relatively high share of immigrants. In 1990, people born outside the country accounted for 7.8% of the national population; for the cities with over 200 000 inhabitants, this was 20.4%. More than 40% of the total immigrant population lived in the four biggest cities (Amsterdam, Rotterdam, The Hague and Utrecht), while only 11.5% of the Dutch population resided there (Dieleman, 1993, p. 123). This high degree of concentration in the cities largely determines their housing situation. The tenure structure of the urban housing stock is severely biased towards rental housing, since home-owners account for only 10% (in Amsterdam and Rotterdam) to just over 30% (The Hague and Utrecht). Within those cities, the residential patterns of the immigrant groups are fairly similar to those of Dutch households with a comparable income and household structure (p. 124). This reflects the improvements in their housing situation since the early 1980s. Thus, even though the immigrants live in the cheaper parts of the housing stock, they are by no means marginalised in the Dutch housing market (p. 124). In other words, they are no worse off than similar Dutch (large) family households remaining in the cities.

Family reunification became common during the latter part of the 1970s. By that time, the guestworkers from Morocco and Turkey had gradually improved their housing conditions. Initially barred from social rental housing by regulations that discriminated against newcomers, they moved out of lodgings into other poor-quality dwellings in the late-nineteenth-century working-class neighbourhoods (Dieleman, 1993, p. 124). These were mostly private rental dwellings; in Utrecht (and in the medium-sized cities), however, these areas contained numerous cheap owner-occupier houses. Although cheap rental housing was formally regulated, in reality few households on the waiting lists would accept this housing because of its poor quality. Furthermore, private landlords resorted to various strategies to gain control over allocation and reap the financial benefits (van Weesep, 1984). Where the older neighbourhoods consisted pre-dominantly of multi-family housing, condominium conversion became widespread, offering the guestworkers (and other households with low priority) an opportunity to circumvent the housing allocation rules (van . Weesep, 1984).

By the early 1980s, changes in the allocation rules gave immigrants access to social rental housing. Gradually, immigrants became more prevalent in neighbourhoods with inexpensive social housing, especially in districts built between 1906 and 1930 and directly after 1945. Blauw (1991, p. 54) cautions that these changes may not have improved their housing conditions greatly. First, immigrants moved into post-war areas following their rejection of better but more expensive renovated housing in urban renewal areas. Secondly, they became concentrated in the neighbourhoods built in the 1950s, where large and inexpensive flats are found; but many of these no longer meet the generally accepted standards. The dwellings lack modern amenities such as central heating and complete bathrooms. Many are poorly insulated against the weather and sound. Vacancies and turnover rates in such blocks of flats are often very high. The elderly tenants pass away and those indigenous Dutch families that can afford a single-family house in a new town or suburb move out (p. 54). This high turnover provides opportunities for Moroccan and Turkish families. But it also implies that they stay one step behind the Dutch population at large in regard to the improvement of housing.

On occasion, the emergence of new concentrations of guestworkers has provoked violent reactions from the indigenous population. In an effort to pre-empt hostility and to promote social integration, a series of inadequate efforts were made to disperse the immigrants throughout the social housing stock. Officially or informally, several towns set a quota for immigrants per building or complex (Mik, 1991, p. 183). This restricted the immigrants' housing opportunities. When challenged, these policies were ruled discriminatory and in violation of the constitution by the courts in the early 1980s and were subsequently abandoned. However, in one form or another, both the policies and the debate resurface from time to time.

The Amsterdam area provides a clear picture of the dynamics of immigrant housing and the political debate. Amsterdam's policies reveal that the desire to promote integration of immigrants and provide equitable housing opportunities is inherently incompatible with the reality of the persistent concentration of guestworkers. Within the city, there is some dispersal of the Turkish and Moroccan population, but in many areas these groups remain strongly overrepresented (Table 11.6). They have become less predominant in some of the older neighbourhoods, while their share has risen in districts built in the 1950s. They remain virtually absent in the newest neighbourhoods (van Kempen, 1992a). At the regional scale, the rapid growth of the Moroccan and Turkish population in Amsterdam has led to an increasing contrast between the central city and the surrounding municipalities, although several of the latter accommodate numerous ethnic households.

In 1983, there were only four areas in Amsterdam where immigrants (Moroccan, Turkish and Surinamese) accounted for more than 25% of the population; by 1990, there were 10. These included the four early concentration areas, but six more districts with sizeable numbers of immigrants in 1983 had crossed the 25% mark. The striking drop in the share of immigrants living in the older neighbourhoods and their growing presence in post-war areas do not imply a dispersal. Rather, it indicates a shift in the concentration areas (van Kempen, 1991). The shifts in the pattern are strongly related to the greying of the Dutch population and its

Table 11.6. Distribution of Turkish and Moroccan population of Amsterdam by neighbourhood type, percentages

Neighbourhood types	Turkish		Moroccan		Total population	
	1983	1990	1983	1990	1983	1990
Inner city	2.4	2.2	3.5	3.5	8.4	10.9
Pre-war high status	2.5	0.8	2.0	1.2	8.9	7.9
19th-century working class	21.7	16.2	25.8	18.7	16.6	13.9
1906–30	45.7	43.1	42.3	37.5	24.0	21.0
1931–45	10.0	13.5	8.3	11.5	6.6	7.0
1945–60	10.9	14.9	10.9	17.7	13.2	12.5
1960s	4.8	5.7	4.6	6.3	13.1	10.1
New neighbourhoods	1.5	3.3	2.2	3.2	7.9	15.5
Mixed neighbourhoods	0.5	0.3	0.4	0.4	1.3	1.2
Total (= 100%)	15 900	21 800	23 700	31 600	678 700	689 300

Source: Adapted from van Kempen and de Klerk (1993).

mobility; the shifts are not only a consequence of the infiltration of immigrants. In the post-1945 areas, many dwellings are vacated by the ageing Dutch population. The largest of these dwellings are particularly suited to the families of low-income immigrants. Young Dutch households do move into these areas, but they depart again quickly, as they pursue better housing. The immigrants comprise the stable population groups in the neighbourhoods (van Kempen, 1992a). They are much more positive about living in these districts than Dutch households.

The Federal Republic of Germany

The guestworkers in West Germany also became increasingly concentrated in the big cities. In 1986, when foreigners accounted for 7.4% of the national population, their share in Frankfurt had reached 25%; in several other big cities (Stuttgart, Munich, Düsseldorf and Cologne) over 15% of the inhabitants were foreign-born. Within these cities, the immigrant population is found largely in two types of residential areas. Most of the underprivileged immigrants are concentrated in centrally located neighbourhoods, often urban renewal areas. However, since the mid-1980s, more have started to filter into the large housing estates on the urban periphery built during the 1960s and 1970s (Friedrichs and Alpheis, 1991, p. 120).

The continued growth of the number of guestworkers in the old neighbourhoods is now more related to their characteristically high birth rate than to immigration. But the increasing concentration is largely due to the outmigration of the native German population to the suburbs rather than to the rapid increase in the number of foreigners.

The general housing situation of immigrants in Germany is poorly documented in the literature. But case studies have presented overwhelming evidence that guestworkers are less well housed than the indigenous population. There are no major differences among the homeowners of the two groups. Yet very few of the guestworkers have ascended to the owner-occupier sector. This is hardly surprising, in view of their place on the bottom rungs of the labour market. The guestworkers are hard hit by the changing qualification requirements for jobs and by the downturn of the German economy after the political reunification of the country. They have had to cope with a drop of over 20% in jobs available to them (Friedrichs and Alpheis, 1991, p. 123). Guestworkers find themselves trapped in the worst of the traditional working-class neighbourhoods; within such dilapidated areas, they live in the worst housing.

Underprivileged foreign workers have to accept the apartments that cannot easily be rented to others: poorly maintained, substandard units in damp, run-down and cramped buildings (Arin, 1991, p. 208). These apartments tend to be old and small, and consequently many guestworker households live in overcrowded conditions. Housing data at the national level show that foreign-born households of all sizes are concentrated in buildings constructed before 1918 (Table 11.7). In 1979, over 60% of foreign households lived in dwellings without complete plumbing and amenities, as opposed to less than 45% of the German households. Case studies from several cities show that they are much more subject to overcrowding than the indigenous population. For example, in Augsburg, the standard of 1.4 persons per room was exceeded by 72% of the foreign households but only 15% of the German households (Friedrichs and Alpheis, 1991, p. 128). Moreover, migrants often pay excessive rents due to ignorance of their legal rights or difficulties in dealing with the authorities. Often they cannot protest about unfair rent increases since they are afraid of getting into conflicts; they put up with what they are offered and try to avoid trouble (Arin, 1991, p. 208).

The weak position of the guestworkers in the housing market is partly a result of overtly discriminatory regulations. As a group, they are still subject to various legal restrictions. Although they are no longer forced to rotate back to their home countries, their living conditions are highly dependent on their ability to hold down a job; there is a direct link between their work permit and their residence permit. Foreigners are also restricted in the exercise of basic rights. With respect to housing, they are often subject to quotas for a given neighbourhood (i.e. the type of restrictions that were declared unconstitutional in the Netherlands). Berlin, for example, enacted a special ordinance in 1975, banning underprivileged foreigners from 3 of the 12 boroughs. These are traditional working-class districts where early concentrations of guestworkers emerged. The ordinance was passed by progressive politicians, to prevent an overload of

Table 11.7. German and foreign-born renter households in the FRG, by size of household and age of building, 1978

Household type	Number	Construction period of building			
		Before 1918	1919–48	1949–54	After 1955
One and two persons					
German	8 917 000	22.2	15.1	38.7	23.9
Foreign-born	446 000	36.4	11.5	30.1	21.0
Three and four persons					
German	3 759 000	18.4	12.8	36.9	31.9
Foreign-born	413 000	37.9	13.1	27.8	21.2
Five or more persons					
German	700 000	21.8	13.9	32.1	32.3
Foreign-born	138 000	44.2	13.0	24.3	18.4
All households					
German	13 376 000	21.1	14.4	37.9	26.6
Foreign-born	997 000	38.1	12.4	28.8	20.7

Source: Adapted from Friedrichs and Alpheis (1991, p. 129, Table 6.8).

the social infrastructure, which could have hindered integration (Arin, 1991, p. 205). The ordinance did not lead to the dispersal of the ethnic minorities to other boroughs. However, it did stabilise the foreign-born population of the three districts.

Throughout Germany, efforts have been made to regulate the housing market further, in order to protect foreigners from substandard housing conditions. The legislation prescribes that if minimum standards (including the amount of space per person) are not met, the dwelling will be condemned and must be vacated. But it does not specify who is responsible for replacement housing. Consequently, migrants are blamed for their poor housing conditions. Enforcement of this legislation means that guestworkers must obtain a legal lease for any dwelling that conforms to the requirements. For the guestworker it is more important to have a bona fide lease than a suitable dwelling. Only guestworkers possessing a valid lease can bring their dependants into the country. They also need a lease to extend their residence permit. Rather than improving their housing conditions, the efforts at regulation tend to restrict their housing choice and weaken their housing market position (Arin, 1991, p. 205).

The vast majority of guestworkers in Germany are still housed in the private rental sector. The social rental sector remains largely closed to them. This is not so much a matter of formal exclusion through regulation; the immigrants do have access to the waiting lists. But the opportunities are disappearing rapidly; the sector is shrinking as privately owned social apartments are converted to owner-occupier or luxury dwellings. Thus, the poor housing conditions of the guestworkers may be largely explained by the reluctance of many private owners of standard properties to rent to the large families of foreign labourers. They would much rather select their tenants among two-person households with two incomes than large families dependent on a single wage-earner. The owners of dilapidated turn-of-the-century housing are willing to accommodate these foreign families because of lack of alternative demand. Overcrowding and disinvestment still guarantee them attractive returns. Being thrown back upon the whims of the private sector implies that the guestworkers remain disadvantaged in the housing market.

Some students of housing maintain that the difference in socio-economic status is responsible for the discrepancies between German and foreign-born households, rather than direct discrimination on the part of the landlords (Friedrichs and Alpheis, 1991, p. 127). They also cite a lack of evidence for the contention of others that the outmigration of Germans from the concentration areas is a reaction to the increasing presence of foreign workers in those neighbourhoods. But others have identified clear signs of discrimination. The study of the housing pattern of the deprived foreign-born population in Berlin is a case in point. Like elsewhere in Germany, the guestworkers are the worst-housed population group in this city.

Before the reunification of Germany, Berlin counted 240 000 foreigners among its 2 million inhabitants (12.5%); half of these were Turkish. Since then, the city has experienced a rapid population growth, as ethnic Germans were resettled from eastern Europe. The number of households has increased even more rapidly. Accounting for 50% of all households, the proportion of singles is relatively high. The group consists mostly of pensioners on low incomes. Together, singles and two-person households comprise 80% of all households (Arin, 1991, p. 202).

Among West Berlin's housing stock of just over 1 million dwellings, half are so-called old units built before 1949; four out of 10 were built in the 1860s to 1890s. No less than 280 000 units are still in urgent need of rehabilitation. A large proportion of the old units are small; almost two-thirds are one- or two-bedroom dwellings. Many of these apartments are still inexpensive, even though rent control in Berlin ended in 1987. In spite of the huge number, inexpensive housing is still in short supply, given the large proportion of low-income households. There are also indications that the rents will escalate and that gentrification will run rampant. This happened in Munich and Hamburg, where rent control was terminated in the 1970s. The reunification of the city, along with its new status as the capital of Germany and future seat of government, put additional pressure on the housing market. This forebodes severe problems for the guest-worker population.

Switzerland

The cities in Switzerland tend to have even higher shares of foreigners than their immediate surroundings and than the country as a whole. But the differences are less pronounced than in other countries, due to the large number of foreigners living in Switzerland. Geneva, with its many international organisations, has by far the highest concentration of foreigners, accounting for over one-third of its population. With rates slightly above 17%, Zurich and Basle are also (just) above the national average of 15%, but the cities of Berne and Lausanne remain below it (Arend, 1991, p. 157). The proportion of foreigners in the cities increased slightly during the 1980s, mostly because of the suburbanisation of the indigenous population.

At first glance, the general housing conditions of the Swiss and the foreigners differ very little. There are some discrepancies, but overall both groups enjoy roughly the same quality of housing. The only significant difference lies in the tenure distribution. Two-thirds of the country's households are renters; yet among the foreigners, the share of renters is over 90%. In all other respects, the statistics show that the groups are quite similar. The housing costs of the two population groups are virtually identical (Gerhauser and Sartoris, 1988, p. 46). On average, each paid approximately 19.5% of their household income for housing in 1986. What they get for their money is also similar. Of the Swiss, 67% live in fully equipped dwellings; this applies to 58% of the foreigners. Only 10% of the foreigners live in dwellings without central heating and without a kitchen of their own. While this is a low rate by any standard, it is still twice that of the indigenous population. Foreigners also have to make do with somewhat less space per person (on average 34 m² versus 45 m² for the Swiss). Yet these differences are not so much the result of differences in dwelling size. They are largely the consequence of variations in their respective household size. One in three of the foreign households consists of four or more persons, compared to one in five among the Swiss (p. 47).

However, the broad similarities between the groups conceal important differences that emerge when the situation is studied in more detail. The two groups are different in household size. With a similar household income, the foreigners therefore have 21% less income per capita than the Swiss (Gerhauser and Sartoris, p. 48). In other respects as well, the aggregate figures mask major differences. The figures are seriously distorted by the statistics for the single-person households. The foreigners in this category earn more than the Swiss, mostly because there are many widowed elderly persons in the latter group. If the singles are ignored, the differences in the housing conditions between the Swiss and the foreign population become much more pronounced (p. 50).

A second caveat applies to differences within the category of foreigners.

Table 11.8. Aspects of the housing situation of Swiss households and underprivileged guestworkers, percentages, 1980

	Swiss			Underprivileged guestworkers		
	Single	Families		Single	Families	
		With children	Without children		With children	Without children
In rented apartments	76.6	54.3	48.5	93.8	90.0	89.5
Less than 0.5 person/room	76.8	47.0	8.7	52.2	16.5	1.3
Apartments with kitchen	89.2	98.2	98.6	74.0	93.1	97.6
Apartments with own bath	88.5	94.8	96.4	74.8	89.1	92.4
Apartments built after 1970	15.4	16.5	23.5	13.3	15.2	15.8
Annual rent < SF 3600	39.0	22.4	13.9	57.5	35.2	27.6

Source: Adapted from Arend (1991, pp. 158–159, Table 8.3).

With respect to their general status, Arend (1991, p. 158) lumped the Germans, French, Austrians, British, Americans and Dutch together as the "privileged Westerners". They are well-off in all respects, including housing. The Italians, Spanish, Yugoslavs, Turks, Portuguese and Greeks are designated as the "underprivileged guestworkers", who are in a much less enviable position.

As far as housing is concerned, the latter category is relatively deprived (Table 11.8). This is obvious when we look at the figures on overcrowding. Among the guestworkers, 31% live in accommodation with more than one person per room, compared to barely 8% of the Swiss. Differences in the amenities of the dwellings do exist, but are less striking. Yet the fact that more than 25% of the single guestworkers live in dwellings without baths and kitchens seems to be significant (Arend, 1991, p. 160). These differences correspond to the lower rents paid by the guestworkers.

With its 360 000 inhabitants, Zurich is the largest city in Switzerland. The foreigners in this city are hardly segregated from the Swiss population in general. But the guestworkers are clearly concentrated in the older parts of the city, in the less popular neighbourhoods near the centre. They occupy the housing that cannot be rented to the indigenous population, or at least not at the rates that the guestworkers (can afford to) pay. Arend (1991, p. 163) notes that on average the foreigners do not live in cheaper dwellings than the Swiss of similar socio-economic status. Instead, they look for apartments that they can afford, and select the cheaper ones among these.

Direct discrimination in the housing market does not seem to be the underlying cause of this pattern. The Swiss pride themselves on their easy coexistence with the foreigners, whom they perceive as very similar to themselves (Arend, 1991, p. 163). Arend notes that the foreign population in Zurich contains a large proportion of Spanish and Italians, who look less "foreign" to a Swiss than a Turk does to a German. In addition, the general lack of residential segregation is attributed to the constrained spatial extent of the city (and its small size). The city's compact form has prevented the emergence of clearly demarcated districts with their own homogeneous population.

Instead, the spatial housing pattern of the guestworkers is largely determined by differences in access to various parts of the housing stock. Essentially, the more properties owned by the state and by co-operatives in neighbourhoods, the lower the number of guestworkers in those areas. Social housing and co-operatives are rarely accessible to foreigners (Arend, 1991, p. 163), largely because of the low mobility rate of the Swiss. The inhabitants of Zurich are very attached to their traditional neighbourhoods. Consequently, there are few vacancies in the older housing stock for foreigners to take advantage of. Difficult access to the older stock also explains why relatively many foreigners live in new buildings on the urban periphery (p. 163). Thus, while housing segregation between the privileged and the underprivileged foreigners increased during the 1970s, it changed only slightly between the underprivileged and the Swiss population.

The coexistence of the indigenous population and the foreigners did not create tensions as long as each group had clearly different aspirations. The guestworkers came and went, rotating back to their home countries. While living in Zurich, they created demand for housing that was not attractive to the Swiss. But this situation may be changing. The socio-economic developments precipitated by the restructuring of the economy also affect Swiss cities. Economic change may usher in a sharper social segmentation (Arend, 1991, p. 164). As more Swiss are confronted with an increasing cost of living and stagnating incomes, there will be more demand for low-cost housing on their part.

A FUTURE IN THE MARGIN OF THE HOST SOCIETIES?

The developments in guestworker housing in the three countries are determined by two sets of factors. On the one hand, there are the strategies of the households, reflecting their immigrant status and their social position. On the other hand, the changing housing conditions and the nature of the housing markets in the respective countries exert an influence. The interplay of these factors determines the current housing conditions of the (former) guestworkers and their future perspectives. We set out to discover whether their situation has become more similar to that of the indigenous population. Can they improve their situation as time goes by? Or will their future be to remain in a marginal position in the housing markets of their host societies?

When the guestworkers were recognised as immigrants in the Netherlands, they gained entry to the vast social rental sector. They occupied
dwellings in the older post-war neighbourhoods which had lost favour
with many of the more affluent indigenous family households. Taking up
the rejects does not necessarily imply that immigrants have a weaker
housing market position than members of the indigenous population with
a corresponding socio-economic status. This step up the housing ladder has
more to do with their household characteristics and the high mobility rates
in this part of the social housing stock as elderly households are dissolved
and families move from the cities to the suburbs. The guestworkers simply
were allocated housing where the most (suitable) dwellings became
available. Large numbers have thus vastly improved their housing conditions. Yet, in some ways, they remained one step behind the indigenous
population, even though the broad patterns suggest similarities. They do
occupy the least attractive parts of the stock. The existence of a time-lag is
also suggested by the allocation mechanism; the guestworkers can now
turn to the municipal housing officials and the social housing associations
for dwellings. In contrast, Dutch families turn increasingly to the private
sector as they move into new rental and owner-occupier dwellings. The
housing future holds threats for all low-income households. Dutch housing
will depend increasingly on market principles, and the growth of the social
rental sector will diminish. This policy change can jeopardise the slow but
steady progress that the guestworkers have made.

In Germany, the housing situation of the guestworkers has deteriorated
in recent years, due to the increasing competition from other underprivileged newcomers. Little help is to be expected from the authorities,
who have to deal with a dwindling social rental stock and the upgrading
of the private rental stock. In many areas, the guestworkers themselves
have been made responsible for resolving their housing problems. If they
are unable to secure appropriate housing, they may even face the loss of
their residence permits. Although the housing situation has improved
when seen in a long-term perspective, the slow progress that was being
made has now been stopped in its tracks by shifts in housing
opportunities. Obviously, the housing market position of the guestworkers
in Germany remains weaker than that of the indigenous population (Arin,
1991, p. 210). And the continuing acts of hostility towards the guestworkers
bode ill for the future.

Because of the enforced rotation back to their home countries, the stay of
guestworkers in Switzerland was temporary, until very recently. This
meant that they could not improve their housing situation through
successive steps up the housing ladder. Due to their short-term perspective
and the need to save their money for when they would return to their
home country, they accepted the worst units in the least attractive neighbourhoods. Thereby, they guaranteed the occupancy of dwellings that

would otherwise have remained empty or be used under very different circumstances. Because of their presence, the value of the remainder of the housing stock was boosted (Lischner, 1988, p. 106). But in the event that more foreigners will be allowed to stay permanently, they will increasingly look for the same housing as the Swiss. The direct competition between the two population groups will also increase because of the sharp rise of housing costs throughout the country, which may entice Swiss households to move into less expensive dwellings. The housing situations will thereby tend to become more similar, but the conflict over access to this stock may become more acute; it may threaten the current peaceful coexistence of disparate population groups.

In all three countries, the spatial structure of the housing stock and the role of the gatekeepers reinforced the differences in housing quality as well as the segregation tendencies resulting from the mobility strategies of the immigrants. When guestworkers became immigrants, they initially looked for housing in the neighbourhoods where they once lived in cramped temporary accommodation. When the employers ceased to provide housing, they often had to fall back upon information and help from family members or people from the same village or region in their country of origin. While they have now also entered other neighbourhoods as vacancies became available, the overall pattern of concentration within the cities remains intact. The indices of segregation between the population groups are still (much) lower than elsewhere (e.g. the USA; cf. Huttman, 1991), but the pattern reveals segregation none the less. This may have some benefits for the guestworkers, as long as they have not become fully integrated in the host societies. But it may also complicate attempts to rectify inequities in their housing situation.

As new categories of disadvantaged foreigners are emerging and the housing systems are under increasing stress, the housing perspectives for the guestworkers are becoming much bleaker than they seemed only a few years ago. They are being joined by large numbers of political (and economic) refugees, competing with them for shrinking resources and disappearing jobs. There is little hope for a turnaround in the economy that will boost their position. If anything, the present migration tendencies will relegate the older guestworkers to increasingly marginal positions. Newcomers have rapidly bypassed the previous groups of migrants. In contrast to the 1960s and 1970s, the major flows of labour migrants in Europe no longer consist of guestworkers. Economic and political changes have meant that we are no longer looking at a redundant population of agricultural and unskilled workers. People now move for advanced education and professional opportunities. The guestworkers of yesterday have largely been replaced by highly educated professionals, moving within internal networks.

As the new groups of migrants leave the older ones behind, and as the guestworkers remain marginal, their only hope for catching up is long term. It may be a slim hope at that; they may gradually improve their situation if the economy picks up again and the welfare state retains its basic programmes. But will they catch up with the indigenous population and stay ahead of newcomers? If not the second generation, possibly the third generation will slowly blend into the host societies. But before this integration is complete, if ever, many years in the margins of the new Europe still await them.

REFERENCES

Arend, M. (1991) Housing segregation in Switzerland, in Huttman, E.D., Blauw, W. and Saltman, J. (eds), *Urban housing segregation of minorities in Western Europe and the United States*, Duke UP, Durham, NC, pp. 155–167.

Arin, C. (1991) The housing market and housing policies for the migrant labor population in West Berlin, in Huttman, E.D., Blauw, W. and Saltman, J. (eds), *Urban housing segregation of minorities in Western Europe and the United States*, Duke UP, Durham, NC, pp. 199–214.

Blauw, W. (1991) Housing segregation of different population groups in the Netherlands, in Huttman, E.D., Blauw, W. and Saltman J. (eds), *Urban housing segregation of minorities in Western Europe and the United States*, Duke UP, Durham, NC, pp. 43–62.

Blotevogel, H.H., Müller-Ter Jung, U. and Wood, G. (1993) From itinerant worker to immigrant? in King, R. (ed.), *Mass migration in Europe: the legacy and the future*, Belhaven, London, pp. 83–100.

Dieleman, F.M. (1993) Multi-cultural Holland: myth or reality? in King, R. (ed.), *Mass migration in Europe: the legacy and the future*, Belhaven, London, pp. 118–135.

Dieleman, F.M., Hooijmaijers, A.B.C.M. and Van Kempen, R. (1993) *Veldtocht tegen de scheefheid; een onderzoek naar de effecten van scheefheidsbestrijding op lokaal niveau*, Faculteit Ruimtelijke Wetenschappen, Universiteit Utrecht.

Friedrichs, J. and Alpheis, H. (1991) Housing segregation of immigrants in West Germany, in Huttman, E.D., Blauw, W. and Saltman, J. (eds), *Urban housing segregation of minorities in Western Europe and the United States*, Duke UP, Durham, NC, pp. 116–144.

Gerhauser, F. and Sartoris, E. (1988) *Neue Aspekte zum Wohnen in der Schweiz. Ergebnisse aus dem Mikrozensus 1986*, Schriftenreihe Wohnungswesen 40, Bundesamt für Wohnungswesen, Berne.

Ghékiere, L. (1991) *Marchés et Politiques du Logement dans la CEE*, La Documentation Française, Paris.

Gurtner, P. (1992) Die Wohnbauförderung des Bundes, Paper for the Seminar Subventionen und Controlling, Berne.

Huttman, E.D. (1991) Housing segregation in Western Europe: An introduction, in Huttman, E.D., Blauw, W. and Saltman, J. (eds), *Urban housing segregation of minorities in Western Europe and the United States*, Duke UP, Durham, NC, pp. 21–42.

Jaedicke, W. and Wollmann, H. (1990) Federal Republic of Germany, in Van Vliet, W. (ed.), *International handbook of housing policies and practices*, Greenwood, Westport, CT, pp. 127–154.

King, R. (1993) European international migration 1945–90: a statistical and geographical overview, in King, R. (ed.), *Mass migration in Europe: the legacy and the future*, Belhaven, London, pp. 19–39.

Lischner, K.R. (1988) *Siedlungswesen in der Schweiz*, 3rd rev. edn, Schriftenreihe Wohnungswesen 41, Bundesamt für Wohnungswesen, Berne.

Mik, G. (1991) Housing segregation and policy in the Dutch metropolitan environment, in Huttman, E.D., Blauw, W. and Saltman, J. (eds), *Urban housing segregation of minorities in Western Europe and the United States*, Duke UP, Durham, NC, pp. 179–198.

Nota (1989) *Nota Volkshuisvesting in de jaren Negentig; van bouwen naar wonen*, SDU Uitgeverij, The Hague.

Parkinson, M., Bianchini, F., Dawson, J., Evans, R. and Harding, A. (1992) *Urbanisation and the functions of cities in the European Community*. A Report to Commission of the European Communities, DG XVI, European Institute of European Affairs, Liverpool.

Tomann, H. (1990) The housing market, housing finance, and housing policy in West Germany: prospects for the 1990s, *Urban Studies*, 27, pp. 919–930.

Ulbrich, R. and Wullkopf, U. (1993) Housing affordability in the Federal Republic of Germany, in Hallet, G. (ed.), *The new housing shortage; housing affordability in Europe and the USA*, Routledge, London, pp. 98–127.

Van Kempen, R. (1991) *Lage-inkomensgroepen in de grote stad; spreiding en concentratie in Amsterdam en Rotterdam*, Stepro rapport 103b. Faculteit Ruimtelijke Wetenschappen, Rijksuniversiteit, Utrecht.

Van Kempen, R. (1992a) *In de klem op de stedelijke woningmarkt? Huishoudens met een laag inkomen in vroeg-naoorlogse en vroeg-20ste-eeuwse wijken in Amsterdam en Rotterdam*, Stedelijke Netwerken, Utrecht.

Van Kempen, R. (1992b) Dutch housing policy in the 1990s: the effects on low-income households, in Korcelli, P. and Van Weesep, J. (eds), *Housing and urban policy in transition*, Institute of Geography and Spatial Organisation, Polish Academy of Sciences, Warsaw, pp. 17–33.

Van Kempen, R. and De Klerk, L. (1993) Randgemeenten open voor allochtonen? *Rooilijn* 93/5, 222–227.

Van Weesep, J. (1984) Intervention in the Netherlands; urban housing policy and market response, *Urban Affairs Quarterly*, 19, 329–353.

Van Weesep, J. and Van Kempen, R. (1993a) Low income and housing in the Dutch welfare state, in Hallet, G. (ed.), *The new housing shortage; housing affordability in Europe and the USA*, Routledge, London, pp. 179–206.

Van Weesep, J. and Van Kempen, R. (1993b) Housing policy, gentrification and the urban poor: the case of Utrecht, the Netherlands, Paper for the ENHR conference Housing Policy in Eastern Europe in the 1990s, Budapest, Hungary, 7–10 September 1993.

White, P. (1993) Immigrants and the social geography of European cities, in King, R. (ed.), *Mass migration in Europe: the legacy and the future*, Belhaven, London, pp. 65–82.

Wohnen (1993) *Wohnen in der Schweiz 1992*, Documentation paper for the 54th session of the UN/ECE Commission on Human Settlements, Geneva, 21–23 September. Prepared by Bundesamt für Wohnungswesen, Berne.

Part IV

CONCLUDING COMMENTS
AND OPEN QUESTIONS

12 Where Have Urban Movements Gone?

C. G. PICKVANCE

University of Kent at Canterbury, UK

What is the link between urban movements and marginality? One possibility is that urban movements are the creation of groups who are marginal in society, and who feel excluded from political parties and pressure groups. Another possibility is that urban movements are mobilisations of those who are spatially marginal in location.

In this chapter it will be argued that neither of these linkages is well founded. The image of urban movements as representing the deprived, the underprivileged, the "underclass", is a long way from reality, and the idea that urban movements are typically made up of those occupying spatially marginal positions also seems without evidence. Urban movements are not to be defined in terms of the social or spatial marginality of their members, but at most in terms of the "marginality" of their political form. In other words, urban movements are a less frequent occurrence than other types of "interest aggregation" such as parties and pressure groups.

What then is their significance and why have they increased and decreased in activity in different societies at different times?

In this chapter we shall address this question in the following stages. Firstly, we define urban movements and discuss the pattern of their incidence over time. Secondly, we explore the numerous explanations which have been advanced for the existence of urban movements. We shall assume that both increase and decrease in urban movement activity can be explained by the same range of theories. Thirdly, we discuss some of the methodological problems of studying the changing level of activity of urban movements and draw some general conclusions about their decline (but not disappearance).

DEFINITION

All choices of terminology express theoretical and other assumptions. The term "urban movement" cuts up reality in a different way from terms like community group, citizen action or voluntary association although the

Europe at the Margins: New Mosaics of Inequality. Edited by Costis Hadjimichalis and David Sadler
© 1995 European Science Foundation. Published in 1995 by John Wiley & Sons Ltd

social groups designated by these terms overlap. Choice of the term "urban movement" makes a connection with the wider category "social movement" of which the ecological, women's and peace movements are also examples. It implies an interest in social change and a claim that social movements of different kinds are an important source of social change. However, the degree of cultural critique embodied in social movement demands is variable — being lower typically in the case of urban movements than in the case of peace movements. Moreover social movements cover a variety of aims (anti-abortion, anti-tax, nationalist as well as those mentioned) and the social change they seek is not necessarily "progressive" from a left point of view. (We do not follow writers such as Eder (1993, p. 107) who restrict the term social movement to those movements which directly contribute to the "modernisation" of society.)

Terms such as "urban movement" or "women's movement" operate at two levels. On the one hand they refer to a broad category of social force and on the other they refer to specific organisations which concretise that force. If we are interested in the rise or decline of urban movements this ambiguity has important implications. If we focus on "social movement organisations" as they are often referred to then their rise or fall could be measured by their number and the level of activism. On the other hand if we focus on a particular type of social movement in general, its rise and fall are to some extent independent of the number of social movement organisations involved. For example, if the number of urban movement organisations declines but the ideas they advocate are incorporated into government policy or accepted by public opinion we might claim that the urban movement, viewed as a set of challenging ideas, had not declined at all but had been successful. In this sense urban movement organisations would be a means to an end and their rise or fall would be less important than the absorption or not of their ideas.

In this chapter we will use the term "urban movement" as an abbreviation for urban movement organisations. This choice does not mean that we shall ignore the question of the penetration of movement ideas. But rather we shall treat this as a separate issue from that of the organisational fact of urban movements.

We define urban movement (organisations) as mobilised groups, which make urban demands which challenge existing policies and practices, which make some use of non-institutionalised methods and which do not take the form of political parties. Unlike interest groups which press for modifications to policies and which have routine access to government, urban movements are challenging groups. However, the degree of challenge is a continuum and the distinction between urban movements and pressure groups which are more institutionalised is hard to make in certain cases. This definition does not refer to the organisational form which urban movements take or their success. Some writers have argued that social movement organisations are always informal and network-like (Diani, 1992) but this is certainly not generally true: some are informal, some are not. The question of the success of urban movements is quite separate from that of their definition. Attempts to incorporate level of success in definitions have caused great confusion. For example, Castells (1977) distinguished three levels of success ("urban social movement", "protest" and "participation") but then went on to use the first term as a general one. The problem is that the success or otherwise of a movement can only be decided some time in the future, so there is a tendency (as with Castells) to judge success by "potential for success" which is much more subjective.

Finally in order to specify the character of urban movements we need to define what is meant by an urban demand. As is well known, the delimitation of the urban has been hotly debated among urban sociologists. Authors such as Castells (1977), Dunleavy (1979), Pickvance (1985) and Saunders (1986) agree that the term does not refer to the geographical location of movements but rather to the objects of their demands. Four categories of demand can be distinguished. Three have been widely recognised:

1. Demands about "collective consumption" (e.g. the existence and eligibility for, and costs of, access to housing, health and education facilities);
2. Demands that neighbourhoods should be protected from physical or social threats, e.g. road building, redevelopment;
3. Demands for a greater say in the running of local political institutions and services provided by such institutions.

In addition recent years have seen a fourth category gain in importance: anti-local tax movements.

EXPLAINING THE RISE AND FALL OF URBAN MOVEMENTS

Having defined what we understand by urban movements we now proceed to examine the reasons for their rise or fall.

This topic has been a widely examined issue in the general literature on social movements, and a variety of theories about it exist. In the 1950s and 1960s sociologists studying community action and citizen groups generally saw them as examples of voluntary association (Pickvance, 1986a). The focus was on their social base and internal functioning, and participation in voluntary associations was taken as a measure of the plural distribution of power. From the late 1960s a more political viewpoint was forced on social scientists by the growing strength of students', peace, civil rights and women's movements whose challenging character was intrinsic to them.

The work of Castells and his colleagues on urban movements in France in the late 1960s introduced the term "urban movement" to the urban sociological literature. He was inspired by a combination of Touraine's "sociology of action" which treated social movements as the main creative force in society, and Althusser's structuralist Marxism. However, the isolation of the Castells-inspired work on urban movements from the wider literature on social movements hampered its development, though some attempts were made to introduce alternative approaches. Conversely, the interest in state theory among writers on urban movements was much less common among writers on other types of social movement.

We now examine the main theoretical approaches and how they tackle the rise and fall question.

Deprivation theory

This theory stresses the importance of "objective" urban phenomena such as physical threats to housing or neighbourhoods connected with urban renewal, or rises in transport fares or housing costs. The assumption of this theory is that those experiencing the most deprivation will be most likely to take part in urban movements. It would explain a rise or fall in urban movement activity as due to an increase or decrease in deprivations.

One use of this theory is to put forward a link between urban restructuring processes and urban movement activity. Examples can be quoted from Canada, the USA, France and the UK to connect the timing of office development or urban renewal with the emergence of urban movements (Caulfield, 1988; Gendrot, 1982; Wates, 1976). Likewise movements against threatening road plans, or land uses perceived as having negative externalities belong to the category of deprivation-based explanations (Mullins, 1987).

There are three difficulties with this theory as a total theory. Firstly, its implication that urban movements are made up of the most deprived (or the most "marginal") is at odds with the evidence that it is those who are least deprived who are most articulate in demand-making. Secondly, it would imply that periods of low urban movement activity occur because deprivation has decreased — a debatable assumption. Thirdly, as we shall see below, the theory simply ignores too many aspects of the mobilisation process to offer a satisfactory explanation of urban movement incidence.

At most it can be argued that deprivations can provide triggers for grievance creation, which if political conditions are favourable lead to urban movements (Fainstein and Fainstein, 1985). But as a general explanation of the rise and decline of urban movements this theory is unconvincing.

Consensus mobilisation theory

The question of whether deprivations are converted into grievances was first tackled through the concept of "relative deprivation" (Runciman, 1966). This drew attention to the subjective evaluation of deprivations and in particular the importance of a person's "reference groups" in deciding whether a deprivation constituted a grievance. However, the identification of reference groups is elusive and the concept of relative deprivation has proved difficult to apply.

The question of the conversion of deprivations into grievances has more recently been approached through the concept of consensus mobilisation (Klandermans, 1991). Clearly since most deprivations do not give rise to any action, there are many obstacles in this conversion process. Social psychologists have focused on the cognitive changes needed to convert deprivations into grievances, and on the role of outside actors in this process.

As a contribution to an explanation of the rise and decline of urban movements this theory stresses changes in the extent to which deprivations are converted into demands. Social psychologists tend to focus on micro-level determinants of consensus mobilisation. The role of external agents such as community workers is also important. However, there are also macro-reasons why grievances emerge to different extents over time and in my view these are more interesting. A significant macro-factor is people's expectations regarding state responsiveness to their grievances. It is frequently observed that if governments can successfully claim that the financial "cupboard is bare", then protest activity in support of greater spending (rather than a halt to a spending project) will be deterred. One way this happens is by discouraging those with deprivations from considering they have a grievance. Conversely, in periods of growth in state spending, demands for higher spending will be greater as the conversion of deprivations into grievances is increased.

Overall this theory contributes something to an explanation of urban movement rise and decline, but it is debatable how far consensus mobilisation is an autonomous process, rather than a reflection of external agents and broader forces.

Class theory

If a body of people with grievances exists, how far is class theory relevant to understanding their actions?

The simplest model would be a structuralist Marxian one, arguing that the working class is the most likely class to undertake collective action on the grounds that it is the most exploited section of the population, and that the more a grievance is concentrated among the working class the more likely it is to be expressed in collective action.

This model was used by Castells and his colleagues in the late 1960s (Olives, 1976). Their theory was that urban movements expressed social contradictions, and that contradictions involving the working class had the greatest transformative potential. They envisaged joint action by urban movements, trade unions and labour parties as having a quasi-revolutionary potential.

Unfortunately, this model did not fit the evidence (Pickvance, 1976). The grievances of urban movements were more often those of the middle class, and manual workers were much less involved than non-manual workers. To cope with this fact Lojkine redefined urban movements as means by which middle-class and *petit bourgeois* interests were allied with those of manual workers, enabling a wide "front" against big capital to be created (see Pickvance, 1977a). But again this "front" was more apparent on paper than in reality. A weakness of both these approaches was that they attempted to move directly from "structure" to action and paid no attention to the question of grievance creation and the mobilisation of the "social base" into active groups (Pickvance, 1977b).

Castells subsequently made a radical revaluation of the potential of urban movements. In *The city and the grassroots* (1983) he argued that the multi-class character of urban movements was essential, that their greatest chance of success was by remaining autonomous of political parties and other groupings, and that they were "reactive utopias" with prospects for low-level change only. This change of view was a reflection of a devaluation of class and a revaluation of culture, and reflected Castells's return to Touraine, his first teacher.

The class theoretical approach which predominates in the interpretation of "new social movements" on the other hand never had any Marxist underpinning, and gives more autonomy to cultural values. It argues that advanced industrial society has led to the emergence of a set of "post-materialist" values among the highly educated minority of the population — these values concern belonging, self-expression and the quality of life. Inglehart (1990) shows that this minority is continuously increasing throughout western Europe and North America and predicts that by 2000 "post-materialists" will be as numerous as "materialists". He also shows that there is a strong correlation between holding post-materialist values and participating in new social movements.

Advocates of this approach identify the highly educated segment of the middle class as playing the leading role in social movements. It is likely that there is an overlap between urban movement participants and participants in "new social movements". Urban movements make concrete demands for changes within the existing social order, and can also be defensive and conservative. But their demands for greater participation and more rights have parallels with the cultural critique of "new social movements". If this is so the rise of the "new social movements" may have reduced the potential support base for urban movements.[1]

It would be wrong to say that members of the working class do not participate in urban movements. Multi-class urban movements exist but usually leadership is by middle-class members. Deprived groups especially are likely to be organised by external activists such as professional community workers.

In understanding the trend in urban movements the expansion of a segment of the middle class attached to post-material values is undoubtedly relevant. But on its own it is a process which would suggest a continuing increase in urban movements, rather than a decline. This implies that it must be subject to countervailing forces, as will be shown below.

Protest participation theory

The question of whether people with grievances are likely to form or participate in an urban movement has been tackled by examining the mobilisation of people into organisations as well as through class and cultural theory. This subject can be broken into two topics: motivation to participate and organisational survival, which are discussed in this section and the next.

There are numerous reasons why people with a grievance do not take part in an existing movement. They may doubt its efficacy, distrust its leaders or dislike its methods; or they may not be able to afford the time or costs of participation (see also Pickvance, 1977b; Dunleavy, 1991). The well-known approach of Olson (1965) is more sceptical still and argues that a rational individual seeking a collective good will not engage in collective action to achieve it. As in the case of a non-trade union member who receives a wage increase won by the trade union and paid to all workers, Olson argues that the rational individual will "free-ride" on the actions of others. This model assumes that a collective action does take place nevertheless. It also advances various propositions about how organisations can counter the tendency to free-ride, e.g. by offering selective incentives available only to members — like free legal advice offered by trade unions. But the main problem with Olson's approach is its assumption about the ubiquity of calculative motivation.

In contrast to this instrumental approach is an alternative approach which argues that people participate in protest as an expressive act, and that calculation is not involved at all. This is the perspective of many writers on "new social movements" for whom the aim of participation is not the securing of benefits, but the expression of their identity and a critique of the social order. Parkin's (1968) study of CND took this view, arguing that CND participation was due to a prior value commitment. Hirschman (1982) argues against Olson that in such movements participation is not a cost but a "benefit" which is added to the value of the ultimate goal.

The question is which of these approaches — instrumental and expressive — is most applicable to urban movements. It was argued above that urban movements were to some extent more concrete in their demands than "new social movements". But this is a difference of degree rather than kind: urban movements not only make demands for more public resources, they also make demands for more rights (e.g. rights to consultation or participation in decisions).

To explain the decline in urban movements in terms of changes in individual motivation we need to know whether "supplies" of expressive and calculative motivation have changed over time, and indeed whether they are substitutable (or whether urban movements rely mainly on calculative indication). We have no evidence on this. Hirschman (1982) has identified a cyclical pattern of protest participation with phases of "public-orientation" and "private-orientation" following one another in time. But his explanation of changes in phase is entirely at the micro-level.

This brings us to the final point about participation, that it is affected by the general protest environment. In periods like the 1960s when protest was occurring over numerous issues, the likelihood that protest would emerge over any issue was much greater. This is because governments were believed to be likely to give in to demands, and because protest movements in one field created resources usable in others. When the protest environment becomes less favourable this reduces people's inclination to take part in protest.

In sum, motivation to participate in urban movements may change over time but as with grievance creation this is likely to be the reflection of wider processes at least in part.

Resource mobilisation and organisational survival

We stated earlier that urban movements were typically not made up of the deprived, but are more likely to be either led by the middle class, or mainly made up of the middle class. A major reason for this is that to maintain an organisation in existence requires resources, and those suffering most deprivations are by definition also deprived of resources.[2] Conversely, those with more resources and with grievances which might seem minor to the most deprived are in a better position to create and maintain an organisation. In addition to the material and non-material resources of participants, resources available via their social networks, workplaces and other institutional attachments will also be brought to bear. Finally, urban movements will seek to mobilise resources among third parties — the "conscience constituency" of sympathisers. (For a discussion of the resource mobilisation approach see Jenkins, 1983, and Mayer, 1991.)

The continued participation of those with grievances is the other key to organisational survival. If resources are in good supply, less time needs to be spent in fund-raising which can demotivate some participants. The existence of expressively motivated participants will also help organisational survival, as will selective incentives for the calculatively motivated. (Such rewards, on Olson's analysis, will help secure the involvement of those who would otherwise calculate that they can free-ride on the activities of others.) Finally, if participants start to obtain rewards from participation itself (rather than from the movement's achievements of its goals) this will help ensure the movement's survival, e.g. when participation brings social rewards.

The supply of resources is a key element in movement survival but there is a debate about its role in the rise of social movements between those (like "new social movement" theorists) who emphasise cultural orientations and those who emphasise material conditions (see Jenkins, 1983). But the idea that a decline in resources is an explanation of the decline in urban movement activity is less plausible. There is no reason to think that the total supply of material resources usable by urban movements has changed, but it is possible that competition from other types of movement has reduced the supply to urban movements.

Institutionalisation

An important process at the level of individual urban movements is their institutionalisation. This refers to a series of changes, though they need not all be found together. They include the formalisation of organisation structure; the decision to put up a candidate at an election and/or form a political party; and the decision to collaborate with the authorities perhaps to the extent of accepting state funding to administer a programme of services which was previously an object of demands.

As we discuss later, all of these processes are likely to be a response to local political contexts and government initiatives, or to a decision by the movement to stand closer to government. However, none of them is inevitable. Some movements collapse. Others lack the stability needed to become institutionalised. In some a decision to institutionalise may itself produce a split between fundamentalists and pragmatists.

Institutionalisation is relevant in explaining the decline of urban movements if more movements choose this course than before. This could occur if either (a) urban movements are more institutionalised from their creation, or (b) become institutionalised more often or faster than before. In the urban sphere, the retrenchment of state social spending since the mid-1970s has certainly provided grounds for both possibilities.

So far we have considered characteristics of the social base of the movement and its mobilisation into a movement. We have touched on some aspects of the broader context. It is now time to address these more systematically.[3] We consider in turn the effect of regime transitions, state interventionism, state structures and other aspects of the context on urban movement incidence.

Political context

Regime transition

One of the most general findings about urban movements is that they flourish in the phase of collapse of authoritarian regimes and prior to the subsequent formation of political parties. In Spain Castells (1983) has described the role of urban movements in the last years of the Franco regime where the government tolerated "neighbourhood associations". The same phenomenon can be seen in Portugal at the end of the Salazar regime (Gaspar, 1984), in Brazil before the return of democracy in the mid-1980s and in Hong Kong in the final years of the colonial regime (Lui, 1984). The parallel extends to Russia, Hungary and Poland where environmental movements were tolerated in the final years of state socialism in the mid– late 1980s (Pickvance, 1995).

The reasons for this phenomenon are (a) the limited opportunities for political participation by opponents of the regime and (b) state tolerance of movements which are not explicitly political or anti-regime in aim.

Conversely, the emergence of democratic politics leads to an increase in opportunities for political participation with the possibility of opposition party formation. Urban and environmental movements typically experience a partial outflow of activists reducing their level of activity to a more sustainable level (Pickvance, 1995).

The general point here is that the rise and decline of urban movements before and after regime transitions is a specific case, and that it is dangerous to generalise about capitalist societies on the basis of what happens in regime transitions — as I have argued Castells does from the Spanish case (Pickvance, 1985). It is equally dangerous to use cases of regime transition to claim a continuous upward trend in urban movement activity.

Party–movement relations

A second aspect of the political context is relations between parties and movements.

There is an inverse relation between the existence of effective political opposition and the strength of social movements such that movements flourish when opposition parties are considered ineffective (Rootes, 1992b). This is sometimes given a functionalist interpretation which sees urban movements as serving to bring new issues to the attention of existing parties (Fainstein and Fainstein, 1974). Parties then absorb these issues into their programmes, allowing the protest movement to go into decline having achieved its aim. This view suggests that protest movements are inherently transitory and if true would help explain the rise and decline pattern of individual urban movements.

Its implications for aggregate urban movement activity depend on the willingness of parties to absorb new issues, which varies with the nature of the issue and the nature of parties. Some issues are so challenging to the agenda of politics that no major parties will absorb them; for example, the radical ecological view which challenges basic assumptions about economic growth shared by all major parties, and the UK anti-poll tax movement whose non-payment tactic alienated it from all but the Scottish National Party. Other issues such as place-specific urban issues are inherently difficult for parties to take on since they concern one locality only. Nevertheless there are some urban issues which parties will take on, for example the demands of the UK squatting movement in the 1960s had considerable Labour Party support and led to councils licensing temporary housing for squatters, and later to legislation providing housing for the "unintentionally homeless".

The willingness of parties to take on board new issues also depends on the character of parties. This is what Katznelson (1981) refers to as the "cultural meaning" of urban politics. In the USA, parties are aggregates of discrete interests without clear ideological unity, and are more able to absorb new demands. In Europe, class-based parties have traditionally been more common and such parties find it more difficult to take on board protest demands which do not conform to their ideological commitments. Rootes (1992b) points out that the British Labour Party has been very receptive to nuclear disarmament protest but much less so to environmental protest due to party competition.

The relation of parties to movements therefore varies between societies and influences the level of urban movement activity, but only when the relation changes can it explain the rise and fall of urban movements.

The cases of France and Italy are good illustrations of this. After the war centre–right governments were in power in France until 1981 and took on the image among the left of a "one-party state". Not only was opposition by established parties felt to be ineffective but the French state has traditionally been the epitome of a closed system. Its suspicion of intermediary associations goes back to the aftermath of the French Revolution. Given this context the volume of movements was not large, but the level of radicalism was relatively high. Significantly the major change occurred in 1977 when the left had great success at the local elections, leading to a demobilisation of urban movements as many movement leaders became local councillors.

A similar analysis can be made for Italy where the long rule of centre–right parties had the effect of producing very radical urban movements,[4] but where the left-wing successes in local government elections in the mid-1970s led to their institutionalisation (Ceccarelli, 1982).

Openness of government to movements

A related topic concerns the openness or closure of governments to external groups. This varies between countries and over time. Kitschelt (1986) for example has classified the USA as an "open" system with France as "closed". The implication is that open systems favour moderate protest group formation (since the perceived efficacy of protest is higher) but make violent protest less likely since systems which are open are more likely to encourage consultation and compromise. Closed systems on the other hand discourage group formation but may encourage violent protest. Other writers point out that openness varies according to the issue (Rootes, 1992a, b).

In explaining the rise and decline of urban movements changes in the openness of governments, and especially local governments, to movement demands are certainly relevant. For example in the 1980s in the UK the reduction in public expenditure in the social sphere was accompanied by a decreased government willingness to consult and listen to external groups. And in the USA, Fainstein and Fainstein (1985) point to the receptivity of local regimes and the unity of urban élites as key factors affecting urban movement incidence.

The contrast between open and closed governmental systems is sometimes treated as synonymous with that between decentralised and centralised governmental structures. On the whole it is reasonable to argue that decentralised systems are more open since they provide more opportunities for inputs, but there can be changes in "openness" within systems whose structure has not changed, due to policy decision.[5]

State policy, state structure and urban movement success

One of the strengths of research on urban movements is that those involved in it have been particularly interested in state theory. Hence there is considerable evidence as to the importance of state policy and state structure in affecting urban movement existence, forms, demands and success. Over time, the argument that the state is merely an instrument of one or more social interests has given way to the argument that the state has considerable autonomy *vis-à-vis* such interests, which justifies treating it as a worthwhile object of study.

Some of the early work on urban movements saw the state as a "wall" defending capitalist interests which could only be brought down by united action by parties, trade unions and urban movements (Castells, 1977). This was a reflection in part of Marxian theory, but in part of the frustrations of the French left at being so long in opposition.

Anglo-Saxon writers on the other hand were faced with a very different context, in which state authorities could not be portrayed as completely resistant to external pressure. Some city councils and some national governments were controlled by social democratic parties which were often sympathetic to urban movement demands. Urban movement success would depend on the relative strength of different departments within authorities as well as on their own power to mobilise protest (Lipsky, 1970; Pickvance, 1976).

Moreover, in countries with "open" systems, state strategies become an important subject of study. These ranged from dialogue, to participation on government terms, to co-optation, to pre-emption (e.g. by setting up rival groups) to repression. The strategies would affect the likelihood of formation of movements, their chances of survival, their goals, forms of action and eventual success. The question of the choice of these strategies (which influences the level of success achieved by urban movements) thus became central and allows the economic, political and organisational aspects of state functioning to be integrated into the study of urban movements.

The choice of strategy is not given by the openness or closure of the system but also reflects the party in power, the economic situation it faces, and the potential of urban movements in coalition-building. How far central and local state strategy and structure can explain the changing incidence of urban movement activity depends on how far state strategy and structure are seen as autonomous of wider social and economic forces. Only if state strategy and structure are completely determined by external forces would they have no independent role in influencing urban movement incidence and success.

State interventionism and urban movements

One of the most influential theories of the development of urban movements is the early work of Castells (1977). He envisaged that as advanced capitalism depended more and more on a skilled labour force the state would have to intervene increasingly to ensure the provision of a sufficient volume of housing, health, educational and recreational facilities. This was a structural need but also a workers' demand. Castells thus anticipated that just as the labour movement had been brought into existence by early industrial capitalism, so a movement centred on these collective consumption facilities, which he defined as "urban", would be created. The "urban movement" would be a "second front" and would bring together different class fractions, thus further threatening the stability of capitalism.

Castells envisaged that this process would have an accelerating effect. As state intervention in the consumption sphere expanded, two processes would occur. Conflicts with market agents (e.g. landlord v. tenant) would decline and conflicts with the state would increase, making them more politicised. And rising state intervention would lead to continuous pressure for extended state intervention (a frequent complaint among neo-liberals). The only constraints on this process of escalation were due to the "fiscal crisis of the state", viz. the fact that state resources were limited by its taxation capacity and economic growth and by rival demands to subsidise the capitalist sector itself.

In retrospect it can be seen that this theory exaggerated the destabilising forces in capitalism. Castells failed to appreciate the difficulties of mobilisation, the incompatibility between the dynamics of political parties and urban movements, and the ease with which state strategies could weaken urban movements (Pickvance, 1977b, 1985; Saunders, 1979; Lowe, 1986). His later work acknowledges these obstacles and sees urban movements as lacking the potential to destabilise capitalism (Castells, 1983).

The linkage between urban protest and state interventionism is an important one, whatever one's assessment of Castells's argument. In many west European countries the 1950s and 1960s were a period of rising state interventionism both in the welfare state sphere and in the economic sphere. Undoubtedly the former was in part a "functional" economic requirement (it was not restricted to societies with social democratic governments which saw the welfare state as quasi-socialist), but it was also a response to demands for a rising standard of living which required collective spending as well as individual spending. These demands were part of a general rise in demands by citizens for greater participation and equality of rights which fed into the various social movements that took off in the late 1950s and 1960s: anti-nuclear, student, women's, etc.

This leads to an interesting debate about how far the rise in urban movement activity is simply to be seen as part of a more general "post-materialism" and a critical attitude to government, or how far it is due to specifically urban changes (see Harris, 1987, 1988, and Caulfield, 1988, for this debate regarding Canadian urban movements). My own view is that the rise in general activism due to an increasingly well-educated population who realised that many aspects of welfare could not be obtained by individual spending was a significant factor, but that specifically urban triggers need not be excluded.

The rising trend of state interventionism in the social sphere which had been treated as an inevitable concomitant of advanced capitalism started to falter in the early 1970s after the oil shock. The pressure on state spending was partly external but partly internal due to the growing affluent class who formed a constituency for policies which sought to make direct taxation less progressive and cut welfare spending. Neo-liberal theories of deindustrialisation, monetarism and ungovernability all envisaged a reduced role for government in the social sphere. In practice these theories were applied to varying degrees in different societies (Pickvance and Preteceille, 1991) and even where they were applied compromises were reached with vested interests. Hence policy was a mix of old and new priorities.

The impact of the new policy environment for urban movements was sharp. Demands for more spending on collective consumption which had a fair chance of success in the "growth" phase of social spending were no longer realistic. And there is no doubt that the effect of the new environment was to demobilise participation in movements demanding more spending. However, this argument does not apply in the case of movements which are *against* plans involving state spending.

At the same time there was a new emphasis in state welfare policy which had important repercussions for urban movements. One way of making the welfare state cheaper to run was to replace paid employees by volunteers. This meant that state responses to certain urban movement demands (those related to service provision) increasingly took the form of state funding of projects carried out by volunteers rather than state employees. Many movements were able to achieve their demands in such ways. The result was a reduction in demand-making, but an expansion of the voluntary sector. Former activists were willing to act as volunteer project workers as well as in some cases paid project leaders. This pattern has been described by Hamel (1991) as a North American one. But it is equally important in western Europe.

In sum, the early 1970s saw a watershed in the general level of activism and state welfare policy which led to a shift of emphasis by urban movements from demand-making to the administration and execution of welfare projects.

So far we have been referring mainly to movements making demands for an extension of collective consumption provision. However, there are other types of urban movement. The trend in movements defending neighbourhoods from a physical or social threat is largely independent of the pattern of collective consumption and depends mostly on the level of private (and public) investment activity which involves changes in land use. (There is an overlap, however, when local residents protest against houses being converted for community care purposes.) The trend in urban movements demanding a greater voice in decision-making is, however, connected with the 1970s watershed. In the 1960s, demand-making for services was often associated with demands to run or participate in decisions about public services. Since the mid-1970s management has followed watchwords such as efficiency and accountability, with participation becoming a secondary consideration. Given this new environment, urban movements demanding decision-making rights have become less frequent than before. Finally anti-local tax movements have appeared sporadically and with different social bases. Groups opposed to the level of local taxes are found among home-owners, whereas groups opposed to the UK poll tax had a wider social profile — the principle of the tax being more important than the amount.

There are thus numerous links between the economic situation, the change in state policy towards the social sector, and the evolution of urban movements of most kinds.

APPLYING EXPLANATIONS OF URBAN MOVEMENT INCIDENCE

For reasons of space and data availability it is not possible to examine the impact of each of the eleven factors discussed on urban movement incidence throughout Europe. Instead we first discuss the methodological problems of answering the question "where have urban movements gone" or rather why they are less frequent and less radical than before, and secondly summarise our provisional answer to it.

We first need to consider the meaning of this question. If it means that urban movement organisations are less frequent than before, then this does not exclude the possibility that the demands of urban movements have been achieved. This is the question of urban movement success. There is certainly evidence of urban movement leaders being absorbed into institutionalised politics (as local councillors) but this in itself does not prove that movement demands have been successful. The leader may have been "bought off" in order to weaken the movement, or may have put individual advancement above the goals of the movement. The only way to judge success is by looking at prevailing ideas and their translation into policies. Again the question of timing arises. In the short term, established parties may respond to a new demand by making superficial changes in their programme but none in their policies. Only in the medium term may changes in policy come about. But policy changes are always vulnerable to a weakening of the political forces that produced them, and so may be short-lived.

Restricting ourselves to the question of urban movement organisations, we now discuss evidence about trends.

In 1983 Castells noted that "in spite of the absence of reliable systematic information on the development of urban movements throughout history, our own knowledge as well as the amount of existing information suggest a clear comparative upward trend" (p. 328). But he also noted the lack of uniformity in this trend, referring to the "uneven development of urban movements [and of their] expansion to a broader geographical and cultural area" (p. 327). As examples he mentions the strengthening of the Spanish neighbourhood associations in the late 1970s when "the Italian movement was agonizing", the emergence of new urban movements in Brazil, Venezuela and Mexico when the Chilean *pobladores* "crumbled under the terror of Pinochet", and the steady flow of community organisations and neighbourhood groups demanding public services in the USA in the 1970s after the violent protest of the 1960s.

The absence of systematic data makes radically different interpretations possible. Castells takes the view that there is a "clear, comparative upward trend". Others such as Ceccarelli (1982) as well as myself, would argue that he does not recognise the specificity of different contexts and therefore cites different cases as belonging to the same trend when in fact they do not.

The key issue here is how to evaluate the importance of contexts. Castells has often described the contexts in which urban movements operate. However, he is only willing to acknowledge that contexts are relevant to explaining urban movements if it can be shown that "the 'context' *acts* on the movement" and to do this "one has to observe the specific effects of the 'contextual features' on the practice of the movement" (Castells, 1985, p. 59).

In fact as I have written "*one cannot observe 'effects'*: one can certainly observe a contextual feature and an aspect of an urban movement, but the statement that one is the effect of the other is not based on observation alone [but on] theoretical judgement as well" (Pickvance, 1986b, p. 227).

My own approach is to argue that contextual features have important effects on urban movement development, and that it is not sensible to debate whether there is a "clear comparative upward trend" as Castells suggests or whether "large-scale urban social movements have faded out as rapidly as they originated" (Ceccarelli, 1982, p. 261). Rather we need to separate trends within societies whose political contexts have remained constant in the respects identified earlier and trends within societies whose political contexts have changed and where the prospects for urban movements have increased or decreased.

To return to the eleven explanations of urban movement decline discussed earlier, these can be crudely grouped under the headings "movement" and "context". The only features on the movement side which would explain a decline in frequency or radicalism are a reduced belief in the efficacy of collective action, a reduced perception of grievances and institutionalisation — all of which can be seen as responses to a context in which governments are seen as less likely to grant demands, rather than being autonomous processes. There is no obvious decline in the level of deprivations, level of resources, size of the educated middle class, or costs of participation in collective action which if they occurred would explain a decline in urban movement activity.

When we turn to the context on the other hand almost all of the changes observable help explain urban movement decline.

Firstly, those countries which have experienced a transition from an authoritarian to a democratic regime (Spain, Portugal and Greece) have all seen a mushrooming followed by a decline in urban movement activity. Secondly, those countries which saw the end of periods of long-term right-wing domination at central and local levels (France and Italy) have also seen declines in urban movement activity often accompanied by institutionalisation. This supports the argument that urban movements decline in frequency and radicalism in periods when effective political opposition is possible. Thirdly, changes in state interventionism, openness to external pressure, and centralisation have generally been in the direction of discouraging urban movement activity. The main exception is in the one area of complementarity between the welfare state and urban movements, viz. the use of volunteer labour to replace state employees in welfare services. Nevertheless there remain differences in level of urban movement activity in western Europe due to differences in institutional structure (types of welfare regime, presence of corporatism, degree of state centralisation), party control of government, levels of openness to external pressure, electoral rules, etc.

We are not, therefore, advancing a "modernisation" theory according to which all societies necessarily converge around a single type. The argument is rather that contextual features have systematic effects, wherever they occur, and that these are major forces which channel and shape mobilisation around urban issues.

Thus to approach the question of where have urban movements gone we need to deconstruct the question. In particular we should disallow comparisons which put in the same category societies which have undergone major contextual changes and those which have not. The fact that Spain, Portugal, Greece, Brazil, Hong Kong and eastern Europe all showed a sharp increase in urban movements in the final years of their authoritarian regimes does not mean that they have taken on the mantle previously assumed by Italy and to a lesser extent France. Nor, *a fortiori*, does it mean that there is a "clear comparative upward trend" as Castells claims.

Equal attention must be given to countries where urban movements exist with less radical demands, in lesser number and with more amicable relations with state authorities. This is more typical in societies where social democratic parties alternate with conservative parties in power, or are involved in coalitions, and where there is considerable openness of government to external influence. As we have argued earlier, issues such as territorial defence, collective consumption, influence on local institutions and local taxation are not likely to be taken on board by existing political parties and help explain the continuing existence of urban movements.

The implications of the argument of this chapter for the book are clear. Urban movements are a "marginal" political form which has been appropriated by and large by the middle classes. They do not represent an alternative channel for marginal groups who have been excluded from the more institutionalised political channels. Rather, marginal groups are likely to experience a double exclusion. Their response is likely to oscillate between resignation and occasional outbursts of violent protest.

ACKNOWLEDGEMENT

I would like to thank Pierre Hamel for his helpful comments.

NOTES

1. It would be interesting to see how far participation in particular types of social movement overlaps in the present and over time.
2. It is important to point out that Piven and Cloward (1977) argue, using US examples, that the poor have more to gain from creating a movement which makes use of the disruptive power of large numbers of poor people, than one which takes an organised form (see also Lipsky, 1970).
3. It should be noted that the importance of the context is a matter of debate. In the general literature on social movements the concept of "political opportunity structure" has been widely used. But as Kriesi et al. (1992) and Rootes (1992a) have pointed out, it is a catch-all term embracing structural and conjunctural features. In the urban movement field the debate — which is discussed later — has concerned the methodology of assessing the effect of the context.
4. The fact that Italian urban movements in the late 1960s were the most radical in Europe is also argued by Ceccarelli as being due to the failure of Italian political institutions to open themselves to a working class which had grown rapidly through industrialisation. He sees the Italian urban movement experience as due to a failure of adjustment in the transition to advanced capitalism rather than, as French Marxist writers did, to the potential capacity of urban movements in advanced capitalism.
5. Other aspects of the political context are not dealt with here. For example, electoral rules affect the ease with which minorities can gain parliamentary representation, and hence the probability that movements become political parties.

REFERENCES

Castells, M. (1977) *The urban question*, Edward Arnold, London.
Castells, M. (1983) *The city and the grassroots*, Edward Arnold, London.
Castells, M. (1985) Commentary on C. G. Pickvance's "The rise and fall of urban movements", *Society and Space*, **3**, 55–61.
Caulfield, J. (1988) Canadian urban "reform" and local conditions: an alternative to Harris's "reinterpretation", *International Journal of Urban and Regional Research*, **12**, 477–484.

Ceccarelli, P. (1982) Politics, parties and urban movements: Western Europe, in Fainstein, N.I. and Fainstein, S.S. (eds), *Urban policy under capitalism*, Sage, Beverly Hills, pp. 261–276.

Diani, M. (1992) The concept of social movement, *Sociological Review*, 40, 1–25.

Dunleavy, P. (1979) *Urban political analysis*, Macmillan, London.

Dunleavy, P. (1991) *Democracy, bureaucracy and public choice*, Harvester Wheatsheaf, London.

Eder, K. (1993) *The new politics of class*, Sage, London.

Fainstein, N.I. and Fainstein, S.S. (1974) *Urban political movements*, Prentice-Hall, Englewood Cliffs.

Fainstein, N.I. and Fainstein, S.S. (1985) Economic restructuring and the rise of urban social movements, *Urban Affairs Quarterly*, 21, 187–206.

Gaspar, J. (1984) Urbanization: growth, problems and policies in Williams, A.M. (ed.), *Southern Europe transformed*, Harper and Row, London.

Gendrot, S.N. (1982) Governmental responses to popular movements: France and the United States, in Fainstein, N.I. and Fainstein, S.S. (eds), *Urban policy under capitalism*, Sage, Beverly Hills, pp. 272–299.

Hamel, P. (1991) *Action collective et démocratie locale: les mouvements urbains Montréalais*, Les Presses de l'Université de Montréal, Montreal.

Harris, R. (1987) A social movement in urban politics: a reinterpretation of urban reform in Canada, *International Journal of Urban and Regional Research*, 11, 363–381.

Harris, R. (1988) The interpretation of Canadian urban reform : a reply to Caulfield, *International Journal of Urban and Regional Research*, 12, 484–489.

Hirschman, A. (1982) *Shifting involvements*, Martin Robertson, London.

Inglehart, R. (1990) *Culture shift in advanced industrial society*, Princeton Univ. Press, Princeton.

Jenkins, J.C. (1983) Resource mobilization theory and the study of social movements, *Annual Review of Sociology*, 9, 527–553.

Katznelson, I. (1981) *City trenches*, Pantheon, New York.

Kitschelt, H. (1986) Political opportunity structures and political protest: anti-nuclear movements in four democracies, *British Journal of Political Science*, 16, 57–85.

Klandermans, B. (1991) New social movements and resource mobilization: the European and the American approach revisited, in Rucht, D. (ed.), *Research on social movements*, Westview, Boulder, pp. 17–44.

Kriesi, H., Koopmans, R., Duyvendak, J.W. and Gingni, G. (1992) New social movements and political opportunities in Western Europe, *European Journal of Political Research*, 22, 219–244.

Lipsky, M. (1970) *Protest in city politics*, Rand McNally, Chicago.

Lowe, S. (1986) *Urban social movements*, Macmillan, London.

Lui, T.L. (1984) *Urban protests in Hong Kong: a sociological study of housing conflicts*, M.Phil Thesis, University of Hong Kong.

Mayer, M. (1991) Social movement research and social movement practice: the U.S. pattern, in Rucht, D. (ed.), *Research on social movements*, Westview, Boulder.

Mullins, P. (1987) Community and urban movements, *Sociological Review*, 35, 347–369.

Olives, J. (1976) The struggle against urban renewal in the "Cité d'Aliarte" (Paris) in Pickvance, C.G. (ed.), *Urban sociology: critical essays*, Tavistock, London, pp. 174–197.

Olson, M. (1965) *The logic of collective action*, Harvard University Press, Cambridge, Mass.

Parkin, F. (1968) *Middle class radicalism*, Manchester University Press, Manchester.

Pickvance, C.G. (1976) On the study of urban social movements, in Pickvance, C.G. (ed.), *Urban sociology: critical essays*, Tavistock, London, pp. 198–218.

Pickvance, C.G. (1977a) Marxist approaches to the study of urban politics: divergences among some recent French studies, *International Journal of Urban and Regional Research*, **1**, 219–255.

Pickvance, C.G. (1977b) From "social base" to "social force": some analytical issues in the study of urban protest, in Harloe, M. (ed.), *Captive cities*, Wiley, Chichester, pp. 175–186.

Pickvance, C.G. (1985) The rise and fall of urban movements and the role of comparative analysis, *Society and Space*, **3**, 31–53.

Pickvance, C.G. (1986a) Voluntary associations, in Burgess, R. (ed.), *Key variables in social investigation*, Routledge and Kegan Paul, London, pp. 223–245.

Pickvance, C.G. (1986b) Concepts, contexts and comparison in the study of urban movements: a reply to M. Castells, *Society and Space*, **4**, 221–231.

Pickvance, C.G. (1994) Social movements in the transition from state socialism: convergence or divergence, in Maheu, L. (ed.), *Social movements and social classes: new actors and agendas*, Sage, London, pp. 123–150.

Pickvance, C.G. and Preteceille, E. (eds) (1991) *State restructuring and local power: a comparative perspective*, Pinter, London.

Piven, F.F. and Cloward, R.A. (1977) *Poor people's movements*, Vintage, New York.

Rootes, C.A. (1992a) Political opportunity structures, political competition and the development of social movements, Paper to First European Conference on Social Movements, Berlin.

Rootes, C.A. (1992b) The new politics and the new social movements: accounting for British exceptionalism, *European Journal of Political Research*, **22**, 171–191.

Runciman, W.G. (1966) *Relative deprivation and social justice*, Routledge and Kegan Paul, London.

Saunders, P. (1979) *Urban politics*, Hutchinson, London.

Saunders, P. (1986) *Social theory and the urban question*, Hutchinson, London.

Wates, N. (1976) *The battle for Tolmers Square*, Routledge and Kegan Paul, London.

13 Thinking about the Edge: the Concept of Marginality

ANTOINE BAILLY
University of Geneva, Switzerland

ERIC WEISS-ALTANER
University of Quebec, Montreal

INEQUALITY: A DRIVING CONCERN OF SOCIAL SCIENCE

To an important extent, the social sciences have developed through their confrontations with the differences and inequalities that divide (and bind) individuals, groups and areas. The explanation, criticism and justification of such differences have driven the growth of theory and description in social science. Over the past 150 years, geographers, urban and regional planners, economists, sociologists, political scientists and anthropologists have filled libraries with studies of poverty, the *Agrarfrage*, the "housing question" and other manifestations of social and spatial differences. Among others, the concepts of marginality, periphery, deviance, minority, segregation, exclusion and exploitation have all seen service in these efforts to understand the nuances of socio-spatial asymmetry.

In this chapter, we shall examine the merits of "marginality" as a tool for analysis and policy in this area. Marginality's etymology evokes the geometric metaphor of centre and periphery, while its range of reference spans both the physical and the social, thereby heightening the concept's attractiveness for thinking at the same time about the social *and* the spatial dimensions of human differences and inequalities. Although associated with the theory of modernisation in the 1960s, "marginality" has not been welded to any of the modern contending theories of history and society: liberalism, Marxism or other "radical" outlooks — like dependency theory — that, during the cold war, tried to adopt a critical stance towards the institutions of capitalist society without submitting to Soviet Marxism. These traits taken together make the concept of marginality attractive for thinking about the old and new "edges" in the Europe that is emerging from the collapse of the Soviet Union and of the geopolitical constellations of the last 40 years.

Europe at the Margins: New Mosaics of Inequality. Edited by Costis Hadjimichalis and David Sadler
© 1995 European Science Foundation. Published in 1995 by John Wiley & Sons Ltd

MARGINALITY: ETYMOLOGY AND MODERN HISTORY

Since the 1970s, the concept of marginality has enjoyed great popularity in Europe — first in Italy, then in France (Catelli, 1976; Turnaturi, 1976; Ferradotti, 1978; Guarassi, 1978; Bianchi et al., 1979; Barel, 1982). Yet surprisingly little attention has gone to marginality's historical and epistemological underpinnings. The word's etymological lineage is ancient, deriving from the Latin *margo, marginis*: edge, border, frontier. Its earliest recorded usage in French and English is medieval. "Margin" appears, with those meanings, in French in the early thirteenth century (Robert, 1988), and crosses over into England by the sixteenth century (*OED*, 1971). The term first entered modern social science through economics, in the 1870s. It appears with a quite different meaning in sociology: Park's (1928) "marginal man". Although these two meanings dominated marginality's usage in the social sciences until recently, two other early uses of the meaning of "margin" — although not of the word itself — merit mention here: William James's "fringe" in his psychology of perception and the stream of thought (1890), and Ratzel's (1903) distinction of core versus periphery in geography.

Eighteenth- and nineteenth-century discussions on the meaning of exchange value flowered into the "marginalist revolution" wrought by the Austrian and Lausanne schools after 1870. "Marginal analysis" in economics became a framework for studying the reactions to incremental changes in the economic environment of individuals and firms (Machlup, 1946). Liberal microeconomics in particular defined itself around this particular view of marginality — as adjustment to change "at the edge" or "at the margin" of the area or the flow in question. A marginalist paradigm and the metaphor of optimalisation under constraints became central to the *Weltanschauung* of liberal economists.

This emphasis on reactions to incremental change (Machlup, 1946) suffuses marginal analysis. To many economists, it is precisely this outlook that has given economics its scientific *lettres de noblesse*. Von Thünen's (1826) pioneering study of land use is one of the earliest examples of marginalist analysis. Nevertheless, it is not to this usage of marginality that we look when advocating the use of the term for the study of social and spatial differences.

Outside of liberal economics, "marginal" appears fleetingly before the 1960s, with the important exception of Robert Park's (1928) concept of the "marginal man" (*sic*). Most notably as a result of migration, the marginal man straddles two cultures. A modern, urban Janus, the immigrant is drawn towards two centres of attraction, as Park so clearly states in the following excerpt. Park's double-edged concept cuts through the complexity of urban life and cosmopolitanism, and derives from a spatial metaphor of attraction:

When, however, the walls of the medieval ghetto were torn down and the Jew was permitted to participate in the cultural life of the peoples among whom he lived, there appeared a new type of personality, namely, a cultural hybrid, a man living and sharing intimately in the cultural life and traditions of two distinct peoples; never quite willing to break, even if he were permitted to do so, with his past and his traditions, and not quite accepted, because of racial prejudice, in the new society in which he sought to find a place. He was a man on the margin of two cultures and two societies, which never completely interpenetrated and fused. The emancipated Jew was, and is, historically and typically the marginal man, the first cosmopolite and citizen of the world. He is, par excellence, the "stranger" whom Simmel, himself a Jew, has described with such profound insight and understanding in his *Sociologie*. . . . The autobiographies of Jewish immigrants . . . are all different versions of the same story — the story of the marginal man; the man who, emerging from the ghetto in which he lived in Europe, is seeking to find a place in the freer, more complex and cosmopolitan life of an American city. One may learn from these autobiographies how the process of assimilation actually takes place in the individual immigrant. In the more sensitive minds its effects are as profound and as disturbing as some of the religious conversions of which William James has given us so classical an account in his *Varieties of Religious Experience* (Park, 1928, reprinted 1967, p. 205).

Two meanings, two disciplines: "marginal" as *incremental effect* (economics) and as *cultural plasticity* (sociology). Even today, these are the meanings of marginality that register most strongly in the social sciences, if we may judge by those pollsters of technical usage, the dictionaries and encyclopaedias of social science. A comparison of several such compendia reveals mention of:

- the economic meaning alone: Foulquié (1962); Back et al. (1967); Sills (1968); Branciard (1978); Kuper and Kuper (1985); Bullock et al. (1988); Alquier (1990)
- Park's meaning alone: Zadrozny (1959); Thinès and Lempereur (1971); Reading (1977); Grawitz (1981); Koschnick (1984); Reber (1985); Doron and Parot (1991)
- both economic marginal analysis and of Park's meaning: Seligman (1930); Gould and Kolb (1964); Birou (1966); Foulquié (1978).

The topological metaphor of the "edge" also appears in William James's great work, *The principles of psychology* (James, 1890). James uses the word "fringe" — together with a musical metaphor, "psychic overtones" — to express important parts of his theory of perception and thinking, which exerted a strong influence among psychologists and philosophers of his time, John Dewey quite notably among them. In Chapter 8 ("The relations of minds to other things") of the *Principles*, James distinguishes between "knowledge of acquaintance" and "knowledge about" things, or, as he says, between *kennen* and *wissen* or *connaître* and *savoir* (James, 1890, vol. 1,

p. 221). "Knowledge about" an object is mediated by an awareness of the multiple relations that link the object in question with the rest of life:

> Let us use the words psychic overtone, suffusion, or fringe, to designate the influence of a faint brain-process upon our thought, as it makes it aware of relations and objects but dimly perceived.
>
> If we then consider the *cognitive function* of different states of mind, we may feel assured that the difference between those that are mere "acquaintance," and those that are "knowledges-*about*" . . . is reducible almost entirely to the absence or presence of psychic fringes or overtones. Knowledge *about* a thing is knowledge of its relations. Acquaintance with it is limitation to the bare impression which it makes. Of most of its relations we are only aware in the penumbral nascent way of a "fringe" of unarticulated affinities about it (James, 1890, vol. 1, pp. 258–259).
>
> The traditional psychologist talks like one who should say a river consists of nothing but pailsful, spoonsful, quartpotsful, barrelsful, and other moulded forms of water. Even were the pails and the pots all actually standing in the stream, still between them the free water would continue to flow. It is just this free water of consciousness that psychologists resolutely overlook. Every definite image in the mind is steeped and dyed in the free water that flows round it. With it goes the sense of its relations, near and remote, the dying echo of whence it came to us, the dawning sense of whither it is to lead. The significance, the value, of the image is all in this halo or penumbra that surrounds and escorts it — or rather that is fused into one with it and has become bone of its bone and flesh of its flesh; leaving it, it is true, an image of the same *thing* it was before, but making it an image of that thing newly taken and freshly understood (James, 1890, vol. 1, p. 255).

The Jamesian notion of marginal consciousness, or "off-centered" awareness, still registers a century later, as witness Reber (1985), Piéron (1979) and Foulquié (1962).

None of the three meanings of "margin" mentioned so far explicitly evokes differences in *power*. Liberal economics' insistence on adaptation to incremental changes, and James's account of perception and thinking, lie outside the range of meaning that attracts us to the term of "marginality". However, Park's image of marginality as a hesitation between two poles of cultural attraction, as a way-station in cultural evolution, shows a use of the term that builds on the "geometrics" of social distance and differentiation.

Although the German geographer Ratzel (1903) did not use the word "margin", his couplet of *Kernland* and *Nebenland* — core area and adjacent or peripheral lands — constitutes what is perhaps the earliest use in geography of the metaphor of centrality to speak of spatial differences in power and of the articulation of different areas and populations in an interregional hierarchy:

> La formation d'un Etat résulte de l'action de forces politiques tout d'abord concentrées, puis développées sur une plus ample surface, de telle manière que de nouveaux espaces se trouvent ajoutés au noyau initial; on peut distinguer

en tout Etat des *territoires anciens et des territoires récents, des espaces médullaires et des espaces périphériques.* . . . En outre, comme en Italie, ce noyau n'était pas dépourvu du pouvoir de revivifier et de rajeunir la périphérie; c'est en effet de la Perside que partit le mouvement rénovateur des Sassanides. N'importe quelle carte politique porte ce genre de distinctions, particulièrement manifestes dans certains Etats imparfaits comme le Soudan où, privés du lien unificateur d'une frontière englobante, les Etats font l'effet d'agglomérats de cellules. Les Etats dits unitaires sont cependant eux aussi bien loin de constituer un tissu parfaitement homogène. Derrière les divisions arbitraires en départements ou en provinces, se profilent d'anciennes frontières historiques; dans le plus homogène des grands Etats européens, la France, la Corse représente bien davantage qu'un simple département.

Autant l'espace médullaire est essentiellement un et frappe l'Etat de son empreinte la plus authentique, autant les *territoires périphériques* sont fondamentalement divers. Fortement marqués dans leur culture et même dans leur race, ils ont souvent reçu de la nature une position, un climat et un sol tout-à-fait spécifiques (Ratzel, 1903, pp. 169–170).

Ratzel's image of core and periphery was echoed strongly — either through direct borrowing or through independent adoption of the image — in the discussions on world economic development that ensued after 1945. Raúl Prebisch, director of the United Nations Economic Commission for Latin America, developed the "CEPAL school" that insisted on the existence of structural inequalities between industrialised and developing or "peripheral" countries (Prebisch, 1963, 1971). Other Latin Americans developed and discussed "dependency theories" of economic development (Cardoso and Faletto, 1969; Frank, 1979; Chilcote and Johnson, 1983), while the concept of "unequal exchange" coexisted within a notion of unequal development (Emmanuel, 1969; Amin, 1973). The terms "dependency" and "periphery" appear in social science dictionaries, with these meanings, by about 1970 (Birou, 1966; Reading, 1977; Branciard, 1978; Grawitz, 1981; Kuper and Kuper, 1985; Alquier, 1990).

"GEOMETRICS": MATHEMATICAL METAPHORS FOR UNDERSTANDING SOCIETY

The centre as pivot and chief point within a circumscribed space is a metaphor from Euclidean geometry. A circle is defined by its centre and a distance: it is the locus of points that are all equidistant from the centre. The defining importance of "centre" in this geometric construction has ever after offered an image to express gradients of power, influence and attraction. Figuratively speaking, the "centre" of influence within a territory is that place — that City on a Hill — where riches, trade and power meet to prosper and spread. Of course, this location of great economic, political or cultural "intensity" is not necessarily at the geometric centre of the territory (*vide* Moscow, Berlin, London, New York, São Paulo, Buenos

Aires, Beijing, Tokyo, Bombay). The geometrical metaphor of centre–margin gives the centre high points for power, income or indeed any desideratum. Thereby, "centre" and "margin" are liberated from strict adherence to physical distance. "Distance" itself becomes a metaphor, measuring not miles and kilometres but differences or changes along the metrics of whatever desideratum is at issue.

The other terms that social sciences have used in the twentieth century to speak and think of differences also partake of these geometrical metaphors. Thus, poverty (Donnison, 1981), minority, deviance, inequality (Coates et al. 1977) and differentiation highlight deviations from a norm, represented by distances from a "line". Segregation and exclusion focus on barriers to mobility within a physical or a desideratum space. Has the term "marginality" become popular in contemporary social science because the concept can encompass all others, by dint of its etymology and relative freedom from previous ideological attachments? Or does the recent acceptance of the term express the emergence of social and geographical problems that, by their novelty, complexity or intensity have encouraged the adoption of what was a marginally used term? The merits of "marginality" may become more apparent if we compare it to a pair of companion concepts: "periphery" and "minority" (Schilling-Kaletsch, 1979).

PERIPHERY, MINORITY AND MARGINALITY

Geographers and spatial economists use "centre–periphery" much more readily than they do "centre–margin" or "centrality–marginality", even though both margin and periphery derive from Latin words referring to geometrical edges. By the middle of the sixteenth century in both English and French (Robert, 1988; OED, 1971), "periphery" referred more specifically to the line forming the boundary of a curved plane figure or surface. By the eighteenth century, it had acquired the looser meaning in English of a "surrounding area" (compare this with Ratzel's later Nebenland).

Derived from a notion of circumference, "periphery" evokes a position at the limits of a circumscribed space. Periphery contrasts graphically with centre, the point at which power and riches converge within that space. Perhaps "centre" and "periphery" speak more directly to economists' and geographers' intuitional metrics, shaped by their preoccupation with transport costs and market areas. Christaller's "central places" are a case in point. It is not surprising that economists and geographers should use "centre–periphery" when studying such eminently territorial questions as the dynamics of urban centres (growth poles) or when looking at international development as the result of the geopolitical interaction between a centre made up of aggressive and highly industrialised countries and a periphery of less industrialised or agrarian nations. Terminological habit aside, however, "margin" could stand in for "periphery".

"Minority" is a term that has gained importance in sociology and demography, particularly in the United States, where "minority studies" inquire into the life of the country's ethnic, racial and cultural minorities. Any number of traits can distinguish a minority from the majority, but chief among them is that of number. Within the limits of a given territory, the members of a minority can be identified as such by their shared "location" along one or several socially significant dimensions (such as age, sex, religion, ethnicity or language) and because they are outnumbered — sometimes vastly so — by the persons making up the demographic majority along the same characteristics within that territory.

Might "minority" be subsumed under "marginality"? Not without losing some valuable distinctions and advantages from a terminological division of labour. Both concepts can refer to many similar dimensions of social status. However, each term highlights a different characteristic in particular. "Minority" immediately summons up the dimension of relative numerical weakness. "Marginality" evokes relative social, political, economic or cultural weakness. Not all minorities are marginal. Stratification and hierarchical asymmetries are among the oldest features of human society. If the poor shall never cease out of the land, it is largely because the rich will not leave either. Class societies (Paci, 1973) have ever been ruled by minorities in firm control of the commanding heights. Also, nothing in the concept of "minority" — nor of "poverty" for that matter — explicitly refers to space. This may not matter if inquiry focuses, as so many sociologists do, on groups and their characteristics without regard to the geographic distribution of either. Marginality and centrality, however, have both social and spatial dimensions. By extending the metaphor of location from physical space to social "space", these terms make it possible to see the geographic complexity of social differentiation.

Social marginality appears to be found not only at the geometrical periphery of a city or a country or a continent. It is only a verbal paradox to find the "margin" in the nation's economic and political centre. Poverty in the midst of plenty is unfortunately not uncommon. Consider the downtown slums or the suburban *bidonvilles*, or even the vertical differentiation of the nineteenth-century Parisian apartment building, where the tenants' social marginality rose as they climbed the stairs from the *piano nobile* to the artists' and widows' garrets above. Idiographic studies of French regional disparities since 1950 have revealed pockets of poverty both near and far from the nation's capital, in suburban Courneuve and in the Massif Central.

There is no necessary link between geographical and social location. Neither is there any necessary link among periphery, minority and marginality; nor among centre, majority and centrality. Social élites have always been minorities, located in the capital and in no way marginal. Pre-capitalist cities were "held" by agrarian élites whose power originated in the countryside and not in the cities. These remarks are well worth keeping in mind when we look at Europe today. "Marginality" does not necessarily mean "southern and eastern Europe". Social, economic and political marginality can be found in the core of Europe's Big Apples. The usual association between the geographical periphery and social marginality may be a residue of imperialist and colonialist attitudes of the late nineteenth and early twentieth centuries. Colonies and "colonials" were seen as being far away in every sense. Such "metropolitan" world-views paid little attention to the details of colonial reality, preferring to consider those territories as uniformly backward dependencies. Sociologists provided only some relief from this outlook, through their attention to the interaction among groups and individuals (Moscovici, 1979).

Thus, the study of marginality must go beyond simply projecting economic and social dimensions on specific locations. One must look within and without: inside and outside the social group, inside and outside the region. As always happens when space enters the picture, the geographical scale of analysis must be kept in mind, in order to avoid ecological fallacies of composition. La zone can disappear from view when we look at the Paris region "as a whole" within France. Similar vanishing acts can occur when we look at the planet in terms of "North–South relations" and forget the regional variety within those blocs. In fact, almost every centre can be another centre's periphery (see Christaller, 1935; Lösch, 1944). As the song says, "Everybody's somebody's fool". The courthouse square in the county seat may look mighty fine from the boondocks, but up in the state capital it is just a country backwater. And so on up to Gotham City, where (with apologies to doggerel and Boston) the "Lodges speak only to Cabots and the Cabots speak only to God."

These are fundamental questions in Europe today. The economic integration of Europe, the world recession, the rise of newly industrialised countries in Asia and the collapse of state communism and of the former Soviet bloc are unleashing changes that will recast the map of social differentiation. European firms are adopting a continental outlook. Concerned with their capacity to compete in the European and even wider market, many large enterprises are looking to their "vertical" coherence, without regard for the consequences that their plant closures, plant relocations or multi-sourcing decisions may have on the "horizontal" relationships among subnational regions. Caught in the "blind spot" of firms' strategies, these regions may slide into recession, stagnation and marginality, becoming pariahs in the new Europe. How to reconcile the differing geographical scales of the strategies undertaken by multinational (and eventually, also transnational) firms, by the EU, by national and local governments, by national unions and by myriads of other European non-governmental organisations?

INCREASED AWARENESS OF SOCIO-SPATIAL INEQUALITIES AFTER 1945

After 1945, governments and international organisations funded research into regional income and employment disparities, in the developed and in the developing countries. The studies showed that the income and employment gains from the unprecented post-war expansion were not being shared by all. Academics and independent writers also contributed to renewed public and private awareness of existing inequalities and of the marginalisation facing certain groups or regions. The titles speak for themselves: *Paris et le désert français* (Gravier, 1947); *Night comes to the Cumberlands* (Caudill, 1962); *The other America* (Harrington, 1962). The situation was similar or worse in the developing countries. On the basis of his research in Mexico and the Caribbean, Oscar Lewis (1959) proposed the construct of "culture of poverty" to help understand the persistence of urban poverty everywhere.

A generation later, after the end of the *Trente glorieuses* (years of economic growth), the inequalities are still there, and for some groups — such as Afro-Americans in the United States — the future looks grim: *The new American poverty* (Harrington, 1984) and *The truly disadvantaged* (Wilson, 1987). As for the "South" of the planet, the 1960s and 1970s, heralded by the international development community as the South's first and second "development decades", have given way to the "lost decade" of the 1980s.

The evidence of disparities prompted certain writers (Mishan, 1964; Bailly, 1981) to develop the notion of spatial welfare and a geography of welfare, which Mishan (1964, pp. 5–6) defined as being concerned with the ranking of the geographic situation of social groups along specific value scales. They asked, who gets what, where and how? Who consumes and who does not? Who are the "marginals"? Do they stand outside the network of social and geographic relations? The answers to these questions show how the presence of marginality and marginal groups/regions function as a barometer of the pressures being exerted on specific societies, and a harbinger of the transformations that might ensue (Berthoud et al., 1981).

Since 1945, the study of marginalisation became a way of understanding the reproduction, the renewal and the recomposition of societies (Bartels, 1978). The renewed awareness of regional disparities triggered debates in Europe and the Americas that followed two main directions, one liberal and the other Marxist or "radical". Liberal perspectives drew upon neo-classical economics in order to devise policies that would favour economic growth and spread it more fairly among individuals, groups and regions. Marxists and radical critics of liberalism emphasised the mechanisms in capitalist society that, in their view, created and reproduced personal, group and regional inequality. These debates have not lost their relevance, despite the demise of official, Soviet Marxism and the seeming victory of capitalist social designs.

COMPETING THEORIES OF ECONOMY AND SOCIETY

Liberal viewpoints

The liberal framework emphasises market mechanisms, private property, technological and organisational change and shifts in the international division of labour when studying the marginalisation of groups and areas, and when proposing policy initiatives. For example, Myrdal (1957), looking at the Third World, suggested how economic growth and technological change could produce regional income inequalities. In his scenario, capital ownership concentrates itself in the hands of very large and dynamic enterprises, which locate their most important service activities — their headquarters — in certain "world cities". Manufacturing firms that produce "mature" products calling for less technological innovation become footloose, moving towards peripheral areas or countries. Improvements in transport and communication, together with the eager welcome given to foreign investors in many Third World countries since 1945, encouraged multinationals to open branch plants there and to adopt "multi-sourcing" as a production strategy. Multi-sourcing disseminates the stages of production of specific goods throughout the planet: certain parts come from Brazil, others from Taiwan and Ireland in order to produce a final good in Michigan. As a result, certain areas wax and others wane. Employment is concentrated in certain points of the world system, while employers range over the continents in search of profitability. Multinational and transnational firms in particular, and employers in general, enjoy greater mobility, information and bargaining power than local labour forces. Shifts in the demand for goods can reinforce the processes of centralisation and marginalisation.

From the liberal perspective, such changes, heralded through the price system, motivate entrepreneurs, workers and other economic agents to adapt themselves and their resources to the new conditions (Knox, 1977; Smith, 1977). Responses may come through technological innovation, through new allocations of time and other resources, and through territorial mobility. The responses themselves may set off further adjustments. Thus we have the never-ending story of liberal economics: the "invisible hand" is forever disrupting and rearranging. It is an eschatology of equilibrium gained and equilibrium lost, with eruptions issuing from the bottomless pit of individual creativity and market competition.

The liberal framework is large enough to include many lines of inquiry, ranging from very idiographic and descriptive studies to research quite critical of market imperfections and institutional inefficiencies. Social criticism is not a monopoly of Marxist/radical theories (although liberal critics of capitalism do cease and desist before denying — as do Marxists — the moral right of capitalists to profits).

Marxist/radical viewpoints

Marxist and radical writers look "behind" the functioning of markets to the dynamics of class interaction on an interregional and international scale. To them, these are the crucial processes that shape the decisions — concerning the production, circulation, consumption and distribution of wealth and income — that in turn affect the location and relocation of investment, income and employment.

Marxist and radical analysts (Peet, 1991) have drawn greatly on the tools of historical and dialectical materialism in order to understand the "games" people play within a world system and within social structures that are genetically marked by inequality and that pivot on the creation, appropriation and distribution of surplus value. They focus on the domination of labour by capital, which allows capital to exploit workers and thereby garner the profits necessary to its renewal and expansion. In this vein, Edel (1976) used Marx's rent theory to provide a reading of the players, stakes and rules involved in the internal dynamics of metropolitan areas and in the configuration and reconfiguration of the network of world cities. Others have connected the rise or decline of specific English regions with Great Britain's industrialisation and imperial expansion, with its consequent effects on the spatial division of labour and on flows of surplus value. In their eyes, changes in the mode of production — such as the west European transition from feudalism to capitalism or, as perhaps in Russia, from capitalism to state communism and back — profoundly reshape a country's social and spatial order.

Marxist and radical studies of spatial differentiation have also been very heterogeneous. Marxists themselves were split by internal debates — about tactics and strategy in achieving the transition from capitalism to socialism, about the nature of Soviet society and the international communist movement. They were also divided by national intellectual traditions. In France, Althusser's interpretation held rigorous sway in the 1970s (Althusser, 1970; Althusser and Balibar, 1971). Under this influence, Castells (1972) and Preteceille (1975), for example, proposed the hypothesis that cities be seen chiefly in their role in the reproduction of labour power. British and North American Marxists were much less deductive in their methods, and also much further removed from the orthodoxies of Soviet communism.

Radical geographers studying capitalist countries have concerned themselves to a great extent with the weaker links in the chain: lagging industries, minorities and marginal groups of all kinds (Harvey, 1973; see also the bibliography cited by Coraggio et al., 1977). Interest in the poor of mining areas like Lorraine and Wales has fuelled concern for stagnant industrial sectors and the cities of the "first" and "second" industrial revolutions. The plight of women in suburbs and cities, and of immigrants in slums and poorer neighbourhoods have figured prominently among the research priorities of the radical school. For a while, especially in France from the mid-1960s to the mid-1970s (Topalov, 1989), their priorities were in tune with those of European governments, which funded research in order to formulate policies at regional, national and European levels. Other analysts, without explicitly rallying to a Marxist theory of society, have preferred to bring out the many ways in which power and domination manifest themselves in daily life (Di Méo, 1991). They have shown the totalitarian aspects of regulatory institutions created by the industrial and bourgeois state, such as hospitals, prisons and schools. Pioneered in France by Foucault (1975), this research agenda has subsequently spread to the UK and North America.

By emphasising the existence and importance of domination and exploitation in capitalist society, Marxist and radical researchers have tried to look at it "from the outside", in order to criticise its core values and priorities. They have not only measured the presence of inequality, but have suggested that it is a continuing and essential part of capitalism. Where liberals see the hope of surcease from inequality (eschatology of equilibrium), Marxists and radicals see recurrent and persistent — structural — inequality. Thus their eschatology of transcendence, through evolution or revolution.

LIBERAL AND MARXIST/RADICAL PERSPECTIVES ON MARGINALITY

Each approach, liberal or Marxist/radical, offers its own explanations of marginality in Europe, and suggests different policies to deal with the problem. Liberals see the marginalisation of groups and regions as transitional. The mobility of labour, capital and technological knowledge among regions, and among activities and firms, should eventually reduce spatial income differences, which are due — in their eyes — mainly to differences in human or physical capital endowment per worker. Liberal policy recommendations have emphasised incentives to mobility, through direct or indirect subsidies to training, and to transport and communications, confident that laggard regions can thereby become more attractive.

For Marxists, marginality is an unsurprising outcome of the normal functioning of capitalism. As a particular system of places offering different possibilities and limitations to their occupants, capitalism gives disproportionate wealth and power to a minority, while giving the rest of the population much more modest rations of both. Unemployed workers, family members not in the labour force, inhabitants of marginal regions are seen to play an important role in the reproduction of capitalism and in the determination of the profitability of investment. Even if such "industrial reserve armies" are socially marginalised and excluded from consumption, they represent an alternative labour supply, which can dampen the wage demands of employed workers or respond eagerly to business demand for workers during times of economic upswing.

Although a product and a sign of inequality, marginal groups and regions are rarely useless, totally disconnected from the rest of society, making utterly no contribution to global economic growth. Marginality is not limbo. The view that marginality equals afunctionality was debated and strongly criticised in a Latin American debate of the 1970s, summarised by Roberts (1978, pp. 158–177). Not only is marginality consistent with integration into the economy, but integration can reinforce marginality. Kept away from home by the hunt for fleeting, flitting jobs, the poor studied by Roberts in Guatemala City could not form solid ties for collective action either at work or in their neighbourhood of residence. Roberts (1973, p. 335) concluded "that the incapacity of the poor to organise effectively is due to their overintegration into the city and not to their isolation from its political and social processes". The spread of a "parallel", "unofficial", "underground" or "informal" economy in Europe and elsewhere in the world, and the emergence of new occupational statuses (characterised by impermanence and instability: temporary work, short and medium-term labour contracts) are seen by Marxist/radical analysts as contemporary means to maintain the elasticity of labour supply and thereby protect the profitability of investment in a time of technological flux and world-wide recomposition of geopolitical blocs.

Capitalists dominate workers. In a somewhat different way, large capitalists dominate smaller ones and can thereby contribute to the marginalisation of certain regions. Perroux dedicated much effort to studying the asymmetrical relationships among firms of different size. The larger enterprises in a sector of the economy can sometimes impose prices or other conditions which smaller firms are obliged to take as given. To the extent that such asymmetry is prevalent, the cities — usually the larger ones — that are able to attract the larger firms will be favoured, to the detriment of the smaller cities that are unable to entice or retain these larger firms.

Most of the inhabitants of a country or a continent have little voice over the decisions that fix the number, the salary and the location of jobs. Control over investment and resource allocation lies in the hands of minorities whose enterprises have become very footloose. Regions with better transport and communications, with a more varied labour force, with better training, research and development infrastructure, are better able to attract the more dynamic enterprises, which need flexible and affordable access to workers of varied skills, in order to adopt the technologies that are most appropriate to the firm's strategy. Regional disparities can be cumulative, although this is certainly not inevitable. The existing geographical distribution of jobs, investment, equipment, infra-structure, people, knowledge and technology can favour those already at the top (Coffey and Polese, 1987). However, the regional disparities race is never run. Conditions sometimes change in fundamental ways, challenging regional societies to maintain their relative position or to improve it while new technology, new demands or new conditions of supply keep such windows of opportunity still open.

In France, for example, peripheral regions that had remained largely rural have begun to receive subordinate industrial functions, while Paris centralises higher management and leadership tasks. Industry, public administration and the universities tend to choose people with high qualifications. The activities that remain in the centre, that is in the highly urbanised areas characterised by high costs, are the jobs requiring an environment rich in positive externalities and agglomeration economies, low transaction costs and perhaps also sophisticated consumption oppor-tunities. On the other hand, functions that can be satisfied with less skilled labour that is easier to train and cheaper to hire may move to more peripheral, less urbanised and less costly areas. Subordinate functions migrate towards marginal regions and their less skilled, cheaper and politically more pliable workforces. Left behind is an urban infrastructure — roads, warehouses, factory buildings — that, if not recycled and renewed, may deteriorate and become signposts of a new marginality, in the heart of the nation's capital.

Acting in this way, enterprises establish a hierarchy among their workers. Those among them whose cost of reproduction is small will receive lower wage rates. Inversely, the workers whose skills require more inputs to create and to reproduce can win higher wage rates from their employers. When the firm requires more skilled and sophisticated workers, it will only find them in large cities. The hierarchy of occupational status and wage rates among workers is echoed by a hierarchy of places, some of which become marginal because their inhabitants rank low on income and job hierarchies.

Throughout these processes, the pilots "steering" the path of incomes, jobs and technological change follow stars that often reflect only dimly the wishes or the needs of most of the population. Marginality and marginalisation result from those decisions. Marginality is not an accident of history or an unfortunate "dysfunction" of an otherwise benevolent system. It is a continuing by-product of the central mechanisms and "feedback relationships" that drive industrial societies today. European policies meant to help depressed regions have focused on making these areas attractive to capitalist investment once again, rather than trying to change capitalism and risking a general collapse of economic growth. This is the dilemma of many governments in the context of economic liberalism and international mobility of funds, goods, equipment and technology.

CONCLUSIONS

Despite its relatively recent diffusion, the concept of "marginality" is becoming a driving concern of social sciences, through studies of social, economic and spatial disparities. The concept speaks of a reality at least as old as urban society, and the urban riots in Europe and America have a long history . . . leading sometimes to revolution. From whatever point of view, marginality has always been a sign of crisis leading to social, economic and political unrest.

To speak of marginality in a city, in a region, in a country or between nations is to talk of inequalities driven by exploitation and alienation, and to seek the driving factors. Marginality and marginalisation in the city, in rural areas, in the Third World, challenge us to imagine institutions and policies that can prevent its spread, even if international forces are at work.

Although marginality as a scientific concept and as a fact has gained much recognition (and some of its dimensions have been explored in this book), we have not thought fully enough about its causes and consequences for the future of European societies, nor about the conflicts that grow out of society's unequal use of space. After a period when the agenda was concerned with regional disparities, European nations are now looking for new policies to help against new problems. The indications are that the fight against marginality will be one of the main political questions of the twenty-first century, as Europe debates not only a way of life but also how to treat people.

REFERENCES

Alquier, C. (1990) *Dictionnaire encyclopédique économique et social*, 2nd edn, Economica, Paris.

Althusser, L. (1970) *For Marx*, Vintage, New York.

Althusser, L. and Balibar, E. (1971) *Reading Capital*, Pantheon, New York.

Amin, S. (1973) *Le développement inégal*, Minuit, Paris.

Back, H., Cirullies, H. and Marquard, G. (1967) *Polec: dictionary of politics and economics. Dictionnaire de politique et d'économie. Lexikon für Politik und Wirtschaft*, 2nd edn, Walter de Gruyter, Berlin.

Bailly, A.S. (1981) *Géographie du bien-être*, Presses Universitaires de France, Paris.

Barel, Y. (1982) *La marginalité et ses territoires*, Université de Grenoble, Grenoble.

Bartels, Y. (1978) Raumwissenschaftliche Aspekte sozialer Disparitäten. H. Bobek zum 75. Geburtstag. *Mitteilungen der Österreichischen Gesellschaft*, **120**, 2, 227–242.

Berthoud, R., Brown, J. and Cooper, S. (1981) *Poverty and the development of antipoverty policy in the United Kingdom*, Heinemann, London.

Bianchi, A., Granato, F. and Zingarelli, D. (eds) (1979) *Margina e lotte dei marginali*, Angeli, Milan.
Birou, A. (1966) *Vocabulaire pratique des sciences sociales*, Éditions Ouvrières, Paris.
Branciard, M. (1978) *Dictionnaire économique et social*, Éditions Ouvrières, Paris.
Bullock, A., Trombly, S. and Eadie, B. (eds) (1988) *The Harper dictionary of modern thought*, new and revised edition, Harper and Row, New York.
Cardoso, F.H. and Faletto, E. (1969) *Dependencia y desarrollo en América Latina: ensayo de interpretación sociológica*, Siglo XXI, Mexico.
Castells, M. (1972) *La question urbaine*, Maspero, Paris.
Catelli, G. (ed.) (1976) *La società marginale*, Città Nuova, Milan.
Caudill, H.M. (1962) *Night comes to the Cumberlands: a biography of a depressed area*, Little, Brown, Boston.
Chilcote, R.H. and Johnson, D.L. (eds) (1983) *Theories of development: mode of production or dependency?* Sage, Beverly Hills, California.
Christaller, W. (1935) *Die zentralen Orte in Süddeutschland*, Jena.
Coates, B., Johnston, R. and Knox, P. (1977) *Geography and inequality*, Oxford University Press, Oxford.
Coffey, W. and Polese, M. (1987) *Still living together*, Institute of Political Research, Montreal, Canada.
Coraggio, J.L., Noyelle, T. and Schteingart, M. (1977) Spatial organization, social processes and community struggles in capitalist socioeconomic formations, in Rosenberg, S. (coordinator), *Reading lists in radical political economics*, Union for Radical Political Economics, New York, pp. 128–144.
Di Méo, G. (1991) *L'homme, la société, l'espace*, Anthropos-Economica, Paris.
Donnison, D. (1981) *The politics of poverty*, Robertson, London.
Doron, R. and Parot, F. (eds) (1991) *Dictionnaire de psychologie*, Presses Universitaires de France, Paris.
Edel, M.E. (1976) Marx's theory of rent: urban applications, *Kapitalistate*, San Francisco, 4–5, Summer, 100–124.
Emmanuel, A. (1969) *L'échange inégal*, Maspero, Paris.
Ferradotti, F. (ed,) (1978) *Mercato del lavoro, marginalità sociale e struttura di classe in Italia*, Angeli, Milan.
Foucault, M. (1975) *Surveiller et punir. Naissance de la prison*, Gallimard, Paris.
Foulquié, P., with the collaboration of Saint-Jean, R. (1962) *Dictionnaire de la langue philosophique*, Presses Universitaires de France, Paris.
Foulquié, P. (1978) *Vocabulaire des sciences sociales*, Presses Universitaires de France, Paris.
Frank, A.G. (1979) *Dependent accumulation and underdevelopment*, Monthly Review Press, New York.
Gould, J. and Kolb, W.L. (eds) (1964) *A dictionary of the social sciences*, The Free Press for UNESCO, New York.
Gravier, J.-F. (1947) *Paris et le désert français*, Flammarion, Paris.
Grawitz, M. (1981) *Lexique des sciences sociales*, Dalloz, Paris.
Guarassi, V. (1978) *La condizione marginale*, Sellerio, Palermo.
Harrington, M. (1962) *The other America: poverty in the United States*, Macmillan, New York.
Harrington, M. (1984) *The new American poverty*, Holt, Rinehart and Winston, New York.
Harvey, D. (1973) *Social justice and the city*, Arnold, London.
James, W. (1890) *The principles of psychology*, 2 vols, reprinted 1950, Dover, New York.

Knox, P. (1977) *Social well-being: a spatial perspective*, Oxford University Press, Oxford.

Koschnick, W.J. (1984) *Standard dictionary of the social sciences. Standardwörterbuch für die Sozialwissenschaften*, Vol. 1, K.G. Saur Verlag, Munich.

Kuper, A. and Kuper, J. (eds) (1985) *The social science encyclopedia*, Routledge and Kegan Paul, London.

Lewis, O. (1959) *Five families: Mexican case studies in the culture of poverty*, Basic Books, New York.

Lösch, A. (1944) *The economics of location*, 2nd rev. edn, translated by W.H. Woglom with the assistance of W.F. Stolper, Wiley, New York, 1967.

Machlup, F. (1946) Marginal analysis and empirical research, *American Economic Review*, **36**, 4, September. Reprinted in Machlup, F. (1967), *Essays in economic semantics*, Norton, New York, pp. 147–190.

Mishan, E. (1964) *Welfare economics: five introductory essays*, Random House, New York.

Moscovici, S. (1979) *Psychologie des minorités actives*, Flammarion, Paris.

Myrdal, G. (1957) *Economic theory and underdevelopment*, Duckworth, London.

OED (1971) *The compact edition of the Oxford English Dictionary*, Oxford University Press, New York.

Paci, M. (1973) *Mercato del lavoro e classi sociali in Italia*, Il Mulino, Bologna.

Park, R.E. (1928) Human migration and the marginal man, *American Journal of Sociology*, **33**, May, 881–893. (Reprinted in Turner, R.H. (1967) *Robert E. Park: on social control and collective behavior. Selected papers*, Phoenix Books. University of Chicago Press, Chicago, pp. 194–206.)

Peet, R. (1991) *Global capitalism: theories of societal development*, Routledge, Kegan Paul, London.

Piéron, H. (1979) *Vocabulaire de la psychologie*, 6th edn, Presses Universitaires de France, Paris.

Prebisch, R. (1963) *Hacia una dinámica del desarrollo latinoamericano: con un apéndice sobre el falso dilema entre desarrollo económico y estabilidad monetaria*, Fondo de Cultura Económica, Mexico.

Prebisch, R. (1971) *Change and development — Latin America's great task: report submitted to the Inter-American Development Bank*, Praeger, New York.

Preteceille, E. (1975) *Équipements collectifs, structures urbaines et consommation sociale*, Centre de sociologie urbaine, Paris.

Ratzel, F. (1903) *Géographie politique*, translated by P. Rusch, under the scientific direction of C. Hussy, 1988, Éditions Régionales Européennes, Lausanne, Switzerland.

Reading, H.F. (1977) *A dictionary of the social sciences*, Routledge and Kegan Paul, London.

Reber, A.S. (1985) *The Penguin dictionary of psychology*, Viking, Harmondsworth, England.

Robert, P. (1988) *Le Grand Robert de la langue française*, 2nd edn, dirigée par A. Rey, Éditions Le Robert, Paris.

Roberts, B.R. (1973) *Organizing strangers: poor families in Guatemala City*, University of Texas Press, Austin.

Roberts, B.R. (1978) *Cities of peasants: the political economy of urbanization in the Third World*, Arnold, London.

Schilling-Kaletsch, I. (1979) Zentrum-Peripherie-Modelle in der geographischen Entwicklungsländerforschung. Die Ansätzen von Friedman und Lasuen, *Deutsche Gesellschaft für Friedens- und Konfliktsforschung*, **12**, 39–53.

Seligman, E.R.A. (ed.) assisted by Johnson, A. (1930) *Encyclopaedia of the social sciences*, Macmillan, New York.

Sills, D.L. (ed.) (1968) *International encyclopedia of the social sciences*, Macmillan and The Free Press, New York.

Smith, D. (1973) *Human geography: a welfare approach*, Edward Arnold, London.

Stamp, L. (1964) *The geography of life and death*, Collins, London.

Thinès, G. and Lempereur, A. (1971) *Dictionnaire général des sciences humaines*, Éditions Universitaires, Paris.

Topalov, C. (1989) A history of urban research: the French experience since 1965, *International Journal of Urban and Regional Research*, **13**, 4, 625–651.

Turnaturi, G. (ed.) (1976) *Marginalità e classi sociali*, Savel, Rome.

Wilson, W.J. (1987) *The truly disadvantaged: the inner city, the underclass, and public policy*, University of Chicago Press, Chicago.

Von Thünen, J.H. (1826) *Der isolierte Staat in Beziehung auf Landwirtschaft und Nationalökonomie*, Hamburg.

Zadrozny, J.T. (1959) *Dictionary of social science*, Public Affairs Press, Washington, DC.

14 Open Questions: Piecing Together the New European Mosaic

COSTIS HADJIMICHALIS
Aristotle University of Thessaloniki, Greece

DAVID SADLER
University of Durham, UK

In the introduction to this volume, we stressed our concern with those places and social groups which seem to be "missing out" on the margins of the new Europe. We have brought together a set of contributions which, we hope, can move debate about the future of Europe in fresh directions. In these final editorial comments, we do not intend to summarise what has already been discussed. As was to be expected, however, a lot of issues remain unexplored. The purpose of this last chapter is to highlight some of these open questions. It might be asked, for instance, how the EU can appear "open" and "democratic", when it not only tightly restricts movement by outsiders but also does not give citizenship rights to all people resident inside the EU. Is it possible for men and women in both northern and southern regions to have equal access to new opportunities, as suggested in the White Paper, *Growth, competitiveness and employment* (CEC, 1993a)? How can marginality be identified and who has the power to say who is central and who is marginal, or — put another way — how far is marginality an objective category and how far a matter of language and social perception? And finally, how can marginal people overcome their isolation and collectively struggle for their own rights instead of passively waiting for token compensation?

There are many more such questions. The primary reason behind them, however, is the fact that the construction of the EU is at the same time reinforcing the marginality of those places and people which are socially and spatially excluded from the Union. New frontiers are being established *outside* as well as *inside* the EU (Lipietz, 1993). The outsiders face today a similar process to that which involved the *limes*[1] of old empires against the "barbarians" (Ruffin, 1991). Some former socialist states have become dependent upon the West, while others are destroyed by civil war. The

Europe at the Margins: New Mosaics of Inequality. Edited by Costis Hadjimichalis and David Sadler
© 1995 European Science Foundation. Published in 1995 by John Wiley & Sons Ltd

relatively early moves to accommodate further north European applicant states well ahead of those from the East was a clear indication of where priorities lay. Many of the Scandinavian countries in particular had already begun to adopt a conceptual apparatus of integration similar to that of the EU, based on the principles of free trade and open markets around the Baltic (see Lundqvist and Persson, 1993). To the south and east, the *limes* already differentiates a Catholic-Christian core from a periphery of Orthodox Christianity and Islam. By voting very early for the independence of Slovenia and Croatia, Germany expressed its choice for this *limes*, while the intervention of NATO and the EU in Bosnia against the Serbs clearly showed the preferences of the West.

Inside the EU, a new wall of poverty and marginalisation runs right through all the member states. In the early 1990s, 58 million people were considered as "poor" by the European Commission, having less than half the average per capita income of their respective member state (CEC, 1993b). The number of "poor" has increased by 12% since 1985, and they mostly live in urban areas. There were 3 million homeless people officially recorded, and some 15 million formally unemployed in the EU alone. In the under-25 age group there was an average unemployment rate approaching 20% (CEC, 1992). Regional inequalities have started to increase again and by 1990 they were as high as in 1970 (see Dunford, 1994): 14 of the EU's Level II regions had a GDP per capita above 125% of the average, while 158 regions had a GDP per capita less than 75% of the average. These included the whole of Greece, Portugal and Ireland, two-thirds of Spain, the Mezzogiorno and the larger part of the former GDR (CEC, 1991). The "Cohesion Fund" agreed during the Maastricht Treaty negotiations was not only part of the political price exerted by southern states for their support. It also represented a growing awareness of the continuing gulf between north and south, one made all the more acute (if in different ways) by the prospect of further enlargement to the north and east.

There is a tradition of underfunded EU programmes to combat poverty dating back to the 1970s, although social policy has generally been largely the preserve of nation states. Dominant views in the Commission still approach poverty in terms only of low income and residence in regions with a low per capita GDP. The new "Social Exclusion" programme launched in 1993 by the EU is, however, slightly more advanced and elaborated (CEC, 1993b), the product of a classic Brussels compromise. There was pressure from some member governments to legitimate the path of integration by demonstrating concern for the intensification of inequality. In the Commission, there was not only awareness that the Single Market programme could only be sustained if its benefits were seen to be shared widely, but also a recognition of the structural and multidimensional nature of the problem. Background reports, for instance, highlighted the risk of cracks appearing in the social fabric, and used the term "social exclusion" to denote the prospect of a two-tier or fragmented society (CEC, 1992). The resulting programme was designed to give attention to less privileged individuals and groups (young people, migrants, unemployed, women, the elderly) that had been "socially excluded" from education, employment, housing, health and other social services. Emphasis was placed on the local level, and particularly on decaying urban centres. The whole programme was based on the principle of subsidiarity in terms of financing and on a multidimensional approach, with a methodology which embraced active participation on the part of those "excluded".

The problematic described in the "Social Exclusion" programme is perhaps closer to the one of marginalisation discussed in this volume than more conventional or longer-standing EU views on the subject (and it is not without significance that the EU's outlook is perhaps beginning to shift slightly away from the orthodox neo-liberalism that prevailed in the late 1980s; see below). A subsequent Green Paper, *European social policy* (CEC, 1993c) expanded on these themes, asking three questions of its own:

1. Is there a route back to full employment?
2. Should the welfare state be given a new role?
3. What is the next stage towards equality of opportunity?

Our contributors have, however, made important further clarifications beyond the agenda of social exclusion and the Commission's thinking on social policy, questioning both past and present national and EU programmes. They have made clear the distinction between social/spatial exclusion and marginality, the second being a broader and more inter-disciplinary concept. In particular, marginality accommodates a more sensitive geographical dimension, something that is inserted almost as an afterthought in the "Social Exclusion" programme. Different theories of geography, economy and society suggest how "progress" and "integration" produce disintegration and marginality (see Chapter 13 by Bailly and Weiss-Altaner). Poverty is no longer just associated with specific areas, social classes and income groups: economic marginalisation may have as much to do with marginalisation *in* employment as with total exclusion from the labour market (see Allen and Henry (Chapter 10), Pugliese (Chapter 4) and Kesteloot (Chapter 5)). Social and economic margin-alisation does not necessarily and of itself imply geographical marginalis-ation in the sense of being part of a periphery (see Oksa (Chapter 7), Gaspar (Chapter 8) and Sadler (Chapter 9)). Marginalisation as a process always includes social and spatial elements and it would be wrong to prioritise one against the other.

Low employment status, regressive income distribution patterns, gender and cultural differences, and adverse housing conditions are identified as causes of "social exclusion" in EU programmes and policies. Our contributors, however, have uncovered the objective logic of those characteristics in terms of the inherent tendencies of uneven capitalist development and the social division of labour (see Vaiou (Chapter 3), Robins and Aksoy (Chapter 6) and Sadler (Chapter 9)). An important theme of the book is that this is a time when agendas are in transition, and that policy needs to incorporate a much more sophisticated recognition of the importance of cultural, gender, ethnic, racial and other social dimensions. They can no longer be seen as "residual" elements in some kind of base–superstructure metaphor. Social exclusion and marginalisation cannot be reduced to individual "failure" or to "society drop-out", as some neo-liberal proponents of Maastricht seem to argue. Different types of European welfare capitalism at the national and regional levels prepared the ground in a variety of ways so that today, different forms of marginality are rising in these diverse socio-spatial contexts (see Mingione (Chapter 2) and van Weesep (Chapter 11)). Thus, processes of marginalisation must be understood in their totality, in terms of their integral links to the current phase of European integration, and not as separate, fragmented phenomena. The poor, the marginalised, are not simply those who stayed behind, who were bypassed by progress and who remained in, on or around the social, cultural and spatial margins of Europe. They are the losers in a zero-sum game of European integration, in which everybody hopes to gain, but in reality the winners will be few.

The European Commission is of course aware of the prospect of increasing social and spatial inequalities due to European integration. In a contradictory — some might say cynical — fashion, its major allocation of resources is aimed at strengthening competition and market forces as the main mechanisms to bring benefits to the "losers". People and places thereby become social groups and regions "in care". Certainly, transferring money soothes bitterness and limits migration. It does not, in itself, create the much advocated competitiveness of individuals and places. Current national and EU policies seem to ignore lessons from development and underdevelopment theories, in that the very process of market building is in fact precisely responsible for present and future inequalities.

As a consequence, some EU policies regarding the issues discussed in this volume either provoke with their implementation (in for example the case of anti-migration laws discussed by Pugliese (Chapter 4)) or indirectly reproduce existing marginalisation, assuming a reality separate from the functioning of the system of market forces (see Sadler's account of industrial policy (Chapter 9) and Gaspar on transport policy (Chapter 8)). As Vaiou (Chapter 3) pointed out for women of the south, the unequal terms of women's integration into the labour market are not a matter of "bad" policies that can be "corrected"; they are structural features of uneven development in which winners and losers are mutually determined.

Problematising the relationship between integration and marginalisation in these ways is essential, if we are to understand the new dynamics of European capitalism. Two more open questions are relevant at this point. The first concerns who has the political power to say who is central and who is marginal. In the past, the "theory of marginality" — although heavily criticised — was functional for state policies in many dependent societies, and this has been one of the reasons for its persistence. Today, in order to go ahead with building Economic and Monetary Union, the EU must appear "legitimate" with respect to the very real social and geographical costs of integration. An integral part of this process for the EU is to identify, according to its own criteria, who is socially and spatially marginal (or socially excluded in Brussels bureaucratic terminology). Then, by putting marginal people and places "in care", the EU may absorb social and political unrest in exchange for money, goods and services which it alone can provide.

The second question directly relates to the first. Since the process of European integration, like all political projects, is shaped and transformed by the dynamics of social conflict, it might be asked why marginal people and places have remained silent for so long. As we commented in our introduction (and the point is further clarified in Chapter 12 by Pickvance), there is no mechanical correlation among those who are marginal and their propensity to take action to question this position. An important parameter is that until now social mobilisation, if it has taken place at all, has done so at the regional, local or national level. One strand of opposition to present tendencies is to revert to the national scale, and to argue that it is important to influence national state politics. Precisely what form of national policies might emerge given structural and institutional constraints, and how they would relate to broader international economic and political changes, is of course a vital and indeterminate question (see Amin and Tomaney, 1995). Mobilising against EU policies is a rather new development, although a number of important territorial movements have questioned the local–global link in particular places (Hadjimichalis, 1994). It is also important to consider the political, gendered and cultural exclusion of marginal groups and places from the construction of new Europe, in ways which prevent them from being actively involved. Such processes of marginalisation seem to be playing a leading role in the silence of the losers, more important perhaps than their position at the bottom of any social, economic or geographical hierarchy. On the contrary, national or regional working-class organisations and agricultural co-operatives (representing mostly men), students, the officially unemployed, middle-class producers and consumer associations, not to mention various fractions of capital, are all *inside* the project of the new Europe — independently of their economic and geographical position — and are thus frequently mobilised against aspects of it.

A common European policy dealing with issues of marginalisation is, however, likely to remain itself marginal. There is unlikely to be an upwards trend towards higher quality levels, as Mingione (Chapter 2) underlines, because of the high economic costs involved on the one hand (or more properly, in one definition of economic costs) and lack of political will on the part of the winners on the other. The EU, in association with local and national actors, should consider urgently the possibility of implementing new and innovative forms of social strategies, accepting the multiple features of all people in Europe. The politics of marginality depends upon political constraints and historical variants, but its evolution will result from the form and orientation of social action.

Umberto Eco wrote in 1992 that "Europe looks integrated but in reality it is more disintegrated than it has been since the eighteenth century. European politicians and bureaucrats do not use history and geography as 'magistrae vitae' [teachers of life] and cannot visualise the effects should the lid blow off the saucepan" (Eco, 1992). The process of European integration cannot be stopped. Its particular course must change, however, to accommodate the highly uneven consequences of building a Single Market. Those who proclaim the successes of certain social groups and places must finally learn from European history and geography, and accept that this was achieved at the expense of others. The new Europe should no longer be built with so many people and places simply "missing out", if it is to avoid further and more dramatic expressions of social unrest.

NOTE

1. *Limes* is a Latin term in the singular, describing the geopolitical and cultural boundary between the Roman Empire and the "Barbarians".

REFERENCES

Amin, A. and Tomaney, J. (1995) The regional dilemma in a neo-liberal Europe, *European Urban and Regional Studies*, 2.

CEC (1991) *The regions in the 1990s: fourth periodic report on the social and economic situation in the regions of the community*, DG XVI, Brussels.

CEC (1992) *Towards a Europe of solidarity: intensifying the fight against social exclusion, fostering integration*, COM (92) 542, Brussels.

CEC (1993a) *Growth, competitiveness, employment: the challenges and ways forward into the 21st century*, Bulletin of the EC supplement 6/1993, Brussels.

CEC (1993b) *Action Programme to combat social exclusion and to promote solidarity*, DG V, Brussels.

CEC (1993c) *European social policy: options for the Union*, Commission Green Paper, Brussels.

Dunford, M. (1994) Winners and losers: the new map of economic inequality in the European Union, *European Urban and Regional Studies*, 1, 95–114.

Eco, U. (1992) What is the cost of a failing empire? *L'Espresso*, 6 September (in Italian).

Hadjimichalis, C. (1994) Global–local in conflict: the emergence of territorial movements in Southern Europe, in Amin, A. and Thrift, N. (eds), *Globalisation, institutions and regional development in Europe*, Oxford University Press, pp. 239–256.

Lipietz, A. (1993) Social Europe, legitimate Europe: the inner and outer boundaries of Europe, *Environment and Planning D: Society and Space*, **11**, 501–512.

Lundqvist, L. and Persson, L.O. (eds) (1993) *Visions and strategies in European integration: a north European perspective*, Springer, Frankfurt.

Ruffin, S. (1991) *L'empire et les nouveaux barbares*, Lattes, Paris.

Index

accessibility 123–7
agriculture 39–40
Amsterdam 183–4
Anatoliki Makedonia 39
atypical employment 37–42

Berlin 187–9
Brussels 10, 69–85
Bosnia 10, 90, 97–100

Catalunya 38–9
class theory (and urban movements) 201–3
Cleveland 138–9
community 94–7
consensus mobilisation 201
consumption 77–8
contract services 12, 149–66
culture 10, 87–104

deindustrialisation 28
deprivation 200
dualisation 75–6

eastern Europe 3, 59, 87, 95–6
Economic and Monetary Union 3, 9, 45
employment
  conditions 158–60, 162–3
  systems 18–19
environmental concern 115–16
ethnic neighbourhoods 80–3
European Fortress 52, 65–7
Europe of the Regions 4, 92

financial services 151–3
Finland 107–22
flexibility 72–6
foreign direct investment 135–6, 137
France 63

gender 9, 35–49
Germany 63–4, 176–8, 184–7
guestworkers 10, 12, 70–2, 80–3, 167–73, 180–94

high speed trains 124–6
homeworking 41
household structures 21–6, 29, 43–4
housing 12, 70–2, 167–94

identity 20–1, 87–94, 100–3
informal economy 62
information technology 118–20
institutionalisation 205
integration 3, 6, 27–8, 45, 116–17, 240

labour
  markets 53–5, 61–3, 136, 140
  mobility 42–4
Lisboa 39

Maastricht Treaty 4, 5, 44–6
Marche 38
marginality 3–8, 219–26, 230–3, 237–43
migration 9–10, 51–68, 70–1, 171–3
modes of social integration 17

nationalism 92, 96–7, 98–9
nation states 89–90, 94
natural gas networks 126–7
neo-liberalism 5–6, 139
Netherlands 173–6, 182–4
north-east England 11, 135, 137, 142–5
North Karelia 108–10

old industrial regions 133–48

place marketing 142–5
political parties 206–8
Portugal 127–31
post-Fordism 61–3
poverty 9, 15–32, 238
protest participation 203–4

refugees 58

regime transition 206
regional inequality 238
regionalism 92
reindustrialisation 134–9
resource mobilisation 204–5
rural communities 107–22

service sector 28–9, 149–55
Single Internal Market 27, 36
skill (definition of) 161–2
social
   exclusion 16, 238–40
   mobilisation 241
   movements 198
   partnership 37–42
   policy 20, 26–30, 239
socio-demographic transformation 29
south-east England 12, 149–66
southern Europe 35–49
state theory 208–12
Structural Funds 27
subsidiarity 27

suburbanisation 70
Switzerland 178–80, 188–90

telecommunications 127
telecottages 11, 119–20
Third World 55–7
trade unions 138
Trans-European Networks 124–7
transport 123–7

urban
   marketing 76–9
   movements 197–217

welfare
   capitalism 21–6
   state 111–13
   systems 19–20

xenophobia 6, 66

Zurich 189–90

Looking for Europe.
Will it be theirs?